THESE BOYS AND THEIR FATHERS

THESE
BOYS
AND
THEIR
FATHERS

— A Memoir —

Don Waters

UNIVERSITY OF IOWA PRESS, IOWA CITY

University of Iowa Press, Iowa City 52242
Copyright © 2019 by Don Waters
www.uipress.uiowa.edu

Printed in the United States of America
Text design by April Leidig

Printed on acid-free paper

Library of Congress Cataloging-in-Publication Data
Names: Waters, Don, 1974–   author.
Title: These boys and their fathers : a memoir / Don Waters.
Description: Iowa City : University of Iowa Press, [2019] |
Includes bibliographical references. |
Identifiers: LCCN 2019010730 (print) | LCCN 2019019533 (ebook) |
ISBN 978-1-60938-680-1 (ebook) | ISBN 978-1-60938-679-5 (pbk. : alk. paper)
Subjects: LCSH: Waters, Don, 1974—Childhood and youth. | Waters, Don. |
Fathers—United States—Biography. | Fatherless families—
United States. | Masculinity—United States.
Classification: LCC PS3623.A8688 (ebook) |
LCC PS3623.A8688 Z46 2019 (print) | DDC 813/.6 [B]—DC23
LC record available at https://lccn.loc.gov/2019010730

For my daughters

Men go forth to wonder at the heights of mountains,
the huge waves of the sea, the broad flow of the rivers,
the extent of the ocean, and the courses of the stars,
and omit to wonder at themselves.

———

ST. AUGUSTINE, *Confessions*

CONTENTS

THESE BOYS AND THEIR FATHERS

NOV. 3, 1992

Dear Father,

I would really like to get to know you too. I don't think I could have dinner with you on my Birthday because I have previous arrangements.

Well, I'll tell you a bit about myself. I am very active in school. I go to Reed High School here and am in the National Honor Society, the History Club, the Secretary of the Physics Club, and was the Captain of Reed High's soccer team. Next year, I plan to go to college, but I don't know where yet.

I am very outgoing and a basically happy person. Things sure are going by fast since this is my Senior year. But I would really like to meet you.

During the winter I go snowboarding a lot. I used to ski, but the sport got old and boring. I drive a 1989 Toyota Truck and have had it since I was 16.

Last year I was an exchange student in Denmark and had a great Host Family! I traveled across Europe and have many friends from across the world. I love all kinds of different cultures. I am a very open minded person and supported Clinton for President.

I am very much into alternative music and I play guitar myself. I believe music opens our minds and helps us think about how we can solve some of the problems of our troubled world. Well, enough rambling on and on. Please write back. I enclosed a picture for you.

Love,
Donny

p.s. I spell my name with a y and not ie

LEGENDS

THE LATE NOVEMBER forecast predicted a decent swell, and already we're seeing six-foot walls of blue water. It's 10:30 in the morning in Manhattan Beach, California—a warm, hazy day— and from our parked rental van in a lot overlooking the endless strip of sand, we watch the surfers in the lineup, in wetsuits, bobbing like little black buoys. I've finally made it to the same beach my father surfed more than fifty-five years ago.

"Look how the waves stand right up," Robin says. "And so close to the shore."

"Blake said there'd be surf," I say.

"Well, better you than me," she says. She slides on large, bug-eyed sunglasses that make her look like a celebrity.

A middle-aged woman cruises past on a banana bike with a sparkly gold seat. We don't see banana bikes on the Oregon coast. In Oregon, we have dilapidated, moss-encrusted crab shacks and coastal highways lined with tsunami zone warning signs.

"It's like a giant playground around here," Robin says.

"Just wait until the water dries up." I search my pocket for loose change. "Then this place is going to be in trouble."

"Maybe," she says.

"Do we have enough quarters for the meter?" I ask.

"We'll be fine."

"You think Blake will find this lot?"

"You left a message."

"But now he's not answering."

"He's probably busy driving. Stop worrying," Robin says. She sets her hand on my forearm. "Hey, you okay?"

"Yeah, fine."

"Then why are you tensing your jaw like that?" she asks.

Outside the van, the sun presses against a long-developing bald spot on the crown of my head. My father was bald, and suddenly that fact irritates me. I ask Robin to hold my backpack. Then I ease a thirty-eight-pound balsa-wood surfboard from the back of the van. The board is beautiful, just glassed. It's never been surfed. I carry it to a patch of grass, carefully set it down, unwrap a plug of cold-water wax, and begin drawing X's across its surface, tail to nose, welcoming the wax's pleasing coconut scent. A young couple strolls by on the path and gawks at the pristine surfboard. It's a pretty board, sure, but at ten feet long, it's also as big as a door.

"Jeez, look at the size of that thing," Robin says.

"Believe me, I know."

She coughs. She dabs her nose with a crumpled tissue.

"How are you feeling?" I ask.

"You know. Like I survived a train wreck," she says. "But I made it. I'm here."

She is, and that matters. Over the past few years, Robin and I have gone through rough patches in our relationship, preceded by work disasters, punctuated by relocations, and we're still trying to catch our breaths and sort through the debris. We've been together for more than a decade, but now we're living in separate states. Since August, I've been commuting between Portland and Iowa, spending stupid amounts of money to fly west to see her. She didn't want to move again. She wanted to stay put. I couldn't blame her.

This time, when I returned to Oregon, Robin suddenly came down with kidney stones. An emergency room visit gave her a head cold. But she's tough, and she wanted to come to California. The truth is, I needed her to come. She's my best friend, my partner. She knows everything about my past.

We're several streets north of Marine Avenue, my father's true stomping grounds, but this is closer than I've ever been to his boyhood home. The idea of venturing into sixty-degree water with a signature Greg Noll Malibu-chip longboard isn't as daunting as my reason for being here. My father, whose ghost hangs over this pretty beach, abandoned me when I was three years old. Now I've come to his old surfing spot to try to find some connection to the man.

Or at least that's the angle I manufactured when I pitched the idea to

Outside magazine. I'm on assignment. The plan is to write about early surfing history and confront my feelings for my father on a deadline.

Robert Stanley Waters was once known around these parts as Little Bobbie. As a young man, he surfed in Hermosa Beach, Malibu, and Santa Barbara. He hung out with some of the sport's earliest innovators, including early surf film star Dewey Weber and another dude who went by the nickname "No Pants Lance." My father also snuck under the railroad tracks near Camp Pendleton to ride Trestles, but Manhattan Beach was where his love for waves originated.

To the south stands the concrete pier where he once stored his own Greg Noll surfboard. It's also where, in 1952, he passed his swimming test at age ten. I know a few things because of what he left behind. In my backpack is a paper-clipped copy of his unpublished autobiography, as well as a small plastic baggie of his ashes, which I intend to scatter in the water.

Manhattan Beach is a city of surfing origins. In 1949, Dale Velzy opened the world's first surf shop here. It's also where Dennis Wilson of the Beach Boys first paddled into the water. This stretch of coastline is where the sport spread to the rest of the country after arriving from Hawaii.

Yesterday, after landing at John Wayne Airport, Robin and I went hunting for historical crumbs. At the Surfing Heritage and Culture Center in San Clemente, we found a small collection of his old surfing patches, surf-club membership cards, and old black-and-white photographs. The director of the center was a nice guy, and he was happy to help out. Written on the back of one photo, taken when my father was fourteen, it said in ink: "Bobbie Waters surfing Velzy balsa board; Velzy wanted his boards to get exposure by good surfers."

We left the center with a promise from the director that he'd email digital photos of my father's memorabilia. Then we stopped by a surf shop to pick up the surfboard, which was waiting for me.

Later, at our hotel, I sat on the edge of the king bed, squeezing my hands and contemplating the size of the surfboard on the floor. I wondered how those old-timers did it without wrecking themselves. The board was massive. I'd seen plenty of scratchy films featuring barrel-chested, barefoot men glassing across waves on similar boards. But staring at it, rubbing my big toe against its smooth rail, it seemed utterly intimidating. Even the curved, stained, glassed fin was the size of a boat propeller.

A northern breeze whips Robin's bangs against her glam sunglasses.

She brushes hair from her face and surveys the biking path, the manicured shrubs, and the mansions with terracotta roofs, and she says, "I don't know if I could ever live here. Everything's too neat."

Whenever we travel Robin declares whether she could live in a place.

"Oh, come on," I say. "I kind of like it. It's growing on me."

"Not me," she says.

"Imagine waking up every morning with this view, putting on flip-flops, and taking the dog on a walk to a café. You'd have a movie director's life." She shrugs.

After coating the board with wax, I change in the van. My wetsuit is like second skin. Suiting up requires concentrated, bendy, Herculean effort.

Then we wait for Blake. Blake lives up north in Venice Beach. I contacted him a month ago because he surfs and because today, especially today, I want a friend in the water with me.

Blake arrives in his Honda with his board strapped to the roof. He's in a grey hoodie and flashes his usual squinty smile. He gives Robin a hug, and we stand around chatting about writing and books. Blake asks what we've been working on. Robin recently visited New York, schmoozing with editors and her agent, and she just finished another review for the *Times*. And me? I tell him I'm writing about this, about today, about surfing, about my father, for a magazine.

"Sounds cool," he says.

If there's such a thing as an old soul, then Blake is a new soul. Even though he's ten years older than me, he's as animated as an eighteen-year-old. He's an accomplished writer, but he loves romantic gossip, trying new things, and he's a great dinner party guest.

Blake sets a green thermos on the car's roof and says, "Always bring along hot coffee for afterward. Gets cold out there." I don't have any coffee, and he makes a wise-ass remark about it. "Also, I checked the poo report," he says. "No poo. So we're okay to surf."

I retrieve the huge Malibu-chip from the grass, and together we descend the stone steps. Up and down the beach the lifeguard towers are shuttered for the season, but fresh tire tracks in the sand indicate a recent patrol. The weight of the board strains my shoulder.

Near the water Robin drops my backpack on the sand and whips open a towel filched from the hotel. She spreads it out. I stand beside her, and we watch a blond teenager launch off a solid five-footer, somersaulting through the air.

"I feel off," I tell her.

"Really?"

Off isn't how I usually feel at the beach. It's my father. I haven't thought about him this deeply or for such a sustained period of time *ever*. Throughout much of my life, I've avoided thinking about him or talking about him because thinking or talking about him only enhanced his absence. But recently, I *have* been thinking about him a lot and talking about him a lot, and I've entered a weird jet stream of heightened anger and sadness. My chest feels tight all the time, and lately I've been walking around feeling as if I'm always on the verge of crying.

A magazine assignment, I thought, would be an interesting way to face my father head-on. Not to mention, the assignment would pad my resume, but now that I'm finally here, I feel as if I'm marinating in feelings far too complicated to unpack in a magazine story. I want to feel something other than fury and sorrow whenever I think about him. I'm desperate to feel anything else.

I lay the board down, slide down a low, sandy slope, and put my bare feet in the water. It's almost a beautiful day, and there are waves, but I know it's going to be cold, even with a wetsuit.

———————

I NEVER KNEW MY FATHER in any meaningful way. Even at thirty-seven, after a decade of therapy, I still find it painful to acknowledge this truth. Any man whose father leaves can understand the shame, confusion, and anger generated by such a primal loss.

Early on, Mom often joked that she was Mom *and* Dad. I was her only kid, and she provided for me, she managed, but it never kept me from wondering, during those lean years when we shared a bunk in a tiny, one-bedroom apartment in downtown Reno, Nevada, if our situation might have been different with a father around. Along the way she enlisted men from her clerical job at the sheriff's department jail to dole out nuggets of paternal advice. I remember one evening, when I was around eleven, sitting down with a homicide detective who—badge on his belt, holstered gun between us on the dining room table—wanted to talk to me, man-to-man, about sex.

I never knew anything about my father throughout my childhood or teenage years — his whereabouts, what he looked like, what he did for a living, *nothing*. Whenever someone asked about him, I felt ashamed, and I lied. He was faceless, a phantom. His absence grew inside me like an expanding void. The idea of him living in the world, somewhere out there, haunted me. Did my entrance into the world cause him to leave? Was I worth nothing? With him gone I still needed guidance, and I looked to my friends' fathers for cues. I absorbed their attention as leaves did sunlight, and I quietly learned which ones to appoint as role models.

Why he left remains a mystery. Why he stayed away is another mystery. That part of my family history is full of holes and silence. The questions I've asked over the years yield bewildering answers. As unbelievable as it may seem, I've been unable to get any family member on either side to share more than a few scant details.

Whenever I ask Mom, which doesn't happen often because she's built a moat around the subject — adorned with decapitated heads on spikes — she's likely to say, "Why do you dwell on it so much? You're just like your grandmother."

Her mother, my grandmother, never knew her father either. She was illegitimate, abandoned, and raised by nuns.

Over time the topic of my father slid from taboo to never discussed. I was left to unearth my own pieces of truth. Years ago, Mom offered a brief whisper of insight, a quick peek at a long-ago drama before her curtain crashed down. The information spilled out during a fight. It's like that with her: information leaks out slowly, like flammable gas, threatening to ignite if I demand too much too fast. I learned early on to curb my curiosity, bottle it. There have been low murmurs about violence and betrayal, but no one has ever given me a complete or satisfactory story. And stories are important to understanding a life.

Eventually, I decided to do a bit of research myself, going so far as to purchase copies of my parents' divorce papers at the county courthouse in Reno. They cost nine dollars. Here's what I discovered: I was conceived out of wedlock. When I counted backward through the months, I realized I was conceived during the month of February. I don't know how my parents met, but they married in April 1974 in Virginia City, Nevada. It seemed to be a shotgun wedding. According to the documents I gathered, my father was no longer living with us at the time of the divorce three years later. By then he was working as a miner in Arizona. The stranger was free to visit, Mom sometimes told me, provided he contributed financially. That never occurred.

On my eighteenth birthday, he reentered my life via Hallmark card. Tucked inside the card was a check in the amount of fifty dollars. His signature was in cursive. The ink he used: blue.

Few people can recall the details of nearly every moment spent with their father. But I can. I met him five times as an adult, and each time our disconnection was obvious and massive. But those few times we did share are permanently etched in my memory.

The first remains as vivid as a just-seen film.

Lake Tahoe, summer, 1994—we're driving on the two-lane highway that cuddles the frigid, aquamarine lake. My father lowers his window, and the piney aroma of ponderosa fills the car. In Reno, after I knocked on his hotel room door, he quickly suggested a drive into the Sierras. He was eager to leave town. I stood stiff and silent in his hotel room. My throat was dry. My palms were sweaty.

"I'm glad you finally agreed to meet," he says, now turning to study me.

"I guess I want to know you," I say. "Is that wrong?"

"No, no," he says. "Of course not. Why would it be wrong for you to want to know about me?"

Tahoe sparkles through the trees. The road traces the contours of the lake. We pass houses on rocky bluffs, the road curves again, and we emerge on another cliff with an incredible view.

He's traveled to the Reno area for a work conference. So this is convenient, this meeting-his-son thing. At the hotel, I carried with me a thrown-together scrapbook—photos of places I've visited and photos of friends I've lied to about him. Photos of the lost years. He showed little interest. Instead, he suggested a drive around Tahoe in his Cadillac.

"There used to be a great Mexican restaurant around here," he says, tapping the steering wheel. "Want to see if we can find it? Great salsa."

I look at him out of the corners of my eyes. We're about the same height, same wide billboard foreheads, but he's a stranger. I'm trying to square how this man is my father. He's balding—will I bald too? He has a gut. Will I have a paunch like that at his age? How old is he?

And he talks. About himself.

"I've been in Vegas for a while now," he says. "But I spend most of my time out at the worksite. Lots of driving, but I don't mind."

He talks. About Yucca Mountain. About the importance of his work. He explains the intricate details about how to dig tunnels at the Yucca Mountain nuclear waste site.

"Even though a lot of Nevadans hate the notion of storing the country's radioactive junk in their backyard, it's the ideal solution. Yeah, yeah, people protest about it, and you've got these wackos trying to create a smear campaign, but the geology tells the story. It's really the best location to store waste for ten thousand years."

He talks. About women he's known.

"The last woman I dated seriously was Austrian," he says. "A real looker. Special. She posed for *Playboy* way back when."

The highway follows a bend and then straightens out.

"You look like her, you know," he says.

"Your old girlfriend?"

"No, *her*. Your mother," he says. "Same green eyes. Or is it hazel?"

"Oh."

"You remember how I used to take you on walks at the creek near the university?" he asks me.

I'm silent. No, I don't remember. I don't remember anything about him at all.

"Oh, of course you remember," he says.

"I don't."

"What about the small house near the university? I used to play with you on the floor. Remember that?"

Slowly, I begin wondering why I bothered putting on a clean long-sleeve shirt to hide my forearm tattoo, why I removed my earrings, why I cobbled together a stupid scrapbook to show him. He talks, and as I listen, a light inside me dims. Another goes red. He wants me to like him, clearly. He wants to impress. He tells me about a cousin at Harvard, an aunt in Hawaii, grandparents in the Puget Sound, people I've never heard about or met.

I'm waiting to hear the word *sorry*. I'm waiting for long-winded explanations. My stomach is a fist, and the thoughts that float through my head terrify me. I imagine grabbing the steering wheel, yanking hard, and taking us over a cliff and into the lake. My feelings are too much; they could destroy both of us. So, I turn away. I disconnect. I turn numb.

A year passes. I agree to see him again, during summer, hoping he'll provide explanations this time.

I'm back from college, and the mountains around Reno have gone brown. Over the phone he says he feels like having a steak dinner. "How's that sound, kid?" He knows a place inside the Eldorado casino. This time, I don't remove my earrings. And now there's a surgical steel hoop through my nose. I drive downtown and park in the casino's garage.

And there he is, traipsing down a casino corridor lined with fake Roman columns. He's still overweight, puffy, wearing slacks and a buttoned shirt.

"That hurt?" he asks, eyeballing my nose ring.

"Not really," I say.

"Why'd you do that?" He does not sound pleased.

"Because," I say.

"Because why?"

"I didn't give it much thought. I did it with a friend."

"Yeah, well. What about those hoops in your ears? People will get ideas about that sort of thing."

"Plenty of guys wear them," I say.

The restaurant hostess, who looks my age, shows us to a table with pleated, horseshoe bench seating. I can tell my father is uncomfortable sitting in a nice steak restaurant with someone with rings in his face. But I wonder, can the waitress tell how uncomfortable I am sitting beside a stranger who happens to be my father? Every so often, he cases me with his blue eyes, perhaps thinking, *If I'd been there . . .* He stares at me as if he knows me — but he doesn't know me. We are ghosts to each other.

Like our first meeting, he talks. And I listen.

He wants to fill me in on things he forgot to tell me last time.

Dinner arrives — steak, potatoes.

He's in town for another conference. Convenient, then. He doesn't ask about Mom or college or much else, but I hear about his college years, and I'm still waiting for explanations.

After dinner we man-hug in the smoky casino corridor. It's uncomfortable. Then we shake hands once more. On the way to the parking garage, I decide I don't want to see him again. And I don't, not for eight years, and then only twice more.

During our final encounter, in 2009, my father lay in a mechanical hospital bed in a seaside city north of Seattle. The moment I walk into his room, I notice how extremely overweight he is and how bloated. His chin disappears into a pillow of fat that his head rests on. His skin is loose and speckled with purple bruises. An oxygen tube bisects his face.

I walk over and stand beside his bed, waiting for him to recognize me. I've brought along the day's newspaper. I don't know why. I wanted to bring him something, an offering, a gift.

He shifts and winces. A catheter limits his movements. Dangling from a bed rail is a baggie of bright urine. Before I entered the room, a nurse told me they were trying to drain fluids off him by administering a diuretic. He's been battered by multiple illnesses. Wadded tissues litter his blue bedside tray table.

He sees me but doesn't see me. His eyes close and open, and he says in a gravelly voice, "I'm a hostage here. This is a hostage situation."

"You're a hostage?" I ask.

He doesn't recognize me. He needs water, he says, and will I fetch him a tall glass? Please, *please*, will I do it? Will I help a man in need? There's a sign on his door that reads, FLUIDS RESTRICTED.

"You're not supposed to have water," I say. "I'm sorry."

His eyes slide away. His lips are as split as a dry lake bed. He still doesn't recognize me. I sit in a cold, plastic chair, attempting small talk, but he's dazed, his brain too fogged by oxygen depletion to form intelligible sentences. As I did the first time we met, I scan for physical similarities and differences. Same broad forehead. Different colored eyes. Similar cheekbones. He's not the dashing figure I sometimes conjured up during childhood. Seeing him now, crowded by pillows in a hospital bed, squeezes tears into my eyes. His illness dominates the room, as illness tends to do. Hospital rooms demand a sort of chilly reverence. What's left in this antiseptic chamber is a dying, half-crazed man with greasy hair and apple-sized bruises across his arms and legs. Hanging on the wall is a medical chart that reads like some kind of scary encyclopedia, a possible blueprint of my future: diabetes, congestive heart failure, sleep apnea, kidney disease, and on and on. I don't understand half the acronyms. The list terrifies me. Other than our foreheads, I wonder what else we share. For a moment I try to imagine him as an athlete, as the once sporty person his relatives — *our* relatives — have told me about.

My original game plan was ruined the moment I saw electrodes running from his chest to a heart monitor. I wanted to confront him, to finally demand explanations. Now it's impossible. I'm scared I might say something that could literally kill him, though that bitter thought does course through my mind: here's the man who left; here's the man who didn't pay a dime or lift a telephone to place a call; here's the man I want to love and be loved by. I imagine unleashing my pain on him, thirty years of accumulated outrage, and watching the lines on his heart monitor freak out, beeping, beeping, beeping . . .

I stand by the window. It's a grey spring day walled by fog. I turn around. Talking with him is difficult. I have to wait for rare moments when the clouds in his eyes part and he appears to be somewhat cognizant. At the moment he isn't.

"There's a vendetta against me in this hospital," he says quietly. "If you don't act now, I won't be here this afternoon."

His illness creates fear that manifests as paranoia. He describes developing plots. Doctors roam the hallways, he says, conspiring to kill him.

I don't know what to say. For an hour I sit with him and listen to his delusions. Nurses visit the doorway. We talk in low tones about his condition, which seems to elevate his suspicions. His eyes go wide as he watches us talk.

I take my laptop from my backpack and set it on his tray table. I want to show him a slideshow of recent events from my life. A trip to Romania with Robin, my friends, my dog on a Pacific Ocean beach with a tennis ball in her mouth. I want to show him what his son has been doing. But he's not interested. Why do I keep doing this to myself? Besides, he's not really here. And he's unaware that I'm floating. I'm half in the room, bewildered and unnerved to be near him, in his presence. Eventually, he falls asleep.

Another quiet hour passes.

When he wakes up, he turns his head and his eyes land on me, and suddenly his gaze feels alert and genuine. He tears up, and for a moment he's here. He sees me. He says my name. He knows me. He knows who I am.

"Son," he says in a dry whisper. "Hello."

I feel my heartbeat in my head. I stand. I need to speak with his doctor immediately. I need to know what to expect. I need to know what the final countdown will look like. I head to the nurse's station.

The head nurse is a bosomy, long-fingernailed, bright-lipsticked woman who talks fast and seems extremely competent. But I don't care. I ask to speak to his doctor.

She's flipping through a medical chart on the other side of the counter and doesn't seem to hear me. I state my request again.

She says, "Your father's been giving us trouble. He told me earlier he wasn't pregnant."

"Wasn't pregnant?" I say. "What?"

"He lifted his gown, showed me his stomach, and insisted he was not pregnant. But thankfully, we've managed to get him down from 324 to 279. The diuretic is doing its work."

He's not pregnant? I can't handle this shit. "I need to speak with his doctor," I say again. "I want to know what's going on."

"I can answer your questions."

"No, I want to speak with *his doctor*. Not you. His *doctor*."

"The doctor is at lunch," she says, and she reiterates, she can answer any questions. I meet her eyes. I'm not fucking around. I raise my voice. I want his doctor on the phone *right now*. I stalk around the nursing desk, and she stands and takes a step back.

There's still time, I want to say. *There's still time.* She has the doctor on the phone within minutes. But the doctor can't tell me anything either, other than to say my father is only using 23 percent of his heart. His heart is a bruised fruit. "He could die within the week," the doctor states matter-of-factly. "Or he could live six more months. People surprise us all the time."

No one has answers.

When I return to his room, he's sitting upright. Foggy light reaches through the window and accentuates the stubble on his chin. He looks rough. He looks worn. He needs a shave. Another nurse walks in behind me and adjusts his pillows. She glances at an electric razor on a shelf above the bed. Then she looks at me, and unaware of our history, she casually asks if I wouldn't mind.

"He hasn't shaved in a few days," she says. "Want to help out?"

I feel tremendous sorrow for him, and I also feel he's gotten what he deserves. He looks at me with puffy, bloodshot eyes. His breathing is labored. I walk over and grab the razor off the shelf, on which also sits a personal Bible with gold-gilded pages.

"Thank you for visiting me," he says.

He smells ripe, some combination of body oil and dead, dry skin. God,

I hate him. God, I love him — but I have no idea if that's the truth. I know I'll probably always carry around anger and resentment, but I know, as we look at each other, I want to show him, just once, what it means to have a son.

I locate an outlet behind the bed and plug in the razor's cord.

Later that night, his mother — my grandmother — drops me off at a blue-trimmed mobile home in a 55-and-over community called Wheel Estates. His place is across Puget Sound on Whidbey Island, a short ferry ride from the hospital. His parents and his sister relocated from California long ago and live on the island too. Every so often, I can hear faint traces of my grandmother's faded Liverpool accent.

Before I get out, she reaches over and squeezes my forearm. I feel drained, exhausted. "I really think not seeing you for all those years broke his heart," she tells me. "We talked about it numerous times. After his first heart attack, and after the second. We think not seeing you broke his heart. Not having you in his life."

It occurs to me that I've been selfish with my grief. She's watching her son slowly die. I can't imagine her sadness in the face of it. What a sorrowful, incredible phenomenon to bookend your child's life, from birth to death, and to be the living witness to all the joys and complications. I squeeze her hand and thank her. I met my grandmother for the first time when I was twenty-eight, and I've only recently begun to know the rest of his family, but during these rare occasions, I often feel like an intruder.

"Remember," she says, before I shut the car door. "Put Post-it notes on any items you want."

It's clear his home is a stranger's home. It has the smell, feel, and look of a stranger's home. Everything is foreign.

A pink Post-it note pad sits on the kitchen counter. Anything I want? The nautical paintings, the tackle boxes, the fishing poles? I don't want any of it. *Get rid of it all. Sell it all. Burn it.* Even though this is a stranger's house, I snoop around, but I don't cross any serious boundaries because I'm too afraid I'll uncover something unseemly — extreme pornography, a dead body. I leave the medicine cabinet and drawers alone.

Everything is scarily immaculate, with cream walls and faux wood doors and, lit up behind the TV, a Thomas Kinkade landscape painting. A Thomas Kinkade! Supreme hack painter of all time! For some reason there's a diagram in the hallway closet, torn from a *Family Circle*, on how to perform the Heimlich maneuver. That my father keeps instructions on how to save someone from choking strikes me as supremely odd.

There's an open box of Diabeteze candy bars on the kitchen counter. Here and there, I notice framed photos of me as a chubby infant, from a time when he actually knew me. I notice a copy of Robin's book of short stories on his shelf. I don't see mine. There's a typed note on his coffee table listing the magazine subscriptions that will need to be canceled after he dies. I peel off a single Post-it note and set it on a small shelf with various, interesting-looking rocks. They're only rocks, but somehow they seem real and more important than anything else. Then I imagine a father standing in front of me and placing a Post-it note on him. But there's no father here. Instead, on a low table, there's information about car insurance and instructions about *what needs to be done* after he dies. On the dresser in the spare bedroom, where I plan to sleep, there's a small, plastic Christmas tree, lights attached, which he must bring out during holidays.

I spread a blanket across the hard futon, undress, slide beneath, close my eyes, and try to sleep but can't. Instead, I break down in sobs, crying so hard my lungs feel like they're on fire. I force myself to swallow breaths of air. His home is one of the loneliest I've ever been inside. It's too clean, too quiet. After divorcing my mother, he never remarried.

Months later, I'm in the car with Robin when my cell phone vibrates in my pocket. I wrestle it out. It's the phone call. My father is dead. It's a beautiful July day in Oregon, and my father, a man I never really knew, is dead. I ease my foot off the accelerator and pull into a gas station and park.

"He's dead," I say. I don't feel anything. I don't feel anything at all.

"What? What? Who?" Robin asks.

"My father."

"Oh, sweetheart," Robin says.

I feel numb. Numb, again. Robin offers to drive up to Whidbey Island to be near his family, but I don't want that. Instead, I ask her to drive to a nearby river, where I get out of the car, strip off my T-shirt, walk to the edge, and leap in. I need to feel something other than numb, and water always brings me solace.

YEARS BEFORE HE DIED, at sixty-seven, my father wrote a slim autobiography and mailed it to me. He knew I was a writer, and as a final effort to bond, he typed out sixty-eight single-spaced pages separated into nine chapters. Titled "The Story of My Life," it was his attempt "to help my son understand who his father was and help him heal."

Six years passed before I read it. The disappointments from the past were too great, too insurmountable. I internalized the blame for his leaving early in my life. I was still trying to extract that shame through therapy, and though I knew his leaving wasn't my fault, abstract feelings of worthlessness remained with me, buried in my skin like fallout from a bygone war.

His autobiography sat untouched and unread in a cardboard box. It became one of those un-throw-away-able burden items that traveled with me whenever I moved. I was frightened by what the pages might say about him or about me, or what they might reveal about Mom. I couldn't imagine how his clumsy attempt at autobiography might blot out nearly twenty years of total silence.

Then he died. And when his father died a year later, I realized I was the last Waters man in the family line. After my father's death I expected to feel different—better, unburdened, released, or perhaps the way a victim might feel after the perpetrator gets sent to prison. But I didn't feel better. Instead, I felt heavier. I was still angry with him, and I knew I *wanted* and *needed* to move past the feeling.

One night, after a few glasses of wine, I rummaged through the cardboard boxes in the closet until I located his autobiography. I flipped through the pages and meandered through old, dead decades. What I read brought the gauzy contours of his life into better focus.

My father loved the water. As a young man, he was a navy submariner. Later, he crewed aboard yachts in sailing races throughout Southern California. Each chapter signified a different phase in his life. Much of it was on the water. I didn't read the whole document. But I found myself returning to chapter 3. The chapter ran seven single-spaced pages. That night, as I sat on the floor, handling each page as though inspecting the Dead Sea Scrolls, I found myself absorbed by his "Surfing" chapter.

He grew up surfing. I loved water too, but because I was raised in the desert, I never had much access to the ocean as a kid. Despite that, I fell for surfing in my twenties, when a friend in Southern California introduced me to the sport.

Discovering that my father was a surfer amazed me. According to the

"Surfing" chapter, he was raised in Manhattan Beach. He lived several blocks away from a young guy named Greg Noll, a "Los Angeles County Life Guard at the time, and a freelance surfboard maker." Greg gave my father his first surfboard.

My father's beachside youth—and his friendship with Noll—captivated me. I was familiar with the big-wave-surfing pioneer. I'd seen the film *Riding Giants* countless times. Hell, I owned it. In his black-and-white jailhouse trunks, Greg "Da Bull" Noll was legendary for bombing down a massive thirty-five-foot wave in 1969 at a break called Makaha in Oahu. At the time it was the biggest wave ever surfed. Many surfers knew the exact date of Noll's feat.

About Noll, my father wrote: "He was also one of the best surfers in the South Bay and paddled in the Catalina to Manhattan Beach race each summer . . . He lived at home with his parents, and their house was on my way home from school . . . One day he was out in the side yard shaping a balsa-wood surfboard. So, being a kid, I decided to stop by to see what he was doing. As time passed, I stopped by more often."

That my father orbited around Noll intrigued me. He referred to Noll as his "good friend." For the first time in my life, as I reread the "Surfing" chapter, I actually wanted to know more about him—or at least more about that part of his life. Surfing felt like some kind of bridge.

Days passed. I couldn't stop thinking about the "Surfing" chapter. I wondered what Noll might know. Did he have stories about my father, memories? Soon I began fantasizing about riding a balsa-wood board like my father had.

I wanted to breathe deep and exhale my lingering resentments, my fury. In the past, anger had helped keep me focused. Anger was useful. Anger provided protective walls. Anger served as an anchor, but that anchor also dragged me into trenches of depression. It took me well into my thirties before I gathered the courage to open my father's autobiography. It could take me thirty more years, I knew, to even begin to understand him.

Maybe Greg Noll could help me get started. Maybe Noll was a waypoint that could lead to something deeper, something important, and something curative. Was it possible? Even though I knew it was a long shot, I needed to track down Noll. This, I felt, was my own Makaha.

It turned out that Noll liked being left alone. I phoned a mutual acquaintance and asked him to pass Noll a message. He did. Nothing came of it. I turned to the internet and located an email address for Noll's wife. I emailed her — nothing. I also found a street address and a phone number.

The seed for a story began germinating in my head. I contacted a friend and editor at *Outside*. I pitched my idea. He liked it. I thought that having a magazine behind me might serve as a crowbar. It didn't.

For five months I called, left messages, sent letters, postcards, and emails. Noll's silence was so total, I almost admired it. I phoned his son's surf shop in Southern California and left more messages. I didn't hear back. While vacationing in Maui, I sent a postcard to Noll, informing him the surfing was great and would he please respond? Back in Oregon, I drove to the coast and visited the Lincoln City Surf Shop. The owner was a Greg Noll aficionado who collected Noll surfboards. Several hung like trophies from the shop's ceiling. One was a black Waimea Bay Slotbottom Gun, built in 1963. It was a gorgeous big-wave board, ten feet eight inches long.

Finally, after nearly six months of pestering, I heard back from the Noll family, probably because they figured I wasn't going away. The family agreed to a brief visit. Not only that, they granted my other request. Together, we would build a surfboard.

A YEAR AFTER MAILING that first letter, I find myself driving a rental car along the Redwood Highway, headed to my first meeting with Greg Noll, hoping he won't berate me for being an incredible nuisance.

Noll's house is located on the Smith River, ten miles north of Crescent City, a sleepy port town in Northern California, population 7,600, which includes a state prison, Pelican Bay, the city's largest employer.

It's tricky business finding the Noll family compound. My directions tell me to turn at a narrow road off a rural highway. Many of the access roads are nearly hidden and hedged by looming trees, but the hilly, green, wooded scenery is stunning. At last I find the right road. At the end is a high electronic gate, which opens without prompting. I drive into a sizable compound and park behind a motorboat. Right away, I notice Greg sitting in a chair by the house, inspecting a rubber dinghy. He's wearing shorts and a grey sweatshirt with the neck scissored out. He waves at me. I wave back.

I walk over, and Greg casually tells me he's trying to devise a way to attach a fiberglass fin to the dinghy's keel. He talks as though we've reentered some past conversation. He says he wants to try surfing in the dinghy at a local break called Chickenshits. Apparently, Chickenshits only forms waves when conditions get big.

"They call it that because everyone is too chickenshit to try it," Greg says, smiling.

His eyes narrow behind his glasses. At seventy-four, he has thinning white hair and the pasty, scaly legs of an older man, but he still has the gleam of a daredevil in his eyes. For a moment I try to square the man in the chair with the one in John Severson's iconic photo—a young Noll gazing at a mountainous wave at Pipeline, board propped against his shoulder. Forty-seven years have passed since that image was captured.

Greg's wife, Laura, steps outside to join us.

"Greg has orders from his doctor to wear a back brace, but he doesn't," she tells me. She shakes her head. She says Greg recently fractured his tenth vertebra and collapsed his fifth by falling off a stepladder. This news worries me. We have a surfboard to build. I watch Greg bend and inspect the dinghy, and I watch him stand and hunch, as though nothing's wrong. A back brace? During my three-day visit I won't see him wearing a back brace once.

Laura, who's sixty-five, met Greg while she was working as a secretary at his Hermosa Beach shop in the 1960s. She's a pretty woman with glinty hazel eyes and a generous smile. Over the weekend I'll pick up on her sly ability to tuck herself into corners, quietly listening, stepping forward to provide commentary or background information.

"You've got a beautiful place," I say to her.

"We've lived in the same house for thirty-five years," Laura says.

"This landscape reminds me of the northern Oregon coast."

She nods. "We love it," she says. "We moved here in 1974. We were on our way back from Alaska, and we stopped and just decided to stay."

My arrival at the compound coincides with a partial family gathering. Greg's son Jed, who Greg calls Pinch, is here, along with Jed's three-year-old daughter, Trinity. After I shake Jed's hand, something occurs to me: Jed is the same age my father was when he left me. And I was Trinity's age.

My father didn't just abandon us. He also abandoned surfing. In the 1960s—that free love, mind-bendy era—he disapproved of the way surf culture "was beginning to dabble in drugs . . . I was opposed to that."

Leaving surfing is something Greg knows about too. Several years after catching the Makaha wave, and right around the time my father was growing disillusioned, Greg sold his surfboard factory and walked away. He was fed up with Hollywood's tacky exploitation of the sport, so he moved his family north and took up commercial fishing. But unlike my father, Greg slowly found his way back. The sport is too much in his blood. After a while, he began building re-creations of classic wood boards with his son. Now he and Jed handcraft about ten each year. Every two or three months, Jed drives to Crescent City from his shop in San Clemente. Even though Greg makes surgical strikes at trade shows and "Legends" events, he enjoys his privacy, as evidenced by the remoteness of the family compound.

We stand around the dinghy for a while, as though it's a campfire, shooting the shit. I like Jed. I like Laura. I like all of them. They're welcoming, and they don't seem to mind the intrusion of a stranger. And though I'm eager to pepper Greg with questions about my father—did he find him cool? funny? a good surfer?—I don't want to come off as needy or impatient.

The late morning turns to early afternoon. We have work to do if we're going to build a board. Jed leads me across the sprawling compound. The well-tended property strikes me as a bit more SoCal than NorCal. Scattered among redwood trees are a koi pond, an outdoor pool, imported palm trees, and a scarecrow in a wetsuit near the vegetable garden.

Their workshop is a converted, stand-alone, three-car garage with wide doors that swing open. The shop is full of wood, tools, and assorted surfing memorabilia, overhung with vintage boards made by Hobie Alter, Gerry Lopez, and other renowned shapers. The boards are covered with dust and spiderwebs. Any serious collector would drool. Jed tells me the shop has been here for twenty years. It's a true wood shop, with all the expected doodads and messiness. Two outdated calendars show young women in bikinis, one partially nude. This is clearly dude territory, and for a moment, as I take in this surfing Valhalla, I wonder where my father's old surfboards ended up. Everything I have of his fits inside three cardboard boxes—death certificate, mining tools, photo albums, rocks, not much.

Jed has already arranged several long balsa-wood sticks across two sawhorses at the shop's far end.

"It's a bit like an Easter egg hunt," he explains. "You look around the stacks and select wood that matches in weight and grain pattern."

The balsa wood, which comes from Ecuador, is quality stuff, he adds. Once we have the right combination of nine wood sticks, Jed hands me earplugs and a cloth mask and positions the first stick on the surface planer. He wears an industrial mask, and before he lowers it over his face, he says, "We need to correct the widths and clean the sides." Then he flips a switch. Even with earplugs the planer's high whine burrows into the center of my brain.

Because Greg has a broken back, Jed and I perform the majority of the hard labor. Every now and then, Greg appears to give advice and comment on our progress, like a principal architect. For our surfboard, a nine-foot, ten-inch Malibu-chip, the same as my father's, there are about fifteen stages of construction. We'll shape the board at the wood shop, and then Jed will finish by glassing it — applying fiberglass and resin — at his shop in San Clemente.

Jed feeds the sticks through the planer, the blade eats the excess wood, and I ease the boards through the other side. We'll repeat the process until we have nine matching sticks. Jed's right at home with tools and woodwork. The last time I made anything with wood was in middle school shop class, where it took me three months to cobble together a simple cutting board. Jed impresses me, but I'm often impressed by sons who emulate their dads. At thirty-four, he's slipped comfortably into Greg's well-worn sandals. He strikes me as a gentler version of his dad. He's not as boisterous, but he laughs like Greg.

During short breaks we lift our masks to talk.

I learn he's named after Jedediah State Redwoods Park, which is across the river from the house, but his nickname, Pinch, was given to him as an infant. Greg tells me at one point, with a wink, that when Jed was hungry as a baby he'd pinch his mother's breast. The Nolls are a family of nicknames, apparently. Several times I hear Greg call Laura "Lulu."

Jed's childhood was spent outdoors — fishing, riding motorcycles — the typical life of a kid raised next to rivers and forests and an ocean. He maintains the physique of an outdoorsy guy: round surfer shoulders, short strawberry blond hair, and a face freckled by sun. Growing up, the family traveled to Southern California during summers, where Greg earned money as a lifeguard. Jed started surfing in his teens. After his first solid wave, in Haleiwa Harbor in Oahu, he knew he'd inherited the stoke.

When Jed was a boy, his dad made him sweep the shop, which he disliked, but by seventeen his mind had changed, and he found himself on a flight to Japan for an apprenticeship with another skilled shaper. Jed watched his dad from an early age. He served his time apprenticing. Eventually, there came a point when Greg would shape one side of a board and Jed would finish the other side. Later, Jed settled in San Clemente, Orange County's southern hub for surf culture, and opened his own shop.

To end our first workday, we glue the milled planks together. Once we set the vises, our board doesn't look like much. We could be building a simple raft. The glue requires twenty-four hours to dry.

We step outside into the pleasant, seventy-degree weather. The sun is disappearing behind the trees, and the rustling needles throw dappled light all around us. The family's Australian shepherd, Pua, wanders over and sits on my feet.

Jed tells me they never let anyone participate in the building process. Usually, it's just him and his dad.

I admit to him that I'm slightly jealous of his relationship with his dad. "The only thing mine ever showed me was how to vanish," I say.

My speaking so bluntly about my absentee father seems to make Jed uncomfortable. He averts his eyes. We both go quiet. I never know how to casually smuggle the fatherless fact into everyday conversation. Best to avoid it, and usually I do, but my father is the reason I'm here, and lately, I've been thinking about fathers and sons a lot, and I just can't help it.

I steer the conversation back to Greg. I ask Jed how he feels about following in his dad's footsteps.

Jed leans against the shop's wall, slipping his toes in and out of his flip-flop. "The older I get, the more I realize how special it is," he says. "I absolutely understand the uniqueness of it. That I was able to take in the knowledge he gave me."

He smiles. A scar creases over his left eye, and I ask about it. He tells me he earned the scar a long time ago by surfing one of his dad's old boards, a Miki "Da Cat" Dora model, which is a heavy board, a big board, sort of like the one we're building.

YEARS AGO, when I was in my twenties and living in San Francisco, I often drove down Highway 1 to Half Moon Bay to stare at the waves at Mavericks, the notorious big-wave surf break. At the time I knew nothing about my father's past as a waterman, but everything about surfing fascinated me. I liked to keep up-to-date on the competitions, especially the insanity happening at Mavericks, where surfing wizards dropped in on freezing waves with thirty-foot faces.

And me? I paddled out for the first time on a gorgeous day in Huntington Beach, California, a.k.a. Surf City USA, when I was twenty-five years old.

California, 2001 — before the planes hit the towers, before the world went berserk — faint sheets of nearly translucent clouds glide across the sky, and I can feel sunlight warming the hairs on my arms.

"Just stay away from the pros at the pier and you'll be fine," my friend says, before I tramp into the water wearing his wetsuit.

I'm excited. I've always wanted to try surfing. I'm a daily swimmer and close enough in age to an adolescence filled with skateboards and snowboards that I believe my transition to surfing will come naturally.

I stare out at the waves with my friend's board under my arm. He knows what he's talking about. The surfers near the pier are acrobats. They're bronze, yellow haired, and wild looking. Some even look to be thirteen years old. Some probably *are* thirteen years old.

I choose a spot way down the beach, where I feel accepted among the other kooks. I'm comfortable in the ocean, not afraid of getting kicked around, but I'm still frightened about getting my vanity crushed. I *want* to surf. Today, I say to myself, I *will* surf. After I struggle past the first set of breaking shore waves, which pound into my chest, I jump on the board and paddle, only to see another set roaring straight for me. They swallow me and regurgitate me onto the beach.

The waves in my chosen section crumble apart easily, unlike the fuller, triangular mounds near the pier. But waves are waves, and waves break on top of me again and again. I paddle and try to break through more crashing waves, flop, and lose my balance, fall off and feel the ocean inhaling and exhaling and laughing at me. My sinuses are cleansed, my eyes sting. I can't catch a break, much less a wave. When I'm too far inside, waves annihilate me and push me back to shore.

After a while I make it past the breakers and just lie on the board, exhausted. Outside the breakers, nothing happens, and it's like lying on an undulating waterbed. Then I notice an approaching set, and I believe this is it, my time has come, and I try to calculate my entry, paddling into the wave before it crests, as I was told, but the wave rolls me over, the board noses into the trough, and I eat a perfect serving of humiliating shit. And I fall in love.

———

NOLL GAVE MY FATHER his first board in the early fifties. As the decade wore on, my father bought other boards—from some of the same guys whose creations hang in Noll's workshop—and loaded them into his 1940 Ford station wagon, the archetypal woody surf car he bought from a lifeguard for two hundred fifty dollars. My father embraced the lifestyle before the *Gidget* movies turned everything into a cliché. It was a golden time to come of age in Southern California. In Manhattan Beach kids went barefoot on streets without sidewalks. Teenagers packed into auditoriums to watch surfing films with jazz soundtracks.

By 1960, my father had gone from a young "gremmie," odd-jobbing around surf shops, to opening his own on Stearn's Wharf in Santa Barbara. Noll, by then a major figure, supplied him with his inventory of boards. My father even called his shop "Surf Boards by Greg." He and his friends liked to toss their boards off the pier and then leap into the water.

Though by his own admission, he was just having fun, my father was at the forefront of the surfing movement. He shared waves with icons Renny Yater and George Greenough, the surf photographer who invented the modern surfboard fin. My father was one of the earliest members of the exclusive Santa Barbara County Surf Club, which formed to gain access to the Hollister cattle ranch—now famously known as the Ranch. At Hollister, he and his friends hung out in shabby beach shacks, surfing "some of the most perfect waves anywhere in the world."

Nearly always in trouble for ditching school to surf, my father failed to graduate high school with his class.

"I didn't care," he wrote. "I had my friends, surfing, and could care less about school."

Reality soon caught up. The army came calling with a draft notice. He chose to enlist in the navy instead because a friend told him the food was better. On shore leave he surfed in Hawaii and San Diego, where he was stationed, but by the end of the sixties he began turning away from the ocean. According to later chapters in his autobiography, he became interested in geology, in mining, in bedrock and stone. He spent the rest of his years pinballing around Arizona, Idaho, New Mexico, South Carolina,

Ohio, and Nevada as a mining engineer. He last surfed in 1970. He was twenty-eight.

It strikes me as odd how, around the time I entered the world, my father trained his eyes on excavation. It's as though he leaped onto a different set of tracks the moment I was born. The man went from living in California, riding waves, and sailing the Pacific to fathering a son, leaving the son, and then hiding out, literally, underground.

He moved state to state, mine to mine, propelled by "this constant thought in the back of my head that I needed to explore . . . I needed to push myself and confront the unknown." Scattered among his many adventures in his book, he apologized numerous times, but his apologies don't compensate for how, in the span of sixty-eight pages, he barely mentioned having a son.

But there was a time when my father was young—a waterman. I feel a tinge of pride when I reread his "Surfing" chapter, but it's like having pride in an apparition. He was a terrible father, but before I was even a wispy notion in his mind, he fell in love with the ocean, which is the only part of him I understand.

BEFORE FINISHING THE BOARD, Greg and Jed want to show me around the small town.

On our way to scope out Chickenshits, we drive past a local bowling alley called Tsunami Lanes. A tsunami flooded much of the city in 1964. And the same earthquake that hurled tsunami waves at Japan in 2011 also sent waves rolling ashore here. Busted docks sit in heaps around the small harbor. High waves, I learn, damaged boats and closed the highway.

Greg drives to the end of the harbor and stops next to a white plaque with names etched in black. He wants me to take a closer look. Showing me the plaque seems important to him. So I hop out.

"Crescent City is one of the toughest ports to fish out of," he says, with an arm slung out the window. "Fishing is a tense occupation. Just about as dangerous an occupation as you can have." The plaque is dedicated to local fishermen who lost their lives. There's enough open space on it to accommodate more names. I keep forgetting Greg lived another life away from surfing. For years he operated two fishing boats. His crews pulled crabs in the winter and lined swordfish in the spring.

Back in the truck, Greg points to a huge rock poking out from the water several hundred yards from shore. There it is: Chickenshits. The ocean roils around it. It's a long way out. And that water is frigid. To the south of the harbor, near the beach, a dozen surfers are braving it. I ask Greg about the last time he surfed.

"Oh, I don't know. It was sad," he tells me. "But by God, I'm going to put my ass in the dinghy." He looks at Jed in the passenger seat. "I'll catch a wave that way. Right, Pinch?"

It occurs to me that I've never spent time around any other seventy-four year old who uses the word *bitchin'* so often. Or one who laughs about the time he caught a fifteen-foot wave in his twenty-six-foot fishing boat while motoring back into the harbor.

And I've never met a father and son who talk so passionately about wood planers. Greg only uses the Skil Model 100, which is no longer made and which he collects. Jed has gone so far as to enlist a friend to build him a series of prototypes. His latest is the JN2, or "Jed Noll 2." A planer is, father and son insist, a shaper's magic wand.

Greg doesn't know it, but as I listen to him confab with Jed, he's sliding into the role model category in my mind. He's funny. He's cool. And *look*—just *look* how he treats his son.

After the tour we stop for lunch at a roadside Mexican joint. Everyone around town seems to know Greg and Jed. I notice a signed photo of Greg hanging on the wall. "Best Mexican food in the world," it says in his hand-writing. Also affixed to the wall is a sticker bearing the name of the Noll surfboard brand.

When we finish vacuuming our plates, Greg adjusts himself on the other side of the table, apparently preparing for questions. I've left him alone for the most part. Sometimes I like listening to what people will tell me without asking questions. I start by lobbing a cream puff.

Your best wave, I ask.

"You mean, big? Has to be Waimea," he says, referring to Oahu's north shore. "Smaller, but perfect wave? Sunset," he says. Sunset Beach, also in Oahu.

I ask what every curious surfer would want to ask. I ask about Makaha. I want to hear about it. From his mouth. I can tell Greg nearly stops himself from rolling his eyes. One million times, his face says, one million times I've been asked that question. I fold my hands on the table—and wait.

"You have to understand it was a progression," he says. "A stepladder. Each time, you move up a notch. You know from experience what that wave will do. And you learn to control your brain by staying calm. I was thirty-two, and the adrenaline rush from that was hard to believe. My skull was *packed* with adrenaline. There are few bitchin' things like that in life."

He fiddles with his silver watch, explaining how long he's been around the sport and how things have changed. Even the boards have transformed dramatically. It's been like watching a horse buggy morph into a Porsche, he says.

"I started surfing in 1949. I've seen it all," he says. "All the way back to the old plank boards and up to today, with tow-in surfing. Back then, it was just me and Bing Copeland. Nobody else. You knew everyone up and down the coast. But, each year, there were just a few more. And then a few more. There was a whole culture change. You had all these kids who'd just missed the war. And these guys, who were tremendous athletes, were giving the bone to school sports. Instead, they were surfing. And the girls loved them more. There was this huge shift at the time. Surfing became the thing to do."

"It's interesting that Jed is taking up where you left off," I say.

Greg nods. "Jed can shape a world-class surfboard. For someone his age, he knows all the history. I'm so proud of the kid. How can it be better than to have your own son working alongside you?"

He doesn't have to say anything else.

I WAKE UP EARLY on my last morning in Crescent City. An annoying gap between the drapes allows a slim, bright column of light to creep into my eyes. I slept fitfully. My motel room emits a lush mildew aroma. And eighteen-wheelers rumbled along the highway all night long, shaking the bed.

Later, I detour at a roadside coffee shack. I have a free hour, so I head over to the beach, watching the morning surfers scattered along the crescent-shaped shoreline. It's another sunny fall day with nice chest-high waves. I watch a man my age stretching nearby. He stops now and then to adjust his wetsuit.

The moment you join a wave is nearly indescribable. There's a sense of accomplishment, only that comes later; and unity, only that comes before;

but in the moment it's just you and the water and nothing else matters. Watching the man stretch, I understand why he goes through the trouble of tugging on a wetsuit and heading into a cold ocean at nine o'clock in the morning. For a fleeting moment, you touch the ocean's power. You become part of something larger. Of course, it's not all about unity and oneness and other spiritual mumbo jumbo. More than anything, surfing is fucking fun.

"The stoke generated during your first years surfing is the same stoke your dad felt in Manhattan Beach, and it's the same stoke some kid in Japan feels," Greg said to me yesterday. "What else is there that's like it? You know. You understand. Surfing for the pure joy of it."

I sit in the sand and drape my arms over my knees, watching the man carry his board into the water. He's in a full-body wetsuit with only his face exposed. Up north, surfers endure more. Southern California is beautiful, sure. Sun and warm sand and ice-cream cones and freeways and people. But the water is colder up north, the beaches long and barren and absent of lifeguards. Colder water means thicker wetsuits and days surfing alone.

Unlike Southern California beach communities, northern towns like Crescent City are largely unremarkable. I love these tumbledown coastal towns. Crescent City has a working-class vibe, unlike a place like Newport Beach, with its faux Mission-style mansions and manicured boulevards. The open space and emptiness between northern coastal towns feels liberating and extreme. There's also something totally sad yet begrudgingly hopeful about struggling trinket and candy shops with striking Pacific Ocean views.

I sip my coffee, thinking about Jed's relationship with his daughter and Greg's relationship with Jed. Robin and I talk a lot about having children. Lately, that topic seems to be coming up more and more.

"Imagine, if we had a little girl, we could show her the waterfalls," Robin recently said during a hike up to Triple Falls.

I said, "And I'll show her how to play soccer."

"We could also have a little boy. What about the name Ivan?"

"Little Ivan the terror. I'll take him surfing. He'll rule the soccer field."

"She'll rule the soccer field too."

"Yes, she will."

We've removed the obstacles, and we tell each other, well, if it happens then it happens. We're ready. We've been casually trying for some time, even though the thought of failing as a father terrifies me. The top moral defect on my list of all-time top moral defects is being a bad father.

A year ago, I believe Robin had an early miscarriage. She talked about feeling strange for weeks. She talked about feeling nauseated, and she missed her period.

We were ready.

We told each other we were ready.

Then one day she bled, a lot, and she fell into bed with a devastating headache.

I immediately called a friend, an ER doctor, and drilled him with questions.

"Those are all signs of a miscarriage," he told me.

We want a child. We have busy lives, and we're not fanatical about timing everything perfectly, but recently Robin purchased some special thermometer to better monitor ovulation.

At a certain age, when you don't have children, some people begin to feel exposed and conspicuous, especially when you want children and it hasn't happened. It's tougher for Robin, I'm sure. Lately, I've noticed her flinch whenever another woman—always a young mother—asks whether we have any kids.

———————

AFTER DAYS OF milling, gluing, skinning the top, and finding the blank's center point, it's now time to draw the surfboard template. I return to Noll's compound and find Jed sweeping the shop.

Eventually, Greg joins us in the shaping room. He lays a template across the raft-sized blank. I notice markings on the template that read MALIBU . . . LIKE THE ONE I MADE WHEN I WAS TEN YEARS OLD. It startles me. For a moment I wonder whether Greg used a similar one to build my father's first board. Other templates hang on the wall, including a template of the board Greg rode on that fabled day at Makaha.

Greg gives me a pencil and asks me to help trace the board's outline. What remains after sawing around the traced lines is a hunk of wood that resembles a very thick surfboard. I'm glad we're getting somewhere.

"How do you know when the board is finished?" I ask.

Greg pushes his glasses up his nose. "When you look down the board and you see what you have in your mind, that's when you know it's done," he says. "People don't realize how much thought goes into the design. You have to understand the progression of the surfboard, from the Hawaiians until now. You'll find this one is probably more versatile than you think."

Later, Jed shows me how to run the electric hand planer. He eases the "Jed Noll 2" back and forth across the blank. Sawdust rises off the wood in arcs like blown snow.

"Just like that," he says, and hands me the planer. Because I'm new at this, I notch ugly grooves into the nose section, which he corrects when I give the planer back. I lean against the doorframe, watching him work. Every so often, Jed lifts the board to his eyes, gazing down the wood, making sure he's keeping even — making sure it's what he sees in his mind.

The more the blank begins to resemble a surfboard, the more excited I get. It's beginning to look huge.

"Do you have any pointers for when I get out there on this thing?" I ask.

"Just use the weight of the board with the water," Jed says. "Don't worry. You'll see."

We've been at it for days. Building something from nothing is time consuming. I wander around the shop. The air is thick with the smell of woodcuttings. There are signs everywhere of an entire life immersed in the surfing world. Half-finished boards, boards hanging on the walls and from the ceiling. One bears the signatures of a dozen or more surfing luminaries, including Mark Foo, the Hawaiian big-wave surfer who lost his life during the 1994 Mavericks competition.

I leave the shop and look for Greg.

He's not in the yard, but he's around. My first impression of him has pretty much stayed the same throughout my visit. He does not stop moving. During a typical day, you might see him fiddling with a dinghy, calling an old friend, washing boats in the yard, and building a surfboard.

Now I just want to sit down and talk. I've traveled here to learn more than how to build a surfboard. We've been tiptoeing around the topic all weekend.

The kitchen is decked out with hand-built koa cabinetry. There's a beautiful view of the river. That's where I find him.

"Can we talk?" I ask Greg.

We're alone. He knows why I've wandered inside. He nods. When we sit at the table, he sets his hand on my shoulder.

"I think it's great you're doing this," he says. I take out a black-and-white photo of my father from my notebook. We pass it back and forth.

"Your dad," Greg says, "was one of the very first kids to come by my parents' place. He'd stop on his way from school and watch me shape. He was a quiet, bitchin' little guy, and I could tell he had all the makings of a future surfer."

"How so?" I ask.

"Eagerness. A twinkle in his eyes. You can tell."

In my mind I calculate the math. When Greg was fifteen, shaping boards in his parents' yard, my father was maybe ten or eleven.

"One day, I had a board on the heavy side," Greg says. "The shape was no good. Every once in a while, I'd see a kid who didn't have much money. So I gave him the board. Like your dad, I was one of those kids who went around and asked for a free board. Over the years, I'd see him hanging out with the Marine Street gang and surfing at the Manhattan pier."

"Marine Street gang?" I ask.

"Kids who hung out, traveled to surf spots, good friends. Your dad was part of that group."

Greg squints at the photo and goes quiet, as he did at the Mexican restaurant. He can't offer much else. I've spent months banging on his door, and now I've traveled to California, and that's it? That's all? I press him for more details. He calls a friend in Southern California and grills the friend about my father. His friend recognizes the name but nothing else. Greg hangs up. There were so many people circling around him in those days, Greg says, and it's easy to see how he wouldn't remember them all. The conversation leaves me questioning my father's autobiography. Was Noll really a "good friend," or is Greg's memory just hazier than I hoped it would be? I don't know what to think. Suddenly, my father's misspellings and run-on sentences irritate me. Are there other details in his autobiography he inflated or got wrong? Instead of filling in blanks, talking with Greg raises more questions. And I already have enough questions banging around inside my head.

I put the photo away. After a weekend of peering into another family's life, I'm tired. Piecing together the life of a phantom is taxing. Besides, I don't know what information will help me better understand Robert Waters. But later, when I'm alone in the motel room, I'll realize the details aren't as important as the experience. Building the board—and hanging out with Greg and Jed—has helped me create the first positive memory of my father, one that I'll forever associate with him.

Anyway, there's a father in front of me right now—one of the fathers of a sport I happen to love. I ask Greg how he feels about people holding him in such high regard.

"Oh, I don't know," he says. "At this point in my life, looking back, I'm blown away by the impact surfing has had on the world. I'm honored to think the younger generation would want to know about all the dumb shit we did."

"What dumb shit?" I ask.

His eyebrow shoots up. He stands. He asks me to follow him, and he leads me down the hall to his home office. He opens the door to a big, stand-alone safe and removes a small paper Dixie cup. Then I follow him back to the dining room. He plops the cup on the table, lifts it, and reveals a severed thumb encased in a plug of resin. I stare at it. I don't know what to say.

"This friend from my old shop in Hermosa cut it off on a table saw while making a board," Greg says. The thumb disturbs me. The thumb fascinates me. Bits of fat, or something whitish, have bloomed along the detached edge of the fifty-year-old, hacked-off thumb. "The guy wanted the doctor to sew it back on, but the doctor said, sure, sure he could, but the thumb would die and turn black. So, when the doctor was taking care of my friend, patching him up, I slipped the thumb in my pocket. That night, I filled a cup full of resin and plopped it in."

I lean down and inspect it, touching the cold, rubbery, resin cube. Greg has a smirk on his face. I can sense he's waiting for me to say something. So I say, "Bitchin'."

———————

A RUSH OF WATER delivers me to shore. I ride in on my knees. Water drips down my face from my hair. My arms are noodled, and I've been out for so long that I can't feel my toes. The tops of my feet are red and starting to bruise from banging them against the board's hard tail. Robin helps me bury my feet in the sand. After an hour, I haven't caught one wave.

It's a struggle. And frustrating. For months I've been in and out of the water on the Oregon coast, prepping for this day, surfing regularly, but now everything's different. Because of the board's weight, it blasts through oncoming waves like a freighter, but it's difficult to control when faint rips catch the oversized fin and yank the board sideways. And without a leash I have to chase down the board whenever I fall off, which is exhausting. I don't want the Malibu-chip to hit other surfers.

We sit in the sand for a while and stare at the Santa Monica Mountains. A solid three-footer peaks and breaks apart into soup. Blake is still out there, having fun and waiting for another clean ride.

I tell Robin I can't leave my father's ashes in the water. For one thing, I don't know how to transport the plastic baggie outside the breakers without losing it. Also, this isn't the right place. Manhattan Beach is no longer the same city it once was. It's a cushy town now, the sandy beach lined with multimillion-dollar palaces, and around my father's boyhood house on Pine Avenue are few of the trees that gave the street its name. There's little of my father left here.

A few days ago, after landing in Orange County, we drove south to Jed's shop in San Clemente to retrieve the Malibu-chip. Six weeks had passed since my visit to Crescent City.

When Robin and I stepped through the shop's doors, I was speechless. Jed previously mentioned he was aiming for a "storytelling environment" at his shop. The story being told was the story of his dad. The entire shop paid homage to Greg. Greg is the brand's cornerstone, but I wasn't prepared for the number of posters and photos or the film projected onto the wall. Even Greg's ancient Rolodex, containing old five-digit phone numbers of surfing legends, was on display.

I followed Jed down the hall to a shaping room, where I saw our finished board for the first time, snug in a rack, glassed and beautiful. We carefully took it down. I told him I'd try my best not to ding it. He laughed nervously. An identical board sold for around $6,000 and got wall-mounted by collectors.

Now the Malibu-chip is in the sand, waxed up, a ding in the fin, and I take pleasure in returning it to its true purpose.

At the end of his autobiography, my father wrote, "I wish things could have been different, but it was not, and for that I am truly sorry."

I seize the board and head into the water again. I lift the nose over smaller beach-breaking waves, jump on, and paddle. An oncoming wave washes cool water down the neckline of my wetsuit. There's a lull, and the water flattens. Then another set approaches.

It takes half an hour to arrive, and it isn't the prettiest wave or the biggest, but I set a line and paddle. Like my father, I ride goofy foot. All focus is on the mechanics. In the water, on a wave, I feel a euphoria that's more significant than any I felt in my father's presence. Other than our shared name, our shared blood, water is our only connection. It passes through my fingers—invigorating, cold, and baptismal.

When I finally crawl from the sea, wet and calmed, I know more than anything I want more. I want to finally understand.

GYPSY

I RETURN FROM CALIFORNIA stoked by the possibilities.
I want more experiences like I had with Greg and Jed. Maybe I can swap a lifetime of nonexperiences with a father for positive ones created on my own. Maybe, in the process, the unknown will become known. A vague "plan" takes shape: I will use my father's autobiography as a guide to writing a memoir. And through writing a memoir, I'll figure out this absence, perhaps make something out of nothing, and feel whole.

But first I say goodbye to Robin and Portland, board yet another airplane, and return to Iowa.

Like my father, I bounce from place to place, back and forth, restless and unsettled. Over the past fifteen years, I've lived in four different states, seven different cities, and at eleven different addresses. Even though Robin and I have endured our rocky periods and currently live apart, I'm trying to get some footing in my life. Iowa's part of that, even though Robin's not in Iowa.

We met in the Bay Area. Two sensitive writers, opinionated, argumentative, privately brash, and soon in love. A year together turned into two, then five. To pay rent, I was working full time as a director at a nonprofit eldercare facility in Berkeley when Robin accepted an assistant professor job at a small struggling college in Santa Fe, New Mexico. We were excited by this auspicious new desert adventure. New Mexico's state motto promised us a Land of Enchantment. Robin had achieved what she'd set out to do: write and teach. And I figured I could work on my long novel, which was set in the Southwest. So I quit my job. We moved. In Santa Fe, I picked up freelance writing gigs and worked at environmental nonprofits. Our debut short story collections were published months apart. Things were humming along. We spent the academic year in the desert and summer on the Oregon coast. Robin's next book, a memoir, graced the cover of the *New York Times Book Review*.

Everything shifted the moment her college went out of business. Our decisions were soon influenced by panic rather than reason.

Robin was offered another teaching position at a state university in southern New Mexico, a universe removed from the charm of Santa Fe. The MFA program was a step up for her, and the English department offered me some classes to teach. So we relocated again. Then my father died, a month before the job started, which threw me into a state of confused grieving. Then the novel I'd worked on for years failed to sell in New York. And I grew depressed. So did Robin. The English department was toxic, rife with infighting and political maneuvering. New Mexico started to feel more like the Land of Entrapment. After eight months, Robin agonized over whether to quit the job. Her goal all along was to teach and write, but Las Cruces was a difficult place to live for both of us. In the end Robin took a leave of absence, and we washed up in Oregon, her native state, renting a one-bedroom bungalow in Portland, where more troubles piled up.

In Portland, we both found freelance work, and Robin secured another teaching gig at a low-residency writing program, but I was essentially jobless. And I was still quietly grieving the death of a man I never knew. We fought about the difficulties of finding a job in a terrible job market during the Great Recession. Robin was upset I hadn't formed any sort of life plan. I argued I'd been too busy helping her chase a career to build a solid vision of my own. We were stalled, in limbo. We were hurt. We argued. We fought. I was flailing. I wondered how I had ended up in such a precarious place. I had willingly followed her from job to job, place to place, with the foolish belief my novel would sell and I'd land on my feet. It didn't. I had a resume full of disparate skills, but all I really knew was writing. So, in a fit of self-preservation, I did what any jobless, distraught, midthirties male writer in a strained relationship and nearing a nervous breakdown would do: I applied to the Iowa Writers' Workshop. And got accepted. Not only that, the program offered me a top fellowship. It included a living stipend with health insurance for both of us.

I made the decision.

Now that Robin and I have been through couple's counseling and sorted through most of the arguments, we're mending our relationship from a distance.

Robin needed to feel rooted. So, she stayed in Oregon.

I needed to feel the work I'd been doing for years was worthy. I needed validation. So, I left.

My father bequeathed a bit of money to me. Now I'm burning through the inheritance by flying back and forth to visit Robin. With his money, I bought a new surfboard. With his money, I paid off some debts. And with the help of his money, I decide to write a memoir about my relationship to that disappeared man.

———

BACK IN IOWA CITY in my small rental house, I search for the original copy of "The Story of My Life." I find it inside a beat-up cardboard box in the basement. I'd only brought a photocopy to California. I'm glad I did because I spilled cherry-flavored Gatorade on the pages at the beach. But the original, bound by a red report cover, is spotless. It looks the same as it did on that afternoon a decade ago when I stood outside my San Francisco apartment and retrieved it from the mailbox.

Now I carry it upstairs and set it on my desk.

"The Story of My Life" is clumsy, amateurish, and littered with flaws. The format mimics a textbook—dedication page, table of contents, epilogue, etc. Sentences often skip between tenses. My father chose to describe his life in Times New Roman. At the end of each chapter is a completion date. The book has no emotional arc, but it's a solid text—informative, detailed, and unintentionally cruel. The middle chapters, the missing years, are difficult to skim.

As I slowly flip through "The Story of My Life," reading random paragraphs, the sixty-eight pages of paper seem to grow heavier. The document emits vibrations. I set it on my desk and stare out the window. In my small home office, a converted bedroom, there's a black ergonomic desk chair, reading lounger with footstool, forest green walls, wood floors, cheap rug, a framed poster of Greg Noll at Pipeline, closet full of clothes and books, birch midcentury file cabinet, printer, and now a battered cardboard box boiling over with my father's artifacts.

The same apprehensive feeling that surfaced before the California trip returns. It's hard wading around in feelings I've spent my life sidestepping. Thinking about him makes me reenter the same jet stream I just passed through. Abandonment fucks with the soul, and it's challenging to gather the energy to pursue someone who never spent any energy on me.

I've twice attempted to write about him and the other men who briefly auditioned for his role. Both attempts failed. The first attempt at memoir, at twenty-four, stalled at 127 manuscript pages, and the second broke apart around page 116.

What kind of story could I possibly tell when nearly everything's a mystery? Where to begin?

Maybe just begin with a sentence: I met my father for the first time in a Reno casino.

I LEAF THROUGH his autobiography. I uncap a blue pen and draw stars next to potential activities. Perhaps visiting the places he lived will put his disappearance into some kind of understandable context. With the help of Greg and Jed, I untangled his early years. By straining to understand him, I felt a small connection.

He had a wandering life, so I have a lot of options. He was in the navy. He sailed yachts. He was a desert rambler. When he eventually chose a career and settled down, he worked at the Yucca Mountain nuclear waste site in southern Nevada. This is about as much as I know: basics and outlines. But the places he describes in his book are places I'd like to see. The activities he did, I want to do.

According to chapter 4—"Navy"—he was a third-class torpedoman's mate on the USS *Menhaden*, a *Balao*-class submarine that operated around the Pacific. Though I know nothing about military matters, I force myself to get interested.

A computer search turns up two *Balao*-class submarines that allow visitors to sleep aboard. One is in Oklahoma, the other in San Francisco. For a moment I wonder whether there's another man out there seeking connection to his lost father, a man who wants to sleep on a replica of his father's old submarine? Probably not. Anyway, it could be a semi-interesting excursion: board the sub and sleep in the same spot my father did—near the torpedo hold, if that's even possible. Maybe I'll learn something. Maybe I'll *feel* something different.

I write down a short, manageable list.

Next, I'll sail on a yacht.

After losing interest in surfing, my father crewed on yachts in Santa Barbara, as outlined in chapter 5—"Sailing." He competed in races. He was a "master mariner" and earned his advanced piloting license. After retirement he moved to Whidbey Island and bought a Catalina 30 and named her *Zephyr*. So, okay, here's my next journey: locate his former yacht and convince her owners to let me sail on it.

Finally, curious about chapter 8, "Government Service," I consider a trip into the Nevada desert. A visit to my father's former workplace might prove enlightening. The trip, as I imagine it, will take me to the Nevada National Security Site, formerly known as the Nevada Test Site. At the western edge is Yucca Mountain, once designated as the dumping grounds for the nation's nuclear waste. Years of protests and political wrangling eventually quashed that plan. Yucca Mountain borders several military installations. It's about ten miles as the crow flies from Groom Lake, or Area 51. Nearly a thousand underground nuclear tests were conducted nearby on the hydrographic flats. Today, the National Security Site is still home to all sorts of radioactive waste. As I study the area using Google Earth, the flats appear pockmarked from all the detonations. And that's where I want to explore. I just have to convince the Department of Energy to give me access to one of the most heavily guarded and contaminated government installations on the planet, with a notebook in my hand, and a camera.

I study my short list:

> Sleep aboard a submarine.
> Sail on my father's old yacht.
> Take a long, curious, meandering stroll around
> the Nevada National Security Site.

Okay, sure: no problem. After all, I talked Greg and Jed into building a surfboard with me, so how hard could these three things be?

———

THEN DAYS TURN INTO WEEKS. Weeks bunch into a month, and I return to Portland again. As we move through the winter holidays, my initial excitement about the "plan" falls off a cliff. The more I actually think about re-creating my father's experiences and writing about them, the more I procrastinate and avoid. And whenever I audition an opening sentence I realize each is totally melodramatic:

When I received his autobiography in the mail, I was flattered he'd taken the time to tell me about his life, but soon, the document began to scare me, as though it was laced with anthrax, as though it had the power to destroy me, and without the will to read it I felt I was keeping a bomb around my apartment.

One night in mid-January, I broach the topic with Robin after dinner. We're in the bungalow's living room. The lights are dim, the room is warm, and the Flaming Lips drift in from the stereo in the bedroom. For months since returning from California, we've been talking over my memoir idea.

"I'm lost. I don't know how to write this thing," I tell her. "Each start just leads to a dead end. Maybe I should just forget about it."

"What you said about visiting the places your father lived, that sounds interesting," Robin says. "Paying homage."

"But it's not paying homage. Why would I pay homage?"

"Well, what is it, then?"

"I don't know. Stepping into his shoes, I guess. Learning more about him through meaningful adventures. If it can't be meaningful, I don't want to write about it. Surfing felt meaningful. But these other ideas? Traveling to Yucca Mountain? Shit, I just don't know."

Robin published her well-regarded memoir several years ago. I value her advice because she's smart, insightful, and because she sees through my bullshit. Whenever I give her drafts to read, she often tells me to delete this paragraph or that page, which always irritates me, but of course she's often right.

She's on the couch, feet up, knitting. I'm lying on the rug, stretching out a kink in my back.

"I mean," I say, "how in the hell am I even supposed to explore my fury at abandonment? How do you do that?"

"Well, when you do write about it, just remember to stop and open the story up in places," she says. "We both have a tendency toward darkness. Remember to add moments of lightness to your story."

"Moments of lightness?"

"Good memories. You know, scenes with some humor. Give the reader room to breathe." Her clicking needles sound like scurrying crabs.

I return to Iowa City for the spring semester. I forget about the memoir and finish a short story about an aging surfer who meets his son for the first time in Baja California. I attend the required workshop sessions, always thankful I'm not the only thirty-something enrolled in the program. I file the *Outside* story about building a surfboard with Greg and Jed, and while I briefly confront my father in the story, I leave so much unsaid. I bury the memoir idea and keep busy with several book review assignments for the *San Francisco Chronicle*. I slip on running shoes and punish my legs at the university gym. I read other memoirs, deciding every memoir ever written is more urgent, more thoughtful, and better written than anything I could ever write: *The Mistress's Daughter, Son of a Gun, Fierce Attachments, Another Bullshit Night in Suck City, The Duke of Deception, Why Be Happy When You Could Be Normal?*

Excuses plague me. Write a memoir? Me? Sure, I'm comfortable dressing friends and acquaintances in fictional clothing, but the idea of writing a book about my life — the loss, anger, vulnerabilities — strikes me as tacky and self-absorbed and reckless. My pain is no greater than another's pain. I'm not a former child soldier. I didn't escape from a North Korean labor camp. Besides, what's the point? Will the endeavor make me *feel* better? And anyway, didn't the memoir-as-therapy fad peak in the late 1990s?

What's more, I dislike the notion of being thought of as some kind of casualty, as in *Look what the world did to me*, instead of *Hey, look what I did in the world!* So much of memoir, besides, is invention. How can you re-create childhood or even adulthood events and remain accurate and honest? It's impossible. Complicated life events get reduced to token scenes. Fabrication reigns. Too often in memoir the chaos of life gets repackaged into swallowable lessons about "acceptance" and "closure." Also, I'm not interested in writing a memoir with the standard novelistic storytelling arc. The story feels far too complex. Not to mention, the whole idea makes me feel exposed. And, of course, I harbor sick fantasies: I envision you, reader, picking up my book, reading a few paragraphs, and snickering, *Hey, check out this loser!*

In April, I return to Portland yet again for another extended visit. Early one morning, I rise early, make coffee, and sit with my notebook in the bungalow's living room, looking over half a page of memoir notes. I have so little.

After months of kicking around the memoir idea, I finally make the decision: I can't do it. And I give up. For the third time. I just can't do it. I don't know how. Opening the door on the past invites nearly constant pressure inside my chest. My father is a shadow of a shadow. He'll always be a shadow of a shadow. And so I decide to emulate Mom by keeping past events at a safe, manageable distance, content to disregard how the past shapes the present. I shove "The Story of My Life" inside my computer bag. I shove the bag in the closet. I abandon the idea. Like he abandoned me. I feel like a fool for considering it.

Life is moving along fine now. Sure, Robin and I have weathered a lot. Her mother's death, my father's. Despite our arguments, our resentments about how things played out in New Mexico, we've stayed together. Eleven years. That's more or less a marriage. I've never felt closer or more connected to another person. There were certainly some deep ruts in the road early on, including facing my issues with anger and trust and attachment. These days, I've noticed, we're caring for each other in ways that signal we're still a team. At home, we listen to Lucinda Williams and gossip and drink wine and watch stupid reality TV dating shows and dance ridiculous dances in the kitchen while singing along to Air Supply's "All Out of Love." We enjoy taking the dog on hikes at the coast. When I laugh while reading on the couch, it makes Robin laugh in another room. In the past we've vacationed in Tulum, Montana, New York, Maui, and Romania. The rental bungalow where we washed up sits on a quiet street near a park in the hills above downtown Portland, and we both think our dog, Mercy, is the strangest, most incredible animal alive. Sure, we argue about household chores, and even though I complain about feeling aggrieved for doing all of the vacuuming, I also conveniently forget Robin does most of the cooking. It's a partnership, more or less a modern, bohemian life. So why would I want to complicate the balance by wasting time looking for ghosts inside the haunted houses of my past? I need to move on.

The Pacific is about an hour's drive from the bungalow. I head over the coastal range and pull into a parking lot along the highway. To the south, drifting fog makes Neahkahnie Mountain appear shrouded in smoke. I get naked in my pickup and wrestle on my wetsuit. Then I shove a jug of water, an apple, and a plug of wax in my backpack. I free my board from the straps and carry it one-armed along a soggy path cut into a sloping hill dense with ferns, spruce, Douglas firs, and salamanders. Short Sand Creek runs shallow below an arched wooden bridge, and everything smells wet and pregnant. It seems like every fern and shrub is a different shade of green, punctuated here and there with purple flowers bursting from rhododendrons.

The beach appears through the trees. Twin capes form the cove, sheltering it from coastal winds. This area is known as Smugglers Cove. A pirate ship was supposedly spotted here long ago, and the surrounding state park, Oswald West, was named after the governor who fought to keep Oregon beaches public property.

The winds can still whip around the headlands, and today the air smells ripe and briny. It's shivery weather, hovering just above sixty degrees.

Short Sands brings to mind Crescent City—few people, epic scenery, and surfers enduring the same cold water. Before I make my way in, I pass several beachgoers who have staked a camp around a driftwood pile.

One little girl runs toward the surging water with her arms raised. When a wave crashes, she turns and runs back to her mother, giggling. I overhear the mother ask her daughter about the waves, and the girl says, "It's scary."

"It's scary?"

"Yep," the little girl says, clenching her fists.

I set my backpack against a half-buried boulder, strap on the leash, and wade in. From shore the waves don't appear too imposing, but it's different when you move into them. A few people float on their boards around the same area, where incoming swells hit the sandy bottom to form some decently sized waves.

I clutch the nose of my board and pitch it under an oncoming wave. It passes. Another comes. And another. I plunge the nose again and jump on and paddle toward one more, turtle rolling before it collapses and shoves me back. I keep at it for ten minutes, getting thrashed. It's a struggle to get outside. The cold water energizes me, but getting accustomed to the feeling of ice cubes rushing into my suit and across my chest is always gnarly at first.

Finally, an opening. Again, I paddle hard, feeling my back strain, and pop over the lip. The wave crashes behind me. I've made it. I need to rest. Three feet, four feet—the waves are small but powerful and the water is frigid. When I'm lying on my stomach, a three- or four-foot pyramidal wave can seem mountainous. Waves bully you until you learn how to get along.

Forty yards from shore, I join a loose crew spread out along the break. I choose my spot, sit up, shove my hands in my armpits, and wait. Everyone's friendly, which I like. There's an unspoken agreement that if you've made it this far—*if you're out here*—you're due some minor respect. Nearby, a woman raises her gloved hand and claims a wave, and I watch her drop in and carve across it.

There's little wind. The wandering fog reduces visibility to about three hundred yards. It's a marginal swell, and I wait just outside the impact zone, where waves bend into frothy surf. My legs dangle in the green, murky water. I triangulate by choosing a banana-shaped chunk of beach driftwood and the tallest tree on the southern cliff. The idea is to maneuver into the best position to catch a wave. I'm not by any means a remarkable surfer, certainly not like those raised near the ocean. Out of ten attempts, I'll catch three rides if luck's with me, but each ride will push a thrilling tingle up my spine, which makes me return for more. Those other seven attempts? I'll get whipped, crushed, destroyed.

Flotsam drifts by—seaweed, waterlogged branches. It's not unusual for seals to poke their heads above the water and scare the shit out of me. A gigantic concrete dock recently washed up on shore at my other surf spot, Agate Beach, about a hundred miles south of here. I showed up one morning and there it was, beached. Later I learned the dock had drifted from Japan, a remnant of the tsunami. Scientists from Hatfield Marine Center descended with blowtorches, afraid of invasive species, scorching every living barnacle.

Now, out on the water, the girl and her mom look smaller. I wonder how we look to them. Little black specks, Thursday morning escapees.

Before shoving his autobiography inside my computer bag and kicking the bag into the closet, I finished reading through the entire document. I read slowly, knowing I would never read it again. His autobiography told me everything and told me nothing: just a jumbled chronology of facts and anecdotes. He lectured. He summarized. He pontificated on subjects I don't care about and overlooked subjects I do. When something agreeable happened in his life—when he found a job, opened a surf shop—he punctuated these occasions with the phrase "Life was good."

While I read, I looked for similarities in our lives, places of overlap. I wanted to connect our disparate stories. After all, we understand our lives through narrative. We're born. We graduate. Fall in love. Marry. Have children. Stories connect these events. Beginning with our earliest memories, we develop a personal story, and over time that story—how we got from *there* to *here*—accumulates more stories, and the sum of these stories helps us situate ourselves in life's continuum.

In my story, my father is a character who vanished and then made a late reappearance. His absence from the backstory confused my early narrative and still disrupts my present one. Very early on, I learned to manage my story to control my shame. I learned to lie. I learned not to ask Mom.

A central tenet of good parenting is to help your child build self-worth and self-definition through mirroring and validation. Like the mother asking her girl about the waves. By asking, the mom validated. By repeating, she mirrored. My mirrors were warped. Without a father around, I questioned—again and again—my worth as a person and my very existence.

According to childhood behaviorists, children are naturally self-centered little creatures. They're unable to see the world beyond their narrow perspectives. Children believe that anything that happens, good or bad, is a consequence of their own actions. When my father left, my young mind interpreted his disappearance as something I did. It was me: I did it. I did it, and since I did it, I must be horrible. All these years later, even though I talk to a therapist weekly, even though I understand how the young mind processes information, that black cloud still follows me around.

I maintain my position by triangulating between two distant points, easing my hands into the water, paddling forward, backward. I wait for the right wave to guide me back to shore.

———

A MEMORY OF WATER: the river, the beach, water sliding over polished rock. In the Sierras: a gigantic blue bowl cuddled by pine-capped, granite peaks. Downtown: a frigid vein of snowmelt coursing under bridged streets.

In the desert there's little water, so you appreciate it when you encounter it. Water in community swimming pools. Water in casino fountains. Water in the baptismal tubs. Water in the font at the entrance of St. Therese of the Little Flower one bright Sunday in 1980, when I'm seven years old.

Mom dips three fingers in the brass font and crosses herself. I do the same. I follow her down the long carpeted aisle, and soon the organ bleats. The procession begins. Our priest walks behind an altar boy, a boy not much older than me, who carries the cross. I want to be the boy leading the priest, the man everyone calls *Father*. He's father of the church, our Father, a man who looks after us. On some Sundays, Father blesses water and then moves among us and sprinkles our faces.

I sit beside Mom in a hard wooden pew, kicking at the kneeler so it will fall onto my toe. A game I play. Nothing much happens during Mass. Mom grabs my knee, shakes her head. It's early, seven thirty. None of my catechism friends are here. We stand, sit, and kneel as holy songs echo around the clean white nave. Sunlight pierces the faces of the saints in the glass windows. Catechism classes led to my taking holy communion, and when the moment comes I join others in taking the host. I like this part of Mass.

After Mass, Mom lights a cigarette outside and blows smoke into the wind. Her tight brown curls are still damp. We find our yellow Datsun Honeybee in the lot, and she cracks the window, flicking ash as we drive. My job is the stereo, the music. I move the orange radio lever between stations. I want to find that Eddie Rabbitt song. "Drivin' My Life Away."

"Stop there," Mom says. "I like that one."

I keep moving the dial.

"Wait. Go back," she says. "I like that song."

I move the dial to the end until there's static. I turn back to the station Mom wants. I know this one. Linda Ronstadt. "When Will I Be Loved?" I like this one, too.

New neighborhoods far from our downtown apartment have popped up in the desert like dandelions. Mom drives out to one of these developments and parks underneath five poles with colorful, flapping flags.

"Looks like this is it, kiddo," she says.

A paved path connects four model homes, each a different color, each with different floor plans. We walk through the first.

"Not a big fan of these bedrooms," Mom says. "Kind of boxy and not enough light. Wait, there's a half bath near the kitchen, so that's convenient. What's the square footage?" She plucks the flier from my hands. "Hmm. Twelve hundred square feet," she says. "It'd be nice if there was a basement."

Two bedrooms, three bedrooms. It doesn't matter. I love each one. The houses are bright and large and beautiful. The square patches of grass out front look fluorescent green. I imagine running up and down the carpeted hallways. I imagine getting rid of the fake books and cardboard television sets. I imagine playing with my dog, Patches, in the fenced backyard.

I imagine praying alone in my own room, instead of praying with Mom before climbing the ladder to the top bunk of our bed. Our apartment is brick, one bedroom, small. And the fridge broke, and now we're keeping food in a beach cooler on the concrete stoop.

A young woman, a saleswoman, greets us in the kitchen in the last model. It smells like cookies.

It's going to be a lovely neighborhood, the woman says. Good school district, she says. Nice homes, and a grocery store nearby. Convenient. Mom has promised me some day, one day, we will live in a house.

I grab a chocolate chip cookie off the counter, overhearing them discuss money. The woman mentions the minimum down payment, and Mom's eyes dart from stove to fridge to chandelier. Later, as we walk to the Datsun, Mom musses my hair. "Someday, kiddo," she says. We head over to Burger King. At Burger King there's no such thing as down payments.

THE MORNING AFTER surfing Short Sands, I'm up at seven o'clock. I'm usually the first awake — brew the coffee, let Mercy outside. I enjoy mornings. Out the window, Portland's idea of a spring day is comical. The sky is a solid block of grey. This is definitely Def Leppard weather.

I carry a mug into the bedroom for Robin. "Coffee," I say.

"No, no, I'm sleeping," she says.

She's buried beneath tangled sheets. It looks like a bomb went off in our bed. I don't understand how we always manage to thoroughly demolish the bed. I also notice an old, yellowed book on the bedside table called Name Your Baby. I bought it years ago at a yard sale for a quarter, thinking I'd consult it whenever I needed to name a character. Robin's been going through it.

When she emerges, her hair is an interesting shape. She sits up and takes a sip. The dog watches us with her paws curled beneath her head.

"Look at how cute she is," Robin says in her morning voice. "It's amazing humans ever took over the earth. We are not as cute as that."

"How's your morning look?" I ask.

"Still reading those damn story packets," she says. "It's never-ending."

"What about working on your novel for a while?"

"Ha," she says.

Even though her teaching job requires a lot of reading, she's engaged, challenged, and part of a greater community. One reason for going to Iowa, I told Robin, was to improve my odds at securing some kind of teaching job like hers.

I leave Robin in the bedroom with her coffee and the dog.

On the couch, first thing, I decide to update my curriculum vitae. I want to send out a few letters of introduction to low-residency programs. Securing a position in the current academic job market requires an absolutely sparkling curriculum vitae and a dazzling letter. I've also learned it requires some magical combination of pixie dust and outrageous luck.

With my earbuds in, I put on Def Leppard's *Hysteria*, turn on my computer, and locate an online journal database, scrolling down the page, looking for specific journals where my older stories appeared. I'm hunting for exact dates and volume numbers to plug into my CV.

Something odd pops up on the screen. I'm surprised to find my name next to short stories I never wrote. I lean closer. Another writer with my name. Another writer named Don Waters.

It's the first time I've ever noticed him. Several of his stories are aggregated alongside several of mine, or mine alongside his, whichever. At first glance this other Don Waters looks fairly prolific, which annoys me. I browse another online database and notice his name again — our name. At the bottom of a list of his stories is one of mine. It's clearly a cataloguing error, but I'm intrigued by the idea that two writers, in the vague electronic universe of the web, have melded into one.

I spend the morning looking into him. I surf around the web. As weird as it is googling my name — and let's face it, it's a supremely self-absorbed way to pass time — this other Don Waters guy is a wonderful distraction. Better to look into his accomplishments than worry about mine, I figure.

One website contains an extensive list of his stories and the years of publication. I begin a tally on a piece of scratch paper. He published eighty-three stories, articles, and novelettes between 1924 and 1970. If some random website lists eighty-three publications, I know there are bound to be many more.

By the end of the day, I've accomplished little and feel guilty about it. The day is just gone, wasted, when I could have been updating my CV or sketching ideas for a new novel. Instead, I've poked around for info about a dead guy with my name. I decide the whole doppelganger thing is just a coincidence. It's common in the internet age.

That night during dinner, I mention him to Robin, who thinks I spent the afternoon crafting a job letter.

"Another writer with your name?" she says. She seems interested.

"I googled him, his name—our name—over and over, trying different combinations," I say. "I found historical records."

"Someone told me they googled my name and got an accountant in New York."

"Right, right—someone told you," I say. "And how often do you search your name?"

"I don't, it's too weird," she says. "After I read that stupid comment someone wrote about my memoir, I stopped looking."

"I also found an Australian painter," I say. "And a contractor in the Bay Area. And a librarian with the Mellon Foundation. Among others." These others exist in distant universes. They aren't real. They're name-appropriating impostors. "But there might be something here," I say. "With this other guy. Maybe a novel. I don't know."

"But what about your memoir?"

"I don't want to think about writing a memoir anymore."

The next morning, I wake up thinking about him. About Don Waters. Googling only gets me so far, so I head down the wet, rainy hill to Portland State University's library. Overlooking an urban park, the building has a horseshoe-shaped wall of windows that allows grey light to filter into the utilitarian lobby. I stroll through the underlit corridors until I locate the fiction stacks. The book I'm after, an anthology of sea stories published by the *Saturday Evening Post*, lists Don Waters's story in the table of contents. Seeing his name—our name—featured below Ray Bradbury and Jack London gives me a brief, narcissistic thrill. I find an out-of-the-way table and read Don's story, "Vengeance Reef," a sea escapade starring a protagonist named John Pindar. Don's language is somewhat outdated, but I enjoy the story. He wrote about subjects that interest me.

I carry my curiosity about Don back to Iowa City for the final weeks of spring term. I join the local library to access online newspaper archives from both city and university libraries.

I spend the next few days piecing together a partial biography, enough to convince me I'd like to know more about him. Every little scrap of information leads me to believe he led the kind of bitchin' life I dream about living.

Throughout the 1920s and 1930s, Don wrote adventure stories for pulp magazines. I find citations for three adventure novels published in the late '20s. A decade later, he graduated to the "slicks"—the *Saturday Evening Post*, *Collier's*, etc.

But his best-known book was a work of narrative nonfiction.

Gypsy Waters Cruises South was published in 1938 and put him on the map. The *New Yorker* proclaimed the book "sure-fire." Other positive reviews appeared in the *New York Times* and *Chicago Tribune*. It was a "Book of the Week" in the March 6, 1938, edition of the *Washington Post*.

Now, seven decades after publication, Don's book is out of print.

At home, I order *Gypsy Waters Cruises South* from an online antiquarian bookseller for twenty dollars. The book's original price was three. From another bookseller I order the January 20, 1940, edition of the *Saturday Evening Post*, which features Don's story "Man Killer." The accompanying illustration is by Norman Rockwell.

Gypsy Waters Cruises South arrives a week later. And it can't come quickly enough. I spend the week growing convinced my next big writing project will include the other Don Waters—and not my father. The book is cloth-bound, with slight damage to the spine, and the illustrated blue-and-white cover is gorgeous.

I sit in the lounger in my home office and open it.

The book flap corroborates information I've already gathered. In 1931, at the height of the Great Depression, Don put his family on a yacht he rebuilt with his own hands and set sail. Even more incredible, the family lived and sailed on the yacht for a decade, like a seafaring Swiss Family Robinson. Don's daughter, Gypsy, was central to his life. He even named the yacht—their home—"Gypsy Waters" in her honor.

While the family roamed the southeastern seaboard, Don turned their escapades into paying magazine articles, which were collected and published in the book I now held in my hands. I skim the book, choosing random paragraphs, flipping forward, backward, and return to the beginning. They sailed everywhere. Florida, the Keys, Dry Tortugas. They cruised wherever they wanted, wherever the wind carried them, living an extreme oceanic life.

In the front of the book are black-and-white pictures of Don, his wife, Margaret, and their young daughter, Gypsy. Don sits at the wheel wearing a floppy fisherman's hat. Margaret and Gypsy wear sun hats. For a moment

I imagine color blooming on the glossy paper and filling their grey cheeks with life. I envision them stepping off the page. Don was a sailor—like my father. Don loved the ocean—like my father did. But unlike my father, Don was there for his child.

He steered his small family into a roiling ocean, and he kept them together and kept them safe.

Throughout my life I've patched together a sort of imaginary straw father inside me by collecting father figures and emulating the men I admire. That early learned behavior is now a reflex, and even though I'm in my midthirties, even though he's a dead stranger, I nudge Don into that father category. Like I did with Greg. Like I've done with so many older men.

His family's story seems emblematic of all that's missing from mine. The Waters family was a tight-knit, nuclear trio, and as I lean back in the lounger, thumbing through *Gypsy Waters Cruises South*, I realize Don might serve a deeper purpose. His story is the perfect counterweight to the story still dogging me.

———

I RIP DUCT TAPE OFF the cardboard flaps and pour the box's contents on the rug in my office. His family mailed several boxes to me, and I brought them with me to Iowa.

Among my father's artifacts are three photo albums, each arranged chronologically. The albums are like image guides that complement the chapters in his autobiography. Stuck to one page in the middle album is the first letter I wrote to him.

Dear Father,
I would really like to get to know you too.

The albums. Newspaper clippings. Navy patches. Snapshots of a life I never knew about. I'm surprised to find two photos of Mom tucked inside the plastic side pocket. I've never seen them before.

One shows her in a grassy yard, her long dark hair cascading down her back. She's sitting. She has wide-set eyes and a large smile. Robin often says we look alike. In the photo, Mom's wearing a loose yellow sleeveless blouse and reddish orange pants. She holds her bent knee with a hand that also holds a cigarette. She's quite the 1970s postage stamp.

The other is a black-and-white yearbook-sized photo. She looks to be in her late twenties or early thirties, hair severely parted down the middle, and her green eyes turned grey in the colorless photo. I discover handwriting on the back.

> Bob, I've only known you a week — it's been the happiest week in my life. I hope we'll spend many more together. Love, Donna.

It's unbelievable. It's the first and only time I've ever seen a loving gesture between my parents. To think they ever loved or appreciated or even *knew* each other floors me. I don't know how they met. In his autobiography my father only wrote, "I meet your mother, we fall in love, marry, and have a baby together, you. Life is good."

I open the first album, pausing at a photo of the three of us — our small family. It's almost impossible, yet here we are. The generic blue-grey backdrop suggests the photo might have been taken at a department store photo studio. I must be about a year old. I'm in red and sporting a sort of baby mod hairdo. Mom, also in red, wears pearls and a blue-striped blazer. She's squinting. My father, who's heavier than in his surfing days, wears a light blue shirt. Everyone smiles. My father's forearm clutches my hip. My tiny fingers touch his arm.

This same photo was part of my childhood landscape, only I remember it differently because my father was scissored out. There were other photos like this one, each visited by scissors, each bearing a ghostly, uneven outline. In Mom's photo albums my father was gone, cut out, *vanished*. Everything was gone but his hand. Mom would have had to cut part of my tiny body from the picture to remove his hand. So there was his hand. The only image I had of him was a hand. For seventeen years, a hand.

I close the albums. I want facts to explain why he left and why Mom cut out his face.

I set their divorce papers next to "The Story of My Life."

The papers were filed in the Second Judicial District Court two days before Christmas in 1977. Mom cited "incompatibility" as grounds for divorce. She asked my father to "keep in force" a life insurance policy naming me as beneficiary. She asked him for $150 a month "for the support and maintenance of said child during his minority." In exchange for the above, my father would get visitation rights.

On December 27, 1977, he was served a summons at his temporary residence in Kingman, Arizona, where he was working at a copper mine. He signed it.

At a final hearing in March 1978, the "defendant did not appear, and default was entered against him." The court awarded Mom "the care, custody and control of the minor child." The court awarded my father "the stereo, camping equipment and Defendant's personal belongings."

Mom got me.

He got the sleeping bag.

In "The Story of My Life" he moves swiftly past the messy details. He doesn't offer a mea culpa. In his version he comes off as persecuted and a victim of outrageous circumstances.

"I had been handed a raw deal," he wrote. "At the time in the State of Nevada there was no requirement that the other spouse be represented in the court where the divorce was ruled on. That lack of procedure deprived me from having any contact with you until you turned eighteen. Laws have come into existence since then to prevent such abuses."

What does he mean by "there was no requirement that the other spouse be represented?" Is he implying Mom sneaked into court and got a divorce without his knowledge? And that phrase "prevent such abuses." He signed the summons. He knew about the court date. I just don't understand him. If Mom injured him so deeply, why did he keep these photos of her in a special pocket in his album?

And *why* was his not appearing in court justification for Mom to never speak about him, and to erase evidence of his existence?

What the hell happened?

For a moment I try to imagine them—him, thirty-five; her, thirty-four—engaging in an argument of such magnitude that it severed all contact. For thirty-two years, from the day of the divorce in 1977 to his death in 2009, they never spoke another word to each other.

An old, unexpected weight settles in me. Sussing out the full story suddenly seems vital to my well-being. I need to understand what happened. I could care less about writing a memoir. I just need to understand what happened for my own sense of self. So much of what I've privately struggled with has its origins in that distant time period. Everything can be traced back, like emotional and psychological carbon dating. It can be unearthed and examined. I don't understand my parents' relationship.

Even though we have issues with each other, I love Mom. What I don't understand is why she ever loved him. And what I truly don't understand is why an elemental part of me loves him too.

———————

ANOTHER MEMORY: a vanishing. It's November, before Thanksgiving. It's afternoon. And we're moving fast down the hot desert highway. I'm in the backseat. Mom says it's gone. The Datsun Honeybee is gone.

"Gone?" I say.

"Wrecked," she says. "Manny wrecked it."

"Where's Manny?"

"We'll find out," she says.

"Is Manny okay?" I ask.

"I'm sure he's fine," Mom says. Mom's friend drives. She's got striped hair, like a skunk. We keep a lookout for the car. Mom says it's out here. Somewhere in the desert.

"Damn it," Mom says.

Manuel is like family. He's like a dad to me. He's from Mexico, an architect. He unrolls his blueprints for me with trembling hands, lifts me onto his lap, and shows me things he's making. He has black hair and dark eyes and a bushy mustache. We go for walks. He's nice to me. He's nice to Mom.

"Wait, wait. Slow down. It's supposed to be around here," Mom says. She points. "Wait! There it is," she says.

We slow. Mom's friend pulls to the side of the road. Mom's right. There it is. Our Datsun Honeybee is upside down in the ditch.

"Totaled," Mom says. "Damn it." She's silent for a long time. "I can't stop thinking about it. What if one of us had been with him last night?" She turns and stares at me. Her hand grips the plastic seat. "I mean, what if you were with him?"

That night, I'm outside on the concrete stoop when Manuel returns to the apartment. He's limping. There are bandages on his face and dried blood around his ear. He smiles and shoves a fist into his pants. He brings out a handful of quarters.

"For your Ms. Pac-Man game," he says. "Try to stretch it out this time. Sometimes it seems like you lose on purpose so you can ask me for more quarters." He goes inside and I follow, but Mom meets me at the door and tells me to wait outside.

There's nothing to do on the stoop except watch the crab apples fall off the trees in the dirt lot. Through the door I hear Mom and Manuel talking. I hear crying. I wait for almost an hour. I get up and walk around the gravel lane to Carlton's place. I knock. His dad answers the door.

"Carlton, your friend's here," his dad says.

Carlton comes outside, carrying his dad's puffy boxing gloves. "Want to box?" he says.

"Okay," I say.

We walk back to my apartment and sit on the stoop. The boxing gloves hang around his neck by the laces.

"Want to go first? Or me?" Carlton says.

"Maybe me," I say.

"But I want you to go," he says.

We only have one pair of gloves, so one of us puts on the gloves and beats the other. Then we switch. We stop punching when we're out of air, or when the other starts yelling. It's fun.

"My dad says we're gonna choose our own Christmas tree this year," Carlton says. "We're gonna go find one in the mountains and chop it down."

"Cool."

"My dad says you can come if you want."

"Okay."

Carlton slides his brown arms deep inside the gloves. The gloves reach to his elbows. He asks me to get the laces.

"Make them real tight," he says, and I do.

Carlton stands, bounces on his feet. He punches the air. He bobs. I make myself ready. I put my arms up. I don't like being the one without the gloves.

The apartment door opens. Mom's eyes are red. "Hello, Carlton," she says. "Donny, can you please come inside?"

Carlton says, "Ah, man." The gloves fall against his side. "We were about to box."

"I know," Mom says. She looks at me. "But I need you inside, kiddo."

Inside, Manuel is on the couch. He asks me to sit next to him. He smells like onions and beer. Mom sits too.

"We're about to box," I say. "Carlton's waiting."

"He's going to have to wait," Manuel says. "We need to talk to you." He looks at Mom. "I need to talk to you. Look. I have a disease. I need to tell you I have a disease. And the disease made me pass out. And I need to get help."

His eyes are wet. And red. Like Mom's. Manuel says he rolled our Datsun Honeybee. He didn't mean to, but he did.

"We've decided to part ways," Mom says.

Manuel nods. Then he puts his face in his hands and starts crying. Seeing him cry makes me want to cry.

"Why?" I say.

"Because that's what's best," Mom says.

"Manuel isn't going to live with us anymore?" I ask.

"No, he's not," Mom says.

I lean into him. Manuel puts his arm around me. He's warm, so warm. He squeezes me and pats my arm. "You're a good kid," he says. "You're a real good kid."

The next day, Manuel is gone.

———————

TWO BLACK-AND-WHITE PHOTOS glow on my computer screen.

There he is, aboard the *John R. Manta*, one of the last whaling vessels to sail out of New Bedford, Massachusetts. The ship's 1925 manifest lists Don Waters as the "boatsteerer." His age: thirty-eight. He's a year older than me. Height: 5' 6". He's also five inches shorter.

According to my research, the *John R. Manta* set out on its final voyage two years later. Soon after that, the era of American whaling drew to an end.

I locate the photos in the New Bedford Whaling Museum's online archives. I call the museum, wanting more info, but the attendant who answers can't offer anything other than what's already written in the captions.

Don's handsome. There's something special about him, as though he possesses a brand of confidence shaped by stunning feats. The first photo shows him cutting a young seaman's hair: head lowered in concentration, rolled-up sleeves, forearms tense and muscular. This old photo—the players, the setting—is so goddamn *authentic*, as though Ishmael and Queequeg could be hanging out behind the camera.

But I like the second photo better. Don stands on the ship's deck with a group of men, including the captain, steward, and whaling historian

William Henry Tripp. According to the caption, Don was a guest of the captain. At the time the photo was taken, Don was already a popular author of sea stories, and the trip aboard the whaler was, I presume, an opportunity to gather material.

Don gazes at the camera with a crooked smile. His brown hair is swept back. Unlike the others, he doesn't wear a hat, tie, or overcoat. He's the iconoclast. He wears a white sweater with a high neck. He looks friendly, confident, and comfortable in this intrepid setting. He looks exactly like the Don Waters I want him to be: a prime example of mettle and morals and manhood.

I print out the photo and pin it to the wall under my framed poster of Greg Noll at Pipeline.

Over the following days, I research Don's life, shuttling between the library and my rental house, where I build a better portrait by pouring through online newspaper archives, oral history accounts, crew manifests, ancestry websites, city directories, academic archives, school yearbooks, and death and burial indexes.

From online booksellers I order Don's adventure novels and a duplicate copy of *Gypsy Waters Cruises South*. I find digital clips from magazines and clues to possible family members. One surprisingly helpful resource is Family Search, an online genealogical database maintained by the Church of Jesus Christ of Latter-day Saints. Years ago, I published a story called "Mormons in Heat" that took aim at the LDS church. I grew up around a lot of Mormons who tried to push their faith on me, and "Mormons in Heat" was payback, but now, however, I'm grateful for the church's help. The site points me to early census records.

Don was a minor public figure, but it's still a hell of a thing filling in events from more than eighty years ago. He didn't live a stationary life. He moved. He traveled distances.

I collect bits and pieces, shards and snippets, but the whole enterprise is like standing too closely to a Chuck Close hyperrealist painting. Each cell in the grid is meaningless until you step back and take in the whole portrait. To form a cleaner storyline I triangulate between newspapers, public records, and the information contained in *Gypsy Waters Cruises South*. As I'm searching, I feel like an amateur sleuth just sifting through spooky clues of a dead man's existence, drawing half-baked conclusions from partial facts, but then I reorient when I stumble on a new puzzle piece.

Early on in my research, I have no idea Don will dominate my year. I'll become obsessed, looking into him whenever I have free time, mailing away for death certificates in California and Tennessee, tracking down his distant family members, and watching from a cool distance as his family moves around and grows older. Months will pass, and my search will flow through the early twentieth century and into the middle of the century. I'll lose them and locate them again, and then, unexpectedly, I'll uncover a series of odd and disturbing crimes.

But I'm not aware of that yet.

————————

DON WATERS was born in 1887 in Caithness County in Scotland's far northeast, a region of bogs and farms near the North Sea. His parents, John and Annie, left Scotland around 1891 and temporarily settled in Chicago. Not long after, they relocated to a wooded farm in Haw Creek, North Carolina, which is now a neighborhood on the east side of Asheville. In North Carolina, the family grew. Don was the eldest son in a family with four boys and two girls.

Asheville is a smallish town in the Blue Ridge Mountains. The town gets high praise whenever it's mentioned in conversation. People love it. Back then, in the early twentieth century, the town was probably an ideal place to raise a big family. Life was slow, quiet, quaint, and sheltered by beautiful wilderness. Neighbors bumped into neighbors. Horses and buggies ferried people around downtown's cobblestoned Pack Square. Just outside of town, George Vanderbilt had constructed the largest home in America, a 250-room country chateau named Biltmore.

But small-town life wasn't for Don. As a young man, he burned with curiosity. He was Scottish by birth but American in spirit. Presented with an opportunity, he'd jump aboard any agent of forward movement.

And he never seemed to stop.

"I always have either just arrived somewhere or am just starting elsewhere," he once wrote. "I railroaded in North Carolina, jumped north to the St. Paul, then south again to Richmond, beat it down to Florida, built and drove a racing car over dirt tracks, flew a seaplane between the coast and the Bahamas, acquired a thirty-foot sloop."

Don married into an interesting Asheville family. Margaret Batterham —pronounced "Battrum"—was born in 1897 to English immigrant parents. They lived in a large, comfortable home. Margaret's father was the proprietor of a real estate firm, and their house was down the block from Pack Square at 82 Church Street. Margaret, whom people called "Mott," was the middle child in a family of seven kids.

She was, Don said, "a kindred soul."

Margaret was also a writer. In her teens she carried the title of "Asheville's society correspondent" for the *Charlotte Observer*. Later, at Greensboro Normal, a teaching school, she was a member of the literary magazine staff, and after graduating from Ohio State University she published several stories in pulp magazines. But Margaret's writing wouldn't be widely read for decades, not until she eventually became a regular contributor to the *Christian Science Monitor*.

The Batterham family was a lively, intellectual hive. Margaret's sister Rose published a gothic novel titled *Pleasure Piece*. Then I learn that Margaret's brother, Forster, an anarchist, was the common-law husband of the Catholic crusader Dorothy Day. It's kind of a *holy shit* moment for me. Dorothy Day is a hero of mine. She started the Catholic Worker Movement. She was at the forefront of the anarchist, nonviolent tradition in our county. Soon I learn that Margaret's two other sisters, Lily and later Libbie, both married (at different times) the writer and famed literary theorist Kenneth Burke, a central figure in Greenwich Village literary circles and one of the giants of twentieth-century literary criticism. Don and Margaret were related to modernist royalty.

Throughout her life Margaret crossed paths with countless literary figures. And she certainly had opinions about them. After meeting the poet William Carlos Williams, she remarked, "I wonder if you realize how utterly impossible it is for me to realize why he is considered one of the foremost modern poets."

Growing up, Margaret also knew a budding young writer by the name of Tommy. Young Tommy lived with his mom at a boarding house in town. One day, near the town's fountain, she spoke with him about his college plans. At the time she had no way of knowing that Tommy— Thomas Wolfe—would later write *Look Homeward, Angel*, a seminal American novel. Things were like that for Margaret. She floated through literary circles. Even today, the Batterham family plot at Riverside Cemetery sits near the grave of another famous Asheville son—William Sydney Porter, also known as O. Henry.

It doesn't surprise me Don and Margaret found each other. They were seekers and "kindred souls." They set out on a life full of adventure. Decades before Jack Kerouac's and Neal Cassady's jazzy road exploits, Don and Margaret "cruised a couple thousand miles" around the country in a car with "a tent strapped on the running board and a bunch of tin pans and kettles rattling in the back." From Florida to Maine to California to the Valley of the Moon, "among the redwoods of Jack London's country," they were lovers in thrall with each other and a young, wild country.

In 1924 their daughter was born in New York City. They decided to call her Gypsy.

———

DON WROTE for more than four decades, producing stories in serial form, articles, adventure novels, and travel narratives. He lived for a time in California, "writing scenarios for the movies at Hollywood." But he found his first audiences in pulp magazines.

Early in his career, he drew from his experience working on railroads and wrote stories for *Railroad Man's Magazine*. It's an undeniably corny name for a magazine, but it was popular—very popular. The magazine was in print from 1906 until 1970. Anyway, his early serials were collected into an adventure novel and published in hardback in 1928. That same year, he published a second railroad novel, *Pounding the Rails*, followed a year later by a whaling novel, *Black Skin and Brown*.

Pulps peaked in popularity during the 1920s and '30s. For a lot of people, reading pulps was a primary form of entertainment. The pulp industry declined around the 1950s as a result of the rise of television and comics, but the years between the two world wars was a golden period for pulps.

Hundreds of genre-specific titles sold at newsstands and by subscription. *Argosy,* widely credited as the first pulp, had a weekly circulation of seven hundred thousand. Every writer I know would kill for that kind of audience. Seven *hundred thousand.* Imagine it.

Pulps were cheap to produce and often profitable. A typical pulp was roughly the size of a book, made from inexpensive wood pulp (hence the nickname), and bound by a flimsy color cover. Inside were pages of black text set in twin columns. For ten or fifteen cents a reader could expect around 190 pages of stories. Advertisements padded the front and back sections, but otherwise *Argosy All-Story*, as the magazine was later called, was all stories.

Competition among pulps was fierce. The market was flooded. When sales flagged, editors adapted. They increased page counts. Or they simply changed the magazine's focus, hopping topic to topic until they landed the right market. Some magazines found a niche early and held on. Whatever one's taste, there was a pulp to satisfy it: detective, western, romance, sports, murder, war, sex, gangs, adventure, airplanes, and on and on.

Of course, many from the educated upper crust considered pulps to be trashy and not real literature. Pulps, in other words, were just flimsy publications meant for plebes. But pulp magazines helped launch the careers of many serious writers, cover artists, and editors. And while most pulp stories are hastily and poorly written, a small number are considered iconic.

Weird Tales published the first story by fourteen-year-old Lanier "Tennessee" Williams in August 1928. *Argosy* introduced Zorro and Tarzan of the Apes. *Blue Book Magazine* gave us Agatha Christie's Hercule Poirot. Dashiell Hammett's *The Maltese Falcon* was first serialized in *Black Mask*, a pulp launched by H. L. Mencken to support his more literary venture, *The Smart Set*. Every pulp magazine had its idols. Crime: Cornell Woolrich, Raymond Chandler, and Dashiell Hammett. Horror: H. P. Lovecraft. Science fiction: H. G. Wells, Isaac Asimov, and Robert Heinlein. Before he broke into the slicks, Don's work was regularly featured in *Argosy*, *Sea Stories*, *Short Stories*, *Adventure*, and *Railroad Man's Magazine*.

With hundreds of magazines publishing on a weekly and monthly basis, the industry needed writers. And, if you were good, if you could rip out a story in a matter of days, you could find work. Some pulps paid up to three cents a word. Most paid one cent, often less. In 1925, a writer could have expected about twenty dollars for a 2,000-word story. Adjusted for inflation, that's around $260 today.

Two hundred and sixty dollars for a 2,000-word story isn't terrible, considering I once spent eight months laboring over an 8,000-word story only to *give it away* to a midlevel lit journal to add another notch to my CV.

Today, publishing a well-crafted story in a literary journal may be considered "honorable," but it probably won't pay for the electricity consumed in writing it. The best one can hope for is a small check and a shaggy nod and (with extreme luck) a reprint in an annual anthology—*Pushcart Prize, Best American Stories*.

I love writing short stories. But I think author Karl Taro Greenfeld was on to something when he remarked in an interview: "I used to joke that you could be a serial killer on the lam from the FBI, publishing your whereabouts in the third to last page of short stories in literary journals and the FBI would still never find you."

Too often I have trouble rationalizing the path I've set out on. Pursuing "the writing life" often seems a grim project in self-deception. Sure, I've published a book of stories. Sure, other stories appear in respectable literary journals, but I've never come close to earning a sustainable living, and sometimes, late at night, I lie in bed, trying to calm a rising panic that squeezes my lungs and makes it difficult to breathe. Many writers suffer the same anxiety. Several writers I know—talented, beautiful writers—stopped writing altogether to give themselves stability and peace of mind.

And then, late one night, in the middle of researching Don, a startling omen pops up on my computer screen. While combing the web for traces of Don's pulp magazine writing—re-googling our name, trying different word combinations—I come across a strange link.

I click. I land on what appears to be a book piracy website. I move deeper into the website and can't believe what I'm seeing. There are thousands of e-books available for free download! Michael Chabon. Alice Munro. Junot Diaz. Cormac McCarthy. Aimee Bender. Stephen King. Just about every contemporary writer.

I search for my book of stories and in two quick clicks download a free copy to my hard drive. Why is this website so easy to find?

I click again. In an instant I download a copy of T. C. Boyle's latest novel, imagining a tiny spark in a New York basement, which spreads into ductwork, traveling upward through floors, leaping to the next building, until flames consume the entire publishing industry. Several days later the website disappears, shape shifting into a new URL, but it's out there, somewhere, like a hibernating cancer cell.

Earning a living as a writer is nearly impossible, especially now that piracy websites offer artistic work for free. And even if you're lucky to land a book deal, the advance won't last long, unless it's significant, or unless you're a wizardly investor.

Years ago, when I tried selling my novel through an agent at International Creative Management, an influential New York agency, I had high hopes. I'd already published a story collection through a university press. My stories had earned awards. I was someone, it was true, who suffered through bouts of feeling worthless, and I harbored deep insecurities about my writing, but the success of Robin's memoir showed me it was possible to dream big. Even though mass layoffs were crippling New York publishing houses at the time, I tried not to pay attention to any of that news. After all, my agent, a smart woman with a stellar client list, called my novel "sublime." Her approval thrilled me. She was excited. I was excited. It was my sixth completed novel but my first genuine attempt at selling one.

Some editors responded quickly—with rejections. They liked the writing and the story, but they worried my topic was unmarketable. They wanted the book to have more sparkly commercial appeal. The rejections were polite yet confusing. Then editors stopped responding. The silence coming from New York soon took on the eerie quality of a cold wind blowing through a long hollow tunnel.

My novel is about a working-class guy who supports himself by becoming a prescription drug mule to the residents at his grandmother's Tucson retirement village. It features a large cast of elderly folks and takes a serious look at what it means to grow old in modern-day America. Much of the research came from my firsthand experiences working with the elderly in Berkeley.

Another month passed. More rejections.

One editor said, "I don't see the audience for the book. People in their twenties and thirties probably don't care and readers in their fifties and sixties may see their inevitable future and be depressed."

Reading his note made me depressed.

Rejections piled up. I spoke to my agent less and less. Even though no more than fifteen people had looked at my novel, it was a damaged good. Poison had spread around the small pond. From beginning to end the process broke my spirit. Eventually, after spending months in a well of self-pity, I contacted a university press. An editor there had previously urged me to submit my book. So I did. She loved the novel. Before I went off to Iowa, she said wanted to publish it. So I made the decision. And now I wait, holding my breath.

That's another reason I like Don. He did it. He wrote. He was a lone wolf. A man apart. A bad ass.

By his own admission, he wrote because it allowed him the freedom to travel and discover new adventures. He sought out adventure to gather material to write about.

In Don's era it was possible to earn a living as a writer. But you had to be good. You needed to sell stories on a consistent basis. And Don was good. During his most productive years he appeared nearly monthly, in issue after issue, writing about sailing, railroading, whaling . . .

For the umpteenth night in a row, I close my laptop. I turn off the desk lamp. My transparent reflection in the window looks like a ghosted second self. Nighttime in Iowa City is often a lonely time for me. I don't attend the late-night dance parties or cruise the bars with the younger workshop students. At night, I miss Robin, and I wish I could listen to her noises as she moves around the house.

I open a desk drawer and take out an old, disintegrating pulp I ordered from the internet. Flakes fall to the floor when I slide the ancient magazine from the clear plastic cover. Time has turned the paper orange. The January 10, 1931, issue of *Argosy* features a profile of Don. He has a story in the magazine alongside Erle Stanley Gardner, the writer of the Perry Mason series. Near the back is a page dedicated to "The Men Who Make the Argosy." Don is the showcased writer. There's a line drawing of him in the center along with a few paragraphs:

"I took to writing simply because it's the one job a man can hold and drift around as he wants to . . . and I'm certainly much obliged to the readers of *Argosy*, for your interest has helped me a lot—to go elsewhere."

BY 1930 DON WAS a veteran of the commercial pulp circuit and the author of three adventure novels. He was now living with his family in the seaside town of Oxford, Maryland, on Chesapeake Bay. In the 1930 census Don listed his occupation as "Writer of Books." He was forty-three. Margaret was thirty-three. Their daughter Gypsy was now six. He'd been traveling and writing for more than twenty years. Five years earlier, he'd been the boatsteerer on the whaling vessel. Now, in middle age, he had a family and a home, but deep tides coursed inside him—"the urge to roam is too strong for me ever to be content in one place."

One day, as he stood on the shore, toeing the ground with his boot, he watched the annual bugeye sailing race on the bay. He gazed out at schooners cruising past and lamented how it had been a "decade since I last sailed blue water." He watched the wind open their sails. He watched the boats cut clean lines. The spectacle "stirred up the salt in my blood."

Inwardly, Don mourned the decline of the working sailor trade and the mythical pirate's life.

"It will not be long before the sharp sails and raking masts of a working bugeye will disappear before the ruthless paw of progress."

The sea was mysterious, wild, and tempting. The water called to him. Years earlier, he'd published a series of articles on nautical history—from Vikings to whalers—and called the series "Man on the Water."

Looking out at those sturdy bugeyes and their twin masts, the sun glinting off the bay, Don knew. He knew, *he knew*: "I wanted one of these sweet sailing craft."

And before long he saw his chance. He tracked down a shabby, beat-up bugeye at a nearby wharf. The boat was rusted and her masts were gone. The boat slugged through the water powered only by its engine. It was a pathetic specimen, but Don saw "something fine there, a faded belle."

He haggled with the owner. They agreed on a price. Soon the boat was his. And it was full of surprises. First, he discovered old gravestone slabs in the belly, apparently used as ballast. He couldn't believe it. He got to work. "The ballast came out," and he hoisted the boat from the water. Next, he skinned off the rust, set the "king posts," and replanked the hull until she was "well fastened" and "water tight." Finally a new mast went up, and "the dream of long, anxious months became a reality."

From the comfort of my lounger, I read the opening chapter of *Gypsy Waters Cruises South* several times, impressed by Don's nautical savvy. I watch him sweat and work on the page, just as I had watched Greg and Jed in their wood shop.

Even though the opening chapter is marvelous and full of nervous energy and anticipation, it bends my mind to imagine the discussion between Don and Margaret about leaving everything behind. They owned a house. They were settled. They had a six-year-old child. Was the decision based on finances? Was it mutual? A decade before, Don and Margaret had roamed the country in a car, a married hobo duo with a shared lust for adventure.

They made the decision.

"My books were moved aboard . . . bedding and clothes were taken from the house." They sold or gave away everything unnecessary. And then in 1931, Don, Margaret, and young Gypsy boarded the beautiful rebuilt fifty-foot bugeye. As the world's financial markets continued their disastrous spasms, *Gypsy Waters* set sail.

"We had cut loose from the land. Our home was to be afloat from now on."

———

AT MY DESK I peruse his "Sailing" chapter with a blend of sadness and wonder. My childhood fantasies of life with a father included the sort of swashbuckling tales he wrote about.

My father's sailing stories surprise me. He actually knew his stuff. His writing and Don's share a common language. He sprinkled nautical terminology into his autobiographical anecdotes — foc'sle, Bristol condition, knots, jibs, wing and wing. My father sailed in races "around the Channel Islands to Ensenada, Mexico, and in the Master Mariners in San Francisco." He sailed aboard a fifty-four-foot schooner named *La Volpe*. To him the water was a second home. He built masts in Morro Bay. He sailed with the deputy secretary of defense to Maui — a "voyage of 2,500 miles" — and cruised from La Paz and Acapulco and up the spine of Baja California.

"One of my most pleasant memories was anchoring in uninhabited shelters along the coast of Baja and being joined by fishermen." He traded the fishermen a box of .22 caliber shells for a dozen lobsters.

The items I inherited include racing ribbons and yacht club membership cards and newspaper clippings. It's unsettling to handle his old keepsakes, and I wonder why he kept them. A friend's baby announcement from the 1980s. Snapshots of sailboats. A note from an old girlfriend. But then, of course, it occurs to me: he was sentimental. Like the other Don Waters. Like me. And sentimental men enjoy raking over the past, like turning warm embers over in a fire.

Lately, I've been wondering what stories he told himself when he thought about me. On my birthdays, did he think about me? Did he even remember? On his birthdays, did he regret I wasn't around? Did he worry over who would care for him as he grew older?

In his retirement years he sailed a yacht around Whidbey Island and across the deep, blue-grey Saratoga Passage. Did he think about me while on the water? I'll never know. My father was a man on an island who was himself an island.

"ROLLING AND PLUNGING, throwing spray off in sheets from her bow, *Gypsy Waters* bucked dead into the running . . . We were back in the days of the Yankee privateer and the Baltimore Clipper."

They did it. They broke free.

Don, a pirate reborn.

Onward the vagabond family sailed, lowering and weighing anchor.

Past Norfolk, begrimed by industry, and into Pamlico Sound.

Past Ocracoke Island, "the scene of Blackbeard's last fight."

Don gave his wife and daughter cute nicknames. Alongside his "Mate" and "Midshipmite," he piloted the yacht past mail boats and hobo sailors down the inside channels—down, down, down to Beaufort, South Carolina, down past Georgia's "waving marsh grasses," until at last they saw "the land of sunshine."

Florida!

The family sailed for a good reason: to maintain a sense of well-being during desperate times. "We'd try to find our pleasure in simple things that have no price and can neither be bought or sold." That year, 30 percent of adults in the United States were jobless. People stood in food lines. The nation was buckling at the knees. "The depression was on . . . but although our bank account was nil, our wallet as though an elephant had stepped on it, we were millionaires of time."

In port they stocked up on essentials—flour, bacon, sugar, and fuel. Out at sea they survived off earth's table with wind at their backs and sunlight darkening their tans. Armed with rods, tackle, and traps, they pulled yellowtail and red snapper and shrimp from the water. Stopping on land, they found orange, kumquat, tangerine, and coconut groves, all low-hanging, fresh bounty sold cheaply by farmers suddenly confronted with exorbitant shipping costs.

To write, Don propped a typewriter next to the wheel on the bridge, surrounded on all sides by nautical charts and books. He mailed dispatches to his editor at *Motor Boating*, a "monthly national sporting magazine" owned by William Randolph Hearst.

The family followed their own time clock. They sailed past lighthouses, fished, swam, and slept under bright moons. In city ports they met new and old friends. Away from the cities, they hugged the shoreline and gazed at "a cleaner, greener land." This was early Florida, before the state was carpeted in tacky urban sprawl, before the state became known for dysfunctional newspaper headlines. By their own wits, they outmaneuvered hurricanes, observed the rituals of Greek sponge divers in Tarpon Springs, and were left bewildered by shell mounds left by ancient peoples.

To solve the issue of Gypsy's education, Don and Margaret visited the nearest city's school superintendent before each academic year.

"We get a list of the current textbooks for the coming year, a schedule of the courses and a study plan to accompany them. Then each morning aboard is lesson time." Margaret, a teacher, kept Gypsy current. "In all the book subjects she is on par with children of her age . . . In the knowledge not found in books, she is far beyond them."

An education, I imagine, like the Montessori Method, or maybe like the unschooling movement, only on the ocean. Her parents also gave Gypsy responsibilities aboard the boat and encouraged her to follow her curiosities.

When docked in cities, Gypsy ran to circuses and local museums. While at sea she learned how to "read the weather signs." During stopovers on uninhabited islands, she learned "the nesting habits of tern and gull, the life cycle of insects, the way of the turtle and the sponge." Along the way she adopted pets. On board at various times were a turtle, a fox, a dog, and a pelican nicknamed "Pely." Gypsy was homeschooled—*boat schooled*—and three years into their phenomenal adventure she'd "never suffered sickness in her life." She was a happy child, her room below deck filled with a "toy airplane, a chemical set, a rubber ball, kiddie car, a shell collection." And no dolls.

Gypsy made friends easily in the dockyards and at playgrounds during layovers. When one local reporter ventured down to the docks looking to write about this curious, seafaring trio, Gypsy impressed him the most: "Mr. and Mrs. Waters are an interesting pair but their extraordinary daughter 'steals the show.'"

As I slowly read Don's book, taking my time, I find myself revisiting several key passages. He's a fine writer, detailed, to the point, casually confident in his descriptions of sea life and not afraid to share opinions or philosophize. Too often, he describes a tropospheric sunset as a "riot of flame," but few passages hold more power than when he slows the narrative and writes about his daughter.

"She is ten years old now, and it takes a good man at the oars to keep up with her when she sends the dinky swirling ashore. How better can a man equip his offspring for the life they will have to lead when he will no longer be there to help them, than to develop self-confidence, initiative and an innate resourcefulness that will meet and cope with conditions as they arise? What better school is there than the classroom of nature?"

THE MONTH OF MAY arrives, and I return to Portland and to Robin for the long summer, hoping to look into Don's life some more. But two events interrupt my research.

I'm in the middle of reading about Don's seafaring adventures when *Outside* magazine publishes the article I wrote about building a surfboard with Greg and Jed. Several days after the article appears, National Public Radio calls me. A producer from *Talk of the Nation* tells me the host, Neal Conan, wants to have me on the show.

"Neal's read your piece twice and likes it," the producer says. "We'd like to focus the conversation on building the surfboard, and of course your relationship—or lack of relationship—with your father." The producer goes quiet. "So. Are you up for it?"

The idea of being a guest on *Talk of the Nation* intoxicates me. I've listened to Neal Conan and *Talk of the Nation* for years. I quickly agree to the interview, but after I hang up the phone a blast of adrenaline mainlines through me, and I feel electrocuted and punchy in the head.

National Public Radio.

My father abandoned me.

Neal Conan.

And how do you feel about that, Don?

Talk of the Nation.

Oh hi, Neal, thanks for taking my call. I'm just calling to ask your guest why he's such a raging pussy?

I need to leave the house immediately. It's going to be nearly impossible working from the bungalow. So I drive over the Burnside Bridge and head to Mississippi Avenue, one of Portland's newly redeveloped neighborhoods.

I park in front of a chiropractor's office with a green hand-painted sign in the window advertising relief for gardening injuries.

Nearby is an utterly twee café. I order a coffee while standing next to a tragic twenty-something sporting a walrus mustache and a green Fidel Castro hat. I sit down to work but can't.

I've been telling lies about him my entire life. Lying about him is part of my nature. I've only recently begun telling the truth. I always had quick responses to questions about him, but when you start readjusting your responses in your thirties and speaking the truth, it feels like walking on shaky ground. In the magazine article I had outlined the basic information about my early abandonment. Outing myself in a national magazine is one thing, because I controlled the content, I controlled the flow of information, but being interviewed on national radio is an entirely different beast. One stray question could fly out of Neal Conan's mouth and disassemble me.

Several mornings later, I drive around the southwest hills, completely lost. It's cold and drizzling. The Oregon Public Radio studios were booked, so I've been dispatched to a hilly, leafy neighborhood to find some dude's house, where there's supposedly a studio. After several wrong turns and dead ends, I finally locate the right address. A path curves around the house to an overgrown backyard, where an open basement door reveals a converted, in-home radio studio. I'll be speaking with Neal Conan from some random basement.

I wander in, and the radio technician is already behind his command center, earphones necklaced around his throat. I look around. He's got all the gadgets.

"Thanks for arriving early," he says. "Let's get you set up. Follow me."

He shows me to an adjoining, dim room. The walls are plated with foamy, furrowed soundproofing, a sort of extra padding, as though this is a room where people might go crazy. He secures headphones around my ears and closes the door, sealing me into an airtight radio coffin. I sit and wait. A window looks onto a lawn glistening from morning rain. In my headphones I hear the broadcast. I hear Neal interviewing the guest before me. Suddenly, the voice of the show's producer, from Washington, DC, comes into the headphones. He wants to check levels. He asks me to say a few words.

"Okay, we're ready to go," his disembodied voice says.

I sit—and wait—wondering how I talked myself into this. This is my struggle: the struggle against silence.

An announcement. Another announcement. Horns introduce the segment, and Neal Conan says, "And we're back."

My heart jumps into my throat. I take a sip of water. Thankfully, Neal is a pro. For twenty minutes he takes me by the hand and leads me down the velvety interview rabbit hole with softball questions, and I answer truthfully and openly as best I can. We talk about my absentee father and my search for connection and building a surfboard with the famous surfer who gave my father his first board.

And then, before listeners' calls, Neal says, "We haven't spoken about your mother. She was there the whole time. What about her?"

My Achilles' heel. He asks the question. About Mom. And I devise a hasty, improvised answer. I say she fully supports my search for answers, but it's not true. Mom doesn't know about the interview. Mom doesn't know about the article. She never said she supports any search for any answers. She's not forthcoming on the topic, and I'm rarely open with her about how that makes me feel. I fear she'll pull away, and then I'll be without any family. After all, she left my father and never talked to him again. She's got a temper, a brittle side. I've covered for her, invented excuses, and put her needs above mine. I'm still protective, and so I mislead Neal on national radio because I don't know how to admit this to him or his audience.

When the interview ends, I remove the headphones and tug open the coffin door. I'm exhausted, spent. The technician cinches his headphones around his neck.

"That was quite a discussion," he says. "Usually I don't listen in, but that was really riveting."

I don't even remember what I said. The whole interview happened in a dream state. Some safety mechanism activated in my brain, and it's quickly blacking everything out.

Again, I feel punchy. Many friends don't even know about my father. Now they will. Suddenly, I feel wildly vulnerable, as though hot rays of sunlight have finally touched a festering wound. I would have been fine never saying a goddamn word. What did I just do?

Warm summer sun arrives in Portland, savior to the pale-faced. Long

May days stretch into longer June days, and I fall into a deep, severe depression—again. It's the same kind of crushing heaviness I felt after my father died.

I've exposed the wound. I feel raw and supercharged by sadness. I've never spoken so openly about personal shit. About my father. About abandonment. About that particular kind of psychic pain. Allowing the public in as witness heightens my shame. I've kept orderly about my massive feelings by sidestepping, by avoiding, by taking it. I'm a dude. I'm supposed to just *take it*, right? But all along I've only been applying masking tape to cracks in a failing dam wall. Now the dam has sprung leaks, creating floodways, and grief gushes through the openings.

An old high school friend hears the radio broadcast and writes on my Facebook wall: "Listened in. You always struck me as a happy guy in high school."

I was a happy guy in high school. I laughed a lot. *I am very outgoing and a basically happy person*, I wrote in that first letter to my father. But back then I was also in incredible pain.

It's unbelievable such ancient pain can still exist. The sky is blue, the sun is out, and suddenly I'm afraid to drive my truck, afraid to leave the house, afraid of hurting myself. I have no idea how brain chemistry works, but it's like all the happy neural pathways dry up. Robin gets worried. Robin gets annoyed. Robin gets angry with me. I sleep late and stay up until all hours binge-watching season after season of *Disappeared*, a mindless television series that recounts through interviews and reenactments the stories of people who have simply vanished off the face of the earth.

I double my therapy appointments to twice a week, further depleting my small inheritance. Then I drag myself to a psychiatrist and load up on antidepressants—and wait. Several times I head to the beach, but the sand and saltwater don't help. My abilities drag in the water.

Eventually, midsummer, I call Mom. I can't tell whether the meds are working yet. She doesn't answer. I leave a message on her voicemail, and she calls back the next day.

"I'm not feeling right," I tell her.

"Why?"

"I don't know. I'm fighting off this, I don't know, *depression*. It's been a tough summer."

"Why's that?" she asks. "There's no reason to be depressed."

"I've been thinking too much about everything I don't know. I need to know the entire story."

"What story?"

"I've been thinking about him."

"Him?"

"My father."

"And why would you ever want to do that?"

"Because it's important. It's important."

"You should see the jalapeños I've got growing," she says. "And the cherry tomatoes? I have three plants, and I get good tomatoes off them. I try to water them as much as I can. You should visit us sometime. You'd love the new outdoor benches."

As I listen, I feel as though I've been lifted into an alternate dimension. Jalapeños? Cherry tomato plants? Isn't she listening?

Robin is right. Neal Conan is right too: What about Mom?

Thinking about my father inevitably leads to my mother, but it's difficult mulling over her decisions or the men she escorted into our lives, which is probably one reason I haven't seen or visited her in a year and a half. But I need some comfort, connection, truth. So I book a plane ticket to Reno, city of beauty and trash.

––––––––––

MOM WAS BORN in upstate New York to Catholic Quebecois parents. Well, at least I know her dad was Quebecois. Grandma's origins remain a partial mystery to me because her father abandoned her.

Following high school, Mom fled small-town life in search of excitement—she had a touch of the same wanderlust that drove Don and Margaret. First, she moved to Boston, where she puttered around the city on a motorcycle. Later, she skipped across the country to Monterey, California, and married a naval officer. For three years they lived in the Philippines near the Subic Bay naval base. Eventually, she landed in Reno in the early 1970s, looking to buy her first easy divorce.

Reno in the '70s blazed with neon. It bled vice and oozed grime and glamour. It must have been something. At the time, brothels were newly legal, and Las Vegas hadn't yet elbowed out the northern city as the state's premier gaming destination. Gambling became lawful statewide in 1931, during the Depression, and took root in Reno first. When Mom arrived,

Reno was still a prime location to gamble, marry, and divorce. The population was around 72,000 and rapidly growing.

Previous decades saw the quick rise and quick fall of grand gaming and entertainment clubs. Long gone was Club Fortune, where Sammy Davis Jr. and Liberace played, but the art deco Mapes Hotel was still operating, sustained by the legends of Marilyn Monroe and Clark Gable, who stayed there while filming *The Misfits*, a movie that highlighted the region's divorce ranches. Poker, slots, race books, roulette, keno, craps—everything was available and legal and imbued with cigar smoke and garish stories. Like the whiskey waterfall that flowed in the Silver Dollar Bar. And early gangsterism. And appearances by Judy Garland and Ann-Margret at the Sky Room. Harold's Club, the Riverside, and Harrah's dominated downtown's corridor, but as the years rolled by newer, bigger hotel-casinos nudged these older establishments to the side. The Reno arch, famous for its slogan "The Biggest Little City in the World," stood at the center of the luminescence.

And this is where Mom settled.

From above, the Sierra Nevada mountains rip my heart out with their beauty. I always choose window seats on airplanes. Now I gaze out the double-plated window as we circle the high valley. To the east the mountains look dry and amber-colored in the summer months, but to the west they are greener, grander, and carpeted with ponderosa pines. An extinct volcano, Mount Rose, at 10,000 feet, hovers above the valley floor.

I like Reno, and I hate it.

Over the past decade or so, I've noticed, the city has been rebranding itself as an outdoor sporting destination. The city offers sun, crisp high desert air, and easy access to Lake Tahoe and some of the country's most spellbinding wilderness. But it remains a landscape of wild contradictions. Provincial libertarian values live cozily alongside a permissive outlaw spirit. The gaming industry attracts transients, fuckups, and losers—like all gambling towns. Microsoft has a local presence, but so does the Mustang Ranch brothel. Coursing through the middle of town, washing away the muck, is the frigid Truckee River. It's fair to say my childhood landscape was a blend of the tawdry and the magnificent.

Landing in Reno is often turbulent because of updrafts off the mountains, and the plane lands bumpily but safely. My stepfather picks me up outside baggage claim in his gigantic GMC truck. I toss my bag on the rear passenger seat. Inside, it reeks of cigarette smoke.

"Hey," I say.

"Hey," Chuck says.

"How's Mom?" I ask.

"Fine."

"How was the flight?"

"Fine. Mom at home?"

"Might be. She was having lunch with some friends," he says. "Or, as I call them, the retired hussies."

"Oh, come on."

Chuck laughs and his throat sounds like it's full of gravel. He loves getting under my skin, putting me off balance. Whether he says crazy shit because he believes it or just to piss me off, I don't know. Probably both. He taps a cigarette from a crumpled pack and down goes his window.

"Can that wait?" I ask.

He doesn't respond.

"Awesome," I say. Mentally, I open the door and hurl myself out.

Chuck steers with his thumb. He's a hefty man with the same ruddy, strawberry blond complexion as Philip Seymour Hoffman. Sometimes I like to imagine him balancing on a stack of wood crates at his old machine shop, expounding to his pals about his innermost feelings. But that would never happen. He's a working-class dude who became a working-class businessman. Without much formal education, he founded a machining business and later sold it to a Japanese company. The American Capitalist Dream, all that. Mom married Chuck while I was away at college in New York, informing me only after the ceremony. At the time I didn't trust him. He was just another man in Mom's home, and I'd been a front-row witness to the species of men interested in Mom. It's not like I ever wanted her to remain celibate and alone, but the kind of men she dated always seemed to be the kind who knew how to fix cars, shoot guns, and steal cable television.

Chuck recently endured his own Shakespearean tragedy, and I've tried my best to convey my sympathy over the phone. His niece murdered his only sister. It was a brutal and gruesome crime. The woman hit her mother over the head with a baseball bat, slit her throat, stabbed her in the stomach, smoked a cigarette while waiting for the woman to die, and then casually phoned the police. Mom asked me to write the obituary. Initially, I didn't want anything to do with it. The murder horrified me. I wanted to distance myself, but I did my duty and wrote the obituary anyway. An undeniable seediness lies below the surface of Reno's streets, and his sister's murder only serves to remind me of the countless sordid stories staining the high desert floor.

As much as Reno mystifies me, this is my city, and I know it well. We pass a billboard advertising lingerie bowling. Another advertises 99-cent breakfasts at the Cal-Neva. It's ninety-four degrees outside with an excellent chance of tacky.

The strip malls and barren dirt lots rustle loose a million stories. That car dealership over there. On customer appreciation days, Mom would pull into the lot, and I'd hop out, head inside, load up on free hotdogs, and we'd speed away. You get creative when you don't have money. And there, Wonder Bar, another story: Sitting in the ill-lit shadows beside Mom and Manuel, their faces backlit by colorful, sparkling bottles. Manuel was the first of many fathers. I loved his wobbly warmth. He tossed me quarters to feed the Ms. Pac-Man machine in the corner of the bar, but my happy supply of quarters ended the day he blacked out and rolled our car into a ditch.

Chuck stops at the house. He flicks his spent butt into the cul-de-sac. "I need you to write me a letter," he says.

"About what?"

"Some asshole's trying to pull some shit over on me," he says.

"What asshole?"

"It's a business thing. There's this asshole, and it has to do with business."

"Can you be a little more specific?"

"Just write me the letter, will you?"

"Fine, fine," I say, opening the door. "Give me the details before I leave."

Another thing, Chuck puts me to work. He likes me to write letters for him, signed in his name, to other business owners who've wronged him, preferably using the most purple, most highfalutin language possible, as though thesaurusy words are weapons and will humble his intended targets. The whole enterprise is so dippy I actually enjoy writing the letters.

Inside, the house is cool and spacious and well lit. Their new house is in a tony neighborhood and overlooks a golf course. The neighbors are a doctor and a retired airline pilot. Chuck did extremely well when he sold his business, but the massive leap in class happened abruptly, which unnerves me whenever I return. The truth is, I carry a vague pride in the working class because my earliest formative years were lived on the outer economic margins, but I don't really share cultural interests or the language of the working class anymore. So my pride in the working class is theoretical, which even now embarrasses me and makes me wonder where I fit in.

"Is that Donny?" Mom says, her voice high and expectant. She rounds the corner with a dishtowel in her hands. "Look at you," she says. Her hazel eyes brighten. Mom likes jewelry, auditory jewelry, jewelry with sound, and sometimes I can hear her big clacking necklaces before I ever see her. Today, three gold necklaces cascade down her neck. She pinches my hair. "I see grey," she says.

"Mom, stop."

"You're getting some grey. I see grey."

Chuck walks into the family room, where he turns on the TV, collapses on the sofa, and starts watching *The View*. He raises the volume.

I follow Mom into the kitchen.

"There were five murders in the city last week," Mom says. "Can you believe it?"

"Huh," I say.

"There was also a stabbing near our old house," she says. "Jeez. Glad we moved out of that neighborhood. Isn't that terrible?"

"Huh," I say.

Mom's nearing seventy and doesn't have a grey hair on her head. These days, she's rocking a sort of curly surfer hairdo that brings to mind Patrick Swayze's wiggy locks in *Point Break*. She's a terminal worrier, loves bling, and loves buying things. Shopping is her sport. She also spent decades working at the sheriff's department jail, an experience that seeped into her bones and made her believe that everywhere is a possible crime scene.

We sit in the family room for a while, watching *The View*, a reunion around a glowing screen, and I listen to Mom—and listen.

She fills me in on local gossip—what's happening at church, what's happening with so-and-so's health, what's going on with Reno's crime rate. Every so often, she drops a nugget about the past. Lately, over the phone, she's been mentioning her past a lot, making sure I have a firm grip on *her story*, which leads me to believe she might open up about my father—about *our story*. I want that story. Of course, I wonder if she ever sees traces of him in me. When I turn this way or that way, does she think, *That's the same chin!* When she does talk about the past, she imbues it with a rosy patina. All around in the family room are Mom's Asian souvenirs and furnishings from when she lived as a naval officer's wife in the Philippines. Mom says, "Did you hear about that terrible man and what he did to his sons?"

"What man?"

"That man. It was on the news."

"What are you talking about?"

"That man who made his seventeen-year-old beat up his thirteen-year-old brother. I mean," she says, "what is the world coming to?"

"Mom, come on. I don't want to hear about these things."

"But it's true!"

The television stays on nearly maximum volume during dinner. Spaghetti, bread, and Fox News. More tragedies, more smokescreens, more reasons to be afraid.

Instead of eating the salad I ran to the store to prepare—mixed greens, sprouts, heirloom tomatoes, avocado, bell peppers—Chuck prefers to eat his iceberg lettuce. Just chopped iceberg lettuce. He hates my salads.

"Your man Obama wants to raise taxes again," Chuck says. "Will someone take this bread?"

"Huh," I say.

"He's a socialist," Mom says.

"Donna, finish my pasta," Chuck says to Mom. "And finish this bread. And I need some water."

"I certainly think wealth should be spread around," I say. "We're becoming like Brazil. It's unsustainable."

"Oh, *Donny*," Mom says. "What are you talking about?"

"Donna, water," Chuck says.

"You're not a socialist, are you?" Mom says.

"Do you know who was a socialist?" I say.

"Who?"

"Jesus Christ of Nazareth."

"Oh, *Donny*," Mom says. "Don't say things like that. That's awful."

"Donna, you need to eat the rest of this bread," Chuck says. "I can't do it. I can't eat all the bread. And I need water." Mom slaps his hand, and a piece of bread drops on the table. "Take it," he says. "Take it. I can't eat it. I can't."

Later, in the family room, Mom flips through the TV channels. She stops on a police procedural.

I'm on the couch, her laptop on my knees. Before I arrived, her internet connection went down and her email stopped working. Now I'm charged with fixing it. "I need your password," I say.

"Well, I don't know it," she says. "We paid a techie guy to set everything up. He knows the password."

"What techie guy?"

"I don't remember."

"Fine," I say. "Let's just create a new gmail account." I cruise over to Google. "Pick a username."

"What's that?"

"Your email handle. You know, a username. Just choose something."

"Why don't you pick one?" she says.

"How about crazy woman?" I say. "Wait. It has to be one word—crazywoman. No caps." The moment my suggestion leaves my mouth and hits the air, I feel awful, like some superior, snotty asshole. But Mom doesn't seem to hear me or mind. She's too busy watching someone get murdered on TV.

"Do you want to attend Mass with me in the morning?" she asks.

"You know I don't attend church anymore," I say.

"Well, you should," she says.

"Remember our old church? The brick one?"

"Of course I do," she says. "That's where you were baptized."

"Well, when they turned that into a bank, I stopped believing."

Mom squints. "I thought I taught you better."

"Here," I say. I hand her the laptop. "You have to set up a username and password. It's easy. Just follow the steps."

"I don't know what I'm doing."

"It's easy. I'll guide you."

"But I don't know how to do it."

"Just follow the steps."

More TV, more crime procedurals, more couch lounging. When would be a good time to ask about my father?

We all have our weird family dramas and traumas and hesitations about asking the important questions, and of course deep, cutting, complicated love for our parents, and some of us go quiet in the face of it all. For years, I did. I buried all my questions and grew angry, grew depressed—and now I'm ready to try this other way. I feel the need to rip open the seals of the past, as much as it might rip me open a little too.

I almost ask a leading question but stop myself. Instead, I pluck an old photo album off the bookshelf. By chance I choose the early years. Here's Mom and strange men, camping, outdoors, at bars. A lot of men. A lot of beer cans. And impossibly tiny shorts, especially on the men. Of course, I'm in a number of photos, in the background, while Mom poses with different dudes. A thought occurs to me: Mom was a party girl. She liked having fun. She was insanely beautiful and had many boyfriends. And I was a product of a particular time. The free-for-all '70s.

It feels odd to be the returning adult son. The only son. My life is wildly different from hers. Sometimes it's a struggle to find common ground. Chuck and Mom enjoy driving their RV into the mountains and tooling around on all-terrain-vehicles, and I like looking down on people who drive ATVs in the wilderness. Still, the thought amuses me: Mom, nearly seventy, driving an ATV. Mom, in her twenties, driving a motorcycle around Boston.

I set the album on the table. "How did you meet him?"

"Which one?" she says, looking at the album.

"My father."

She sighs deeply. "A friend introduced us. But let's not talk about that."

"But I need to understand some things."

"I told you what you needed to know years ago. Besides, let's not think about that. Things turned out okay. Everything's fine, right? All that stuff doesn't matter. Life goes on. We're fine."

"But you didn't tell me what I need to know."

She sighs again, her eyes narrow, and she shoots me a look. Her look. *That* look. "You're like your grandmother," she says. "You can't just let things go. You have to learn to let things go."

"Tell me."

"I already did years ago."

"No, you didn't."

"Donny. Stop it. Why do you want to go back to that time?"

"Why can't you talk about it?"

She looks at me with hard eyes. "Why are you so weird?" she says.

"What? Why am I weird?"

She stands. "I'm going to bed."

Years ago, we screamed at each other in the tiny laundry room at our old house. She was folding towels, and I stomped through the house until I found her. *Tell me.* I begged her to tell me the story. *Why,* she asked. *Why? What's the use?* And then she broke down and I broke down and we cried in the laundry room smelling of chemicals and fabric softener and the little she told me I didn't believe. I couldn't believe it. So I buried those few words and carried on as if I didn't know anything. And actually, I don't know much. Long ago, Mom locked and sealed that box, and now she refuses to open it again. It's buried, under the dirt, lost. Fuck.

I turn the TV off and drift to the spare bedroom, feeling defeated. Maybe Mom will eventually come around and spill everything, but then again maybe that's just magical thinking.

In the hallway hangs a gigantic framed portrait of my high school senior photo. I'm wearing a tuxedo. The size of the photo embarrasses me every time I walk down the hall. The spare bedroom is now Mom's miscellaneous storage room. On the walls hang photos of my Catholic confirmation alongside class photos from grade school. On an antique sewing table sits a stuffed polar bear, a figurine of a wise Asian man, two geisha dolls, a fedora, and a model replica of the stealth bomber.

Why am I weird?

Thankfully, I'd brought Don's book with me.

––––––––––

THEY WERE "transient and casual rovers." They cruised down Hawk Channel, a watery passageway between the Florida Keys and the outer reefs, and drifted southwest along the green necklace of the islands until they rounded Key West, where they turned north toward Cape Sable, the southernmost "tip of the mainland" and "the only part of the continental United States that is really tropical."

In bed, I put the book down. I'm curious. I open my computer and study Google Maps. Cape Sable looks like a remote place, even today, a bright green spit of unpopulated land jutting from the Everglades.

As the family slowly neared the cape, Don noticed the "outlines of a house, a wharf in front." They sailed closer, dropped anchor, and rowed to shore. A man approached as soon as their toes hit the sand. The man lived on the cape alone, he said. His job was to watch over the nearby coconut plantation.

Throughout their travels the family had encountered a handful of peculiar folk who lived far from civilization. Now another stood in front of them. A hermit. The hermit of Cape Sable. From the hermit Don learned there was "no road to civilization" from this distant outpost. The hermit traveled by boat to acquire all his supplies.

There's a photo of the hermit in the book. He's a small man and not much taller than ten-year-old Gypsy. He wears overalls, a dirty shirt with rolled-up sleeves, and has the tussled look of wildness about him. I can only imagine the size of his loneliness on that cape. It must have been crushing. Alone month after month with only coconuts and coconut fronds as companions and views of nothing but water.

Don's description of Cape Sable and the hermit brings to mind the isolated places my father chose to live. He lived by himself in a cabin in the mountains of Idaho. He lived alone in a single-wide trailer "owned by the local Madam" in Battle Mountain, Nevada. He lived alone in apartments in New Mexico, Arizona, Ohio, South Carolina, and Las Vegas. He lived alone on an island.

The unexpected visitors excited the hermit. He was thrilled to show the family around. He gave them as many coconuts as they could carry. "The meat was so rich that squeezed between the hands, the oil ran out in a stream. We loaded our dinky with cocoanuts . . . like the South Sea Islanders."

The family spent a restful week at the cape, much to the hermit's delight. One night, the hermit "cranked up his ancient truck" and showed them a beach where sea turtles emerged out of the water to nest. It was the season when loggerheads scuttled up the sand and clawed open holes to lay eggs. But predators threatened the nests. Out here, in the wilderness of the cape, raccoons and opossums loved dining on turtle eggs. The creatures sniffed out the draglines left during the mother turtle's long crawl up the beach. If the hatchlings managed to survive in the nest, seabirds threatened them on their hustle to the water. Then, in the water, the small turtles confronted barracuda. The life of a young green turtle was full of terror.

The family wanted to help them. At the beach, whenever they encountered a nest, they excavated eggs, dug fresh holes, and "we buried them a foot deep, smothered the place down carefully, obliterated by our footmarks." They wanted to give the young turtles a fighting chance in the world.

THE HOUSE IS SO QUIET it nearly hums. Nearly midnight, and I'm still awake, restless, and need to leave. I get out of bed. I slide Mom's car keys off the granite island in the kitchen, quietly slip out the front door, and drive downtown to our first apartment, hoping the building has been demolished, but of course it hasn't. I turn into the small lot and park.

I don't know what majestic, masochistic force draws me to this one-story fourplex whenever I return to Reno. It's like visiting a place where known ghosts roam. Security bars now cover the windows, and the lot, once dirt, is paved. I step out and peer through the window. Inside, it's gutted, tiny, abandoned. The place brings to mind one of those bombed-out shells in modern-day Detroit. A long time ago, a boy played with his shelter puppy on the floor in here.

The apartment is several blocks up the hill from downtown, with full views of the flashing skyline. This apartment, this exact building, is the reason I feel spiritually connected to the underclass, especially when I remember those deflating weekends spent touring model homes, walking on crisp plastic runners through two- and three-bedroom homes, bowed by their magnificence, my desire as big as their price tags.

Later, we moved to a two-bedroom duplex on South Center Street, closer to downtown's casino corridor and nearer Mom's work. It was a faded brick duplex that Hollywood location scouts would consider authentically down and out. For three hundred a month, we moved in and I was given my own bedroom. At the time it felt like being anointed a prince.

And there's my room: that window on the second floor. Where I dumped ice cubes on my mattress on blazing summer nights. Where I heated my room with a portable kerosene stove in winter.

Idling across the street, I remember that kid, that good kid, curious, studious, and mischievous in the right ways. I spray-painted walls around the neighborhood on Saturday nights and served as an altar boy on Sundays. I'm annoyed how subsequent renters have decimated the small patch of lawn I once mowed. And the plank fence I helped to build? It's in shambles. The six-block walk to Mom's work at the jail took ten minutes as I traipsed past sketchy boarding houses and motels that rented by the month. Mostly, though, I remember him.

We move in, but first thing, Mom fills a bottle with holy water from church and brings it home. She tosses it around my new bedroom.

"A pentagram," Mom says, shaking her head. "A pentagram on your new bedroom floor. I mean, what is it with people?"

The transvestite who moved out left a star-shaped image on the floor, in tape, and at each corner melted candle wax. It smells like something has been recently burned. I used to like Gary-the-transvestite. He works at our grocery store. Now I'm not so sure. When we toured the duplex, there were about fifty stuffed animals on his bed. And now he's left behind a pentagram.

Mom shakes out half the holy water from the bottle. She wipes a hand on her jeans. "Okay, should be fine now," she says.

The duplex is a mansion. Mom finally has space for the souvenirs she brought back from Asia—straw hats, jade elephants, and long scrolls bearing Oriental characters. She gets to work, and soon our new living room resembles a cluttered Chinatown store. I like it. One painting shows an elderly Asian man crouching and holding a staff. He watches over us like a protective shepherd.

I like our new neighborhood too. Two kids from school, Ronald and Edgar, brothers, live a block away. Five people share their tiny apartment, which makes me appreciate the luxury of my own room. Their dad is a casino janitor. I heard him say to Mom one time, "My brother leave for work but never come home. This was in El Salvador revolution. I knew then we move to America. I will sweep the streets of Reno to stay."

Ronald and Edgar and I bike through the downtown alleyways. We skate parking garages. We walk my dog, Patches, around the neighborhood. We roam.

Ray is a former police officer from Las Vegas. I hear his name around the duplex. *Ray. Ray. Ray.* His name appears on scraps of paper by the telephone. *Ray.* His deep voice floats from the message machine. *Ray.*

Mom meets him through a friend of a friend at work. Mom starts talking about Ray in the same happy way she talked about Manuel. Over the next few months, Mom leaves me with her friend during weekends and drives south. Ray drives north. They meet halfway, in the middle of the state, in Tonopah, in the desert.

"What do you do in Tonopah?" I ask Mom, as she's packing the truck.

"We camp," she says. "Ray likes camping."

"Can I come?"

"Not this time, kiddo," Mom says. "We'll all go camping soon. Besides, you can't miss your swim lessons. Those are expensive. But Ray says he'd like to meet you. You'll like him."

I'm shy but curious about this new man. Mom liked Manuel, and I did too, but he rolled our Datsun into a ditch.

"What kind of car does he have?" I ask.

"What's that, sweetie?"

"Does Ray own a car?"

"Of course he owns a car. What kind of question is that?"

"What kind of car?" I ask.

Mom shakes her head. "He's got a couple cars. He's fixing up an old Pontiac Thunderbird." She laughs to herself. "I mean, come on. What kind of car does he have? Ha!"

"Don't laugh."

"He'll be visiting in a couple weeks. You can see for yourself."

Ray has a Thunderbird? That's a cool car. I imagine this stranger speeding on the open hot desert highway on his way to Reno to meet me.

Weeks later, when Ray pulls up at the duplex, he's driving a Chevy El Camino. His tan arm is slung out the open window. I spy on him through the drapes. The El Camino is a mutant car. It wants to be a sedan and a truck at the same time. It's the lowest form of car ever invented. That he drives an El Camino doesn't stop Mom from agreeing to marry him.

RAY IS TALL. Brown hair and wire-rimmed glasses and a thick full mustache, and he's strong too, with hands that remind me of mountains.

During his first visit, he walks around the duplex, putting a foot in the rooms and leaning in to look. Mom follows him, and I follow Mom. The spicy smell of cologne is a new thing in our duplex.

In the basement, where Mom put down loose carpet and I set up a TV area, Ray looks up at the basement windows and says, "Here's where I'll put my desk."

Mom lit incense to cover the damp concrete smell. It's dark down here, but when sunlight hits the rectangular windows, they look like they're glowing.

We go to lunch at a diner, and Ray slings his arm over the vinyl seat. He taps his pinkie on the seat as he talks. And I listen. His plan is to move to Reno and start his own private investigation business. I get interested. He was a policeman, he says. So he knows the ropes.

"I know how things work," he says. "I just need my license and some stationery to make it legit. And a few gadgets."

"What kind of gadgets?" I ask.

"Oh, you'd like them. Real spy stuff."

After lunch, Ray gets up first, and I quickly follow him out the door.

"Hey guys, wait up," Mom says at the cash register.

Together, we drive around Reno. Then we drive into the mountains. I sit between Mom and Ray on the bucket seat, fiddling with the radio, until Mom tells me to stop. Kenny Rogers. "Coward of the County." I like this one.

Later in the day, back at the duplex, I'm upstairs tightening the wheels on my skate deck when Mom calls me downstairs. They're both in the kitchen.

"Care to sit down with us?" Ray asks.

Mom sits too.

"Listen," Ray says. "I asked your mother to marry me. How do you feel about that?"

"Okay, I guess," I say.

"Your mom thinks you should carry the ring during the ceremony," he says.

Mom leans forward. "We both want you to participate," she says. "What he means is . . . We think it's important. It's a good way to start." She puts her hand on mine and says, "He's a good man."

A good man.

A good man, and cool. My very own Magnum P.I. living with us. Ray says we'll go on adventures. Fishing? Camping? Hiking?

"We'll do all that," he says. Ray leans back in the chair and talks about us as family.

The wedding happens on a Saturday. It's not a Catholic church because Ray's not a member of our faith, but a small, generic church along a busy street. Mom's friends from work and Jazzercise arrive, and I watch them through the windows as Mom puts a corsage on my new white suit jacket. Her dress is as white and flashy as the cake they ordered.

"I'm nervous," I say.

"Don't be nervous. You'll be great," she says.

"People will be watching. I just get nervous."

"It's going to be fine," she says.

I go searching for Ray, who's in a separate room by himself. He doesn't have many friends at the wedding.

He digs into his pocket and takes out the rings. "Don't lose these. I'm counting on you not to lose these."

He begins tying the rings to a white satin pillow.

"Why can't I keep the rings in my pocket?" I ask him. I've seen it on TV. I'm a ten-year-old skater. I don't want to carry a white pillow.

"This is just how it is," Ray says. He tightens the thin satin string.

"You'll walk down the aisle first," he says. "We'll follow. Now, when it's over, I'll give you a thumb's up and you'll follow us. Don't do anything until I give you the signal. Okay? It'll be fine."

I can hear my heartbeat in my ears during the ceremony. I'm nervous standing in my white suit in front of Mom's friends. Mom and Ray repeat vows. When the minister looks over, I approach with the white pillow, and he unties the rings. They repeat vows, and then I watch them kiss with disgusting open mouths. After, they turn and start walking, and I wait for Ray's signal. I wait for his eyes to meet mine, but they don't. They walk down the long aisle and the minister trails them. I'm still standing in front of everyone, and I don't know when I'm supposed to leave the pulpit. I stand alone, waiting. I look down the aisle, thinking Ray will give me his signal, but now they've disappeared and people in the pews are laughing, and I stand waiting.

One of Mom's friends whispers, "It's okay, Donny. You can leave the front now."

I can feel my face heating up. I turn and quickly walk down the aisle by myself, carrying the stupid white pillow.

Mom and Ray are alone in some room. I can't find them. Outside, Mom's friend passes out small bags of bundled birdseed. A white limousine waits to take them to the casino for their honeymoon.

"You toss the seed into the air when they come out the doors," the woman says. "Now, when that door opens—"

"I know, I know. I know how to do it. I helped Mom make these things," I tell her.

Her smile turns into a line.

People start gathering near the church's back door. I take a handful of the birdseed bundles, untie them, and wait with two full fists. Seed drops on the hot asphalt.

At last, the backdoor opens.

"There they are!" someone yells.

Mom and Ray quickly move through the line of people and through a spray of birdseed. They're holding hands, laughing. I wait. When they're near enough, I throw the seeds like I'm tossing a baseball pitch. Right at Ray.

He covers his face, but I see some land in his mouth. Soon it's over. The limo drives away. Mom's friend walks over. "You were supposed to throw it in the air. Not right at them."

It's only a weekend honeymoon, and I stay with Mom's friend. When they return, Ray gives me a gift, an empty tiki statue cup. "You can put your school pens in there," he says.

Soon after the wedding, Mom goes back to work at the jail and Ray moves in. He puts a big metal desk in the basement, rearranging the TV room. I didn't realize Ray was also bringing his dogs, two German shepherds. Patches, my little girl whippet, hides upstairs in my room after the bigger dog, Kaiser, bites her.

In the basement, I stand around watching Ray.

"Look what I found," he says. He pulls a green army helmet from a cardboard box. "Don't know why I still have this. You want it?"

I do.

"And hey, check it out." He shows me two fishing poles. He hands one to me. "This one can be yours," he says. "We'll get you a tackle box."

He gives me gifts—gifts, I believe, a father gives a son. And it doesn't take long before I begin adoring him. I want to go where he goes. I want to do what he does.

One day, Ray and Mom sit me down at the kitchen table again.

"Okay, listen," Ray says. "I'm going to adopt you. I've thought about it. And we've talked about it. And that's what's going to happen. How do you feel about that?"

Warmth spreads through me.

Months pass. And though he doesn't mention adoption again, I adopt Ray as my father. I cross out my last name on school papers and use his, and everyone at school calls me by a new last name. His name. The name of a good man.

We're a sudden new family. The way it should be.

One Sunday afternoon after church, we drive to a casino and sit for a family portrait. Mom and I dress in white. I wear the same white blazer and pink shirt I did at the wedding, like Don Johnson in *Miami Vice*. I even wear sandals without socks. Ray wears a sport jacket.

The photos arrive a few weeks later. We hang them in the living room next to Mom's painting of the wise Asian man. A good family. A father. A mother. And me.

———————

BUSINESS IS NOT GOOD. Nobody's calling his private phone line in the basement. After six months Ray's investigation firm is more like a hobby. So he takes a night job as a security guard.

One night, he brings me along. His job is to patrol a dirt perimeter road around the geothermal power plant outside Reno. Around and around, over and over.

"I just need proper business cards. I need to get them in the hands of the right people," Ray says. He taps a thumb on the steering wheel. He's wearing a shirt that makes him look like a policeman. "I told your mother, as soon as the new phone book comes out, I'll start getting more calls."

The smell of sagebrush floats through the cracked window. I listen to the popping sound the tires make when we hit bigger rocks. The power plant looks like an alien spaceship landed in the middle of the desert. Steam rises from huge silos.

"Ace Investigations," Ray says. "You need to stay ahead of competition. Remember, always give your business a name that starts with 'A.' That way, people will see your listing first." He points to his temple. "Smart. You need to think about these kinds of things you ever start your own business."

About an hour into our patrol, we see headlights approaching the front gates. Ray turns around and steers toward the gates. We pick up speed. When we get close, the vehicle drives away. "Kids, probably," he says. "Probably out on a joyride."

A jackrabbit darts into the headlights and then disappears.

We drive, and Ray talks. "Your mom says, last summer, you walked around with a neighbor's borrowed mower and asked people if they wanted a mow."

"Five bucks a lawn," I say.

"See, that's what I'm talking about. Initiative. Are you going to do that again this summer?"

"I was thinking about spray-painting curbs. For the houses with the numbers rubbed off."

"Oh, that's good, that's good," he says. "You should do that."

"Yeah?"

"Of course."

"It's hard to get paint, though," I say. "It's expensive. And the store keeps the cans in a cage."

"Well, let's buy you some paint," Ray says. "You'll need stencils. We'll get the whole set."

"Okay."

"Here's what I'm thinking. Okay, listen. I'm thinking black paint for the rectangular background. And bright orange paint for the numbers."

"Orange?"

"Fluorescent orange. For the numbers. Instead of white. People will be able to see the numbers better at night with orange."

"You think?"

"Oh, I know. I was a police officer. Wouldn't I know these things?"

Orange. It's an interesting idea. When summer arrives, he buys me cans of black and cans of fluorescent orange. I start walking around a neighborhood miles away, the rich neighborhood up the hill. Nobody in my neighborhood cares about faded house numbers on their curbs. My friend Andy comes along, and we knock on doors.

Ray claims most of the basement with his metal desk and drawers. He calls the basement his office. He's been too busy to take me fishing, but I get a license anyway and go to the Truckee River alone. Patches hides under my bed when Ray lets his German shepherds inside. The old one is trained—Ray says police trained—and I begin asking Ray to show me the commands. The commands are in German, Ray says, so criminals can't order the dog to stop once they attack.

I'm making a sandwich one afternoon when I hear Ray yell, "Donny, get down here!"

I head down the stairs to the basement. Ray's at his desk. It's a papery mess. He opens the drawer. He has an old badge in there, and a taser. I like to play with the taser when he's not around. Ray gives me an envelope.

"Will you drop this at the print shop?" he says. "They know what it's about. They're waiting."

I skate the two blocks, drop the envelope, and skate back. As soon as I return Ray calls me down to the basement again.

"Go to the courthouse and ask for this document number," he says. He gives me a piece of paper. Off I go on my skateboard, scouting for private investigator information. I feel like I'm on an important assignment. His chores don't feel like chores because I like helping.

I return with the right document. On my way upstairs, Ray says, "Hey, you never told me how it turned out."

"Huh?"

"Your curb painting business."

"Andy and I went out a few times."

"Yeah, and?"

"We knocked on doors."

"How'd that go?"

"We met that guy from TV. The car dealership guy. His curb needed painting. We didn't know it was his house when we knocked."

Ray laughs. "Oh, yeah?"

"He came outside without any hair. He's bald. He must wear a wig on TV."

"And?"

"He hired us."

"And there you go," Ray says. "I told you. See, I told you."

"But the thing is."

"The thing is what?"

"After painting his curb, he came out to look. When he saw the orange numbers, he threw his hat in his yard and started screaming. He took the black can and painted over our work. He said, what about white? He wanted white numbers."

Ray leans back in his chair. "Huh," he says. "And he didn't like the orange?"

"No."

He tumbles forward. "He doesn't know what he's talking about," Ray says. "Well, we'll never buy a car from him, that's for sure. Did he pay you at least?"

"He wanted his money back too."

"And you gave it?"

"Had to."

"Huh," Ray says. "Why didn't you run?"

———————

TO ADD SOME LEVITY to my after-midnight excursion I turn the car's radio dial to Reno's old country station and raise the volume on Brooks & Dunn's "Boot Scootin' Boogie." I know this one. I sing along. These dudes are so over the top it's kind of hard not to adore them. I roll the windows down and welcome the warm desert air.

It's quiet back at Mom's. I lie in bed, reading about the hermit and empathizing with his high lonesome feelings. What a life: alone on the beach, alone on the cape, alone in a creaky old beach house. As I toss in bed, old scars begin to itch, and I reconsider my decision to drive around town, awakening past memories.

Like that night, twenty-eight years ago, when I'm sitting on the dusty couch in the duplex's cool, dank basement, watching the A-Team on TV. Ray's desk takes up most of the space.

Upstairs, there's arguing. It's louder than normal. Patches looks at me with her big eyes. I listen to them argue and pinch my leg, which helps. I hear Mom shouting. I pinch harder. After a while, I tiptoe up the wooden stairwell, crouch on the top step, and listen.

"There's no money left," Mom says. "You spent it all on your stupid private investigator business."

"It's not stupid," he says. "I just need more time. You won't divorce me."

"What? Who said that? I never said that."

"I know you're planning on divorcing me," he says.

"What?" Mom says. "You're dreaming again. You're a dreamer."

Weeks earlier, they argued about money as we drove home from the craft fair. Ray suddenly slammed the brakes, pulled to the side of the road, and screamed until Mom pushed both of us out. We walked for miles in darkness.

Now I hear Ray say, "But you love me, right? You still love me, right?"

"Stop clipping my heels," Mom says. "You're always clipping my heels."

"But you love me?"

"Yeah, yeah, sure," Mom says. "Just stop following me around."

Silence. The basement door opens. Ray towers above me. The handsome face Mom introduced me to now looks like a hard mask. I stand. Ray stomps down the stairs and clicks through the TV channels. I join Mom on the living room couch. She's looking at her hands, twisting her marriage ring around her finger.

"I don't like this," I say.

"I know, honey," she says.

"We might want to go somewhere else for a while," I say.

"We'll be fine," she says.

"I don't know."

"Everything's fine. Everything's okay. We'll be fine. Like always."

The next day, Ray's nice again. And for a while Mom wraps her arms around him, hangs off him, hoping he'll stay calm. I hope so too. I'm waiting for the father that was promised me. I'm waiting for the good man. I'm waiting for adoption. But too often he bosses me around and keeps track of Mom, asking where she's been and with whom, and I watch him criticize and praise in the same breath. He doesn't allow her to walk freely around the duplex without trailing close, whispering into her ear, which makes Mom's lips tighten into a red button. I hate watching her being bullied. It upsets me. It makes me ashamed I'm not big enough to help. Ray makes me tired. He frightens me. He asks where I'm going by stopping me in the hallway and hammering his finger into my chest.

I don't like being at home in my hot, slanted-ceiling bedroom or in the damp basement, overhearing arguments. So I wander, walking downtown alleyways, skating empty parking garages at night with Ronald and Edgar. The plastic smell of my city keeps me warm.

I'm a faithful Catholic. I believe. Each night before bed, I pray for Mom and Patches. I pray for Mom, especially. I've seen things. I pray to end up in a nice home if Ray kills Mom. Maybe I'll live with friends of hers. Maybe I'll live with distant relatives in New York. Maybe I'll live.

One night, I'm in the living room when I hear loud footsteps climbing the basement stairs. The door opens. Ray stomps into the room and sets a tape recorder on the rug. He presses play. Out whistles my voice, then Mom's. He stands with his arms crossed.

"But Mom . . . I don't like him anymore . . ." That's me. That's my voice. "I just don't want him here."

"I know, dear. I know." That's Mom's voice. "I'm sorry. I'm so awfully sorry for putting you through this. Someday I'll make it up to you. Everything will be fine."

My voice: "But what about him?"

Mom: "You don't have to worry about him. He'll be gone soon."

Mom runs into the living room and throws herself on the tape recorder, stabbing buttons on the machine to make it stop. She looks up at Ray. "You tapped our telephone? You tapped our telephone!" she yells. "You son of a bitch. You recorded us!"

Ray uncrosses his arms. He seems to grow impossibly large. In an instant he piles on top of her. Mom throws the tape recorder against the wall and pieces go flying. Patches runs from the room.

———————

IT WAS DEEP INTO November and the skies were darkening. Don and his family were tied down near a boatyard on the Miami River, waiting out the end of the hurricane season. Several minor repairs needed attention before they set sail again. They got to work and prepped the boat for the next journey.

Don stood on the deck. He looked up. Something wasn't right. There was "a curious feeling in the air." He'd listened to the radio report the day before. He didn't hear anything too ominous. He knew a storm was brewing to the northeast, far from their berth. Storms rarely curved back.

Then Don saw clouds flying through the sky. A funny feeling entered his gut.

"When bunched clouds pop up over the rim of the world as though shot from a gun, there's something sinister urging them along." He checked the gauges. The barometric pressure was rapidly dropping. He flicked the gauge with his finger. It dropped again. He knew. He quickly told his family to secure *Gypsy Waters*. He urged fellow sailors around the boatyard to do the same. The family hustled around the deck, storing oars and firming anchors. He ran around the yard and cleared loose debris. Something big was coming.

He looked at the sky again. He didn't like what he saw.

"The wind increased in force, became gusty, each succeeding puff stronger than the last one." Glass shatters upstairs above me. The barometer plummeted again. The glass is from the long wall mirror in the landing outside my bedroom. Rain drove in hard and angled. I feel my body become cold. It's happening again. The wind was so powerful one boat on the shore overturned. I run upstairs, taking the steps two at a time. The roof on the boat shop peeled off. Mom's bloody hand clutches a shard of mirror. She's using it to protect herself, a weapon.

"We knew! . . . it was a real hurricane."

I know too. Ray threw her into the mirror.

More clouds gathered. The floor sparkles. The floor is beautiful. The floor is horrible. More rain shot down from the sky. I don't understand Mom's words. The sky shook. Her words do not match reality. "And did it blow!" Don, Margaret, and Gypsy hid below deck in the cabin, unable to communicate with each other over the immense sound of the "inferno outside." They heard glass shattering around boatyard. It's the nonsense that comes from a person when life is too much. Don looked through the portholes and saw an unmanned schooner drifting away, joined soon after by a sloop. Boats went adrift. Beyond the pilings, the incoming waves were "like rows of charging cavalry horses."

"Rectangles of corrugated iron, sharp edged, were driving past with force sufficient to cut a man in two should they strike him." He draws back his fist.

It was nature's hell. He connects, and then again. Some strange force takes me over. Telephone poles toppled. I run to her and grab her and lead her down the stairs, away from him, screaming at him to get out of the way. Later, Don would learn the wind measured 138 miles per hour. I guide her into our small bathroom as blood drips on the floor and I wrap my arms around her, gripping the towel rack. I hold her close. I'm another version of myself, looking at myself from a distance.

"The hurricane shrieked and whined." I feel him behind me. I can hear him breathing. I ask Ray to go, to leave us, please, please leave us. I hold her. I hold the towel rack. I do not let her go. I will never let her go. She's everything.

The front door slams shut. The walls shake.

They waited until, at last, the storm passed. When they emerged from below deck, the foremast was gone. The boatyard was in shambles. Debris was everywhere. One building no longer had a roof. Boats were missing. Much of *Gypsy Waters* was broken but repairable. Everything would be okay. His family was safe.

———————

MY VISIT TO RENO only lasts three days. It's disappointing to leave without getting the full story.

Before flying back to Portland, I borrow Mom's car and visit the county courthouse, scrolling through microfiche until I find the right documents. I want to see them, rub my fingers on them. It's a thick stack. The printout costs more than my parents' divorce papers.

"IT IS HEREBY ORDERED that Defendant, RAYMOND THOMAS ———, JR., be and he hereby is enjoined and restrained from threatening, or actually committing bodily or physical harm upon Plaintiff herein, and from molesting, harming, contacting, threatening or otherwise abusing Plaintiff, directly or by telephone, or her minor child from a former marriage . . ."

Et cetera, et cetera, et cetera.

During the short flight I gaze at the white-crowned clouds, thinking about Ray, daydreaming about hiring my own private investigator to track down that one-time, two-bit private investigator, and then my daydream takes a dramatic turn: I envision raising enough cold hard cash through crowdfunding to hire Ray Liotta to break that dickhead's shins with a lead pipe. It's an animalistic fantasy, and sometimes I have them, but then my human side speaks up. And I wonder: what cruelties were inflicted on Ray as a boy? What awful shit had he endured that primed him for that kind of violent behavior? How far back does his violent legacy reach? Over the years, as I've thought about Ray, the imposing image of him standing in the hallway with red balled fists has softened into the heartbreaking image of Ray as a terrorized, frightened child standing with red balled fists.

Along with Don's book, I also brought "The Story of My Life" with me to Reno, but I never opened it. Now I set it on the seatback tray.

I want to locate my father's whereabouts during The Ray Years. I find him in the "Mining" chapter. While Ray was stomping around the duplex and pushing us around, my father was working as a mine superintendent north of Soda Springs, Idaho, blasting for phosphate in "what was called the Caribou range." He loved the mountain solitude. All around were elk, deer, moose, ducks, and coyotes. He drank beers on the weekend with a Mormon named Tom and a Vietnam vet who carried a .45 caliber pistol and "spooked easily." His favorite part? Clean air. Sucked into his lungs, the high mountain air brightened his mind. Life was good.

I look out the window at the clouds. I think about my father leaving. I think about Manuel. And I think about Ray leaving too.

————————

RAY ARRIVES in his El Camino with a trailer hitched to the back. I'm waiting by the window as he parks alongside the duplex. I carry my bicycle upstairs to my bedroom.

Because of the restraining order, two police officers are present. One seems tired and bored as he follows Ray through the duplex. Ray takes his time. He lumbers around in a black mood. He eyeballs everything and thinks everything belongs to him.

"That's most certainly not your bowl," Mom says.

"It is," he says. "We bought it at Mervyn's. I bought it at Mervyn's. It's mine. I bought it."

"Ha! You bought it? That's a story!"

The police officers clutch their belts and silently look at each other. Ray's a former police officer, now watched by other police officers, and for the first time I wonder why Ray no longer works as a police officer.

Ray emerges from the basement gripping two fishing poles.

"One of those is my son's," Mom says.

"They're mine," Ray says. "I bought them. I paid for them."

"But you gave one to him," Mom says.

"And now I want it back," he says.

I hate watching this. I head out the back door to the small fenced yard. Patches is lying in the dirt next to her bowl. She looks up at me with beautiful, kind eyes. She stands beside me as I spy on Ray through slats in the wood fence. Her tail slaps the back of my legs.

I watch Ray walk out the front door and place both fishing poles inside the trailer. I wait. As soon as he disappears inside, I unlatch the gate, sprint to the trailer, grab one fishing pole, and run back to the yard, latching the gate behind me. Then I toss the pole over another fence and into our neighbor's yard, where it'll be safe.

Next, I watch Ray put a green army helmet inside the trailer. He gave that to me too. Again, I wait until he's inside before running to the trailer. Over the fence and into the neighbor's yard it goes. I steal back the things he gave me, the things he promised me as a father.

The back door opens. I turn. It's Ray. He knows I've been spying. An officer stands behind him.

"Where's my bike?" Ray asks me.

From inside I hear Mom shout, "Just give him the damn bicycle, Donny. I'll get you a new one."

I can't look at Ray.

I walk upstairs, slowly carry the bicycle down, and roll it over. Ray won't use it. It's a bike built for a ten-year-old.

"This is mine," he says.

The officers glance at each other.

Ray rolls my bicycle through the duplex and out the front door. I don't attempt to retrieve it. That would be too obvious.

"I can't get it right," Mom says, after Ray and the officers leave. "You need better men than that in your life. Pitiful. Just pitiful."

A few weeks later, I'm roaming the neighborhood after dark with Edgar and Ronald. As we round a corner, Edgar extends his arm across my chest, stopping me.

"Look," Edgar says. Ray's El Camino is parked on the sloped street that has a view of our duplex. The car's dark, but someone's inside. "He's watching," Edgar says.

The car appears more and more around the neighborhood. It's the ugliest car ever made. So it's hard to miss. As the weeks pass, Ronald, Edgar, and I make a game out of it.

We glide around building corners, watching him. We hide underneath bushes, watching him. We watch the watcher.

One night, we see him exit the El Camino. He's carrying something toward the duplex. We watch him heave it over the back fence. We wait. We watch him walk back toward the El Camino. The headlights go on. He drives away.

We run over to see what he left. It's the framed photos from our family photo shoot.

Months pass. Ray continues watching. He leaves Styrofoam cups dangling off our truck's antennae, marked with black X's. He calls. He leaves threatening messages. He sends pleading letters and terrifying letters. He says he's changed. He says he now accepts the word of Jesus Christ. He follows us to Mass and harasses us with his presence. At home I walk around the duplex and inspect the outside phone lines, making sure he's not recording our telephone calls.

Mom keeps the photos from the professional photo shoot. But she cuts out Ray's face. His calls and weird letters continue for years, but in time Ray fades from our daily lives, even though he remains a threat that lingers in the backs of our minds.

Eighteen years after the divorce, Mom enters a department store and sees him. He's near the electronics section. She believes he sees her too. Terror pulses through her. She quickly seeks refuge through a swinging door and waits in the employee lounge. She explains to confused employees why she's hiding. She's afraid he might be waiting in the parking lot, as he often did, long before, fully in breach of the restraining order. But way before any of that nonsense, Ray was one of my fathers.

––––––––––

AFTER MOM'S THIRD DIVORCE, she begins noticing the men around her workplace: sheriff's deputies and detectives and corrections officers. Many are fathers. They're burly, nice, and they're safe because they carry firearms. One of her oldest friends, a homicide detective, already shows up every year on Mom's birthday to take me shopping for her gift. Before one of these mall trips, he sits me down and gives me the sex talk.

There are men at her work, Mom explains. Pleasant men, she tells me, men who lead a scout troop. One of them plants the suggestion. She comes home one night and urges me to join.

"I don't want to," I say. I'm a skater. The Boy Scouts are lame. "Those kids are queers," I say.

"Don't say things like that," Mom says. "You'll like these guys," she says.

"No."

"Just attend one meeting."

"Nope. Everyone knows Boy Scouts are queers."

"Language," Mom says.

One Tuesday night, she orders me into the car and drives to the American Legion Hall and tells me to get out.

"The meeting is in the basement," she says. "It's only for an hour and a half."

"No. I don't want to."

"Get out of the car."

"No."

"Listen, kiddo," Mom says. She has a hard look in her eyes. "Get your damn butt out of the car."

She attends the meeting with me and stands in the back of the basement with the other fathers.

Many of the boys in Troop 1 are the sons of the county's search-and-rescue squad. It doesn't take me long to learn that these men and these boys aren't queers. If anyone's a queer, it's me. For these men, scouting is an excuse to go crazy in the wilderness and bring along their sons.

Mom pushes me toward these men.

These men begin to father me, and in my quiet way I begin to love them. Whatever the hell they want to do, I'll do it. I follow them around and ask questions and listen to what they say.

On daytrips into the mountains, I pay close attention to their instructions. I laugh at their jokes. I always carry more than my share of equipment. I want their attention. I want them to notice me.

When my new friend Brian invites me over to his house for dinner, I'm the perfect gentleman. I want to impress his dad. I like Brian's dad. He leads our troop. He's a detective at the sheriff's department, and he and Brian share inside jokes. He gives Brian the sort of gentle love I see coming from mothers. On visits to their house, I wonder whether my being around interrupts some kind of order.

But seeing the kiss, one summer afternoon, does something to me. We're in the front yard at Brian's house, on the grass, cleaning and folding tents. The sun is above us, spitting heat. Brian's dad takes the hose and sprays us, and we run into the street. His dad laughs. Soon we're drenched and our clothes are heavy.

His dad tosses us towels. We sit on the driveway, burning water droplets from our skin. After a while Brian gets up to help his dad. They're storing the tents in the garage rafters. I watch Brian's dad sling an arm around him and kiss the side of Brian's head. I watch Brian pull away, embarrassed. He shoves his dad. Sitting on the concrete driveway, watching, I'm ashamed for not having access to that kind of embarrassment.

These men, like Brian's dad. These men — and their sons.

I make friends with boys older than me. Nature enters my blood, and it's a sort of savior. Brian's dad often leads us into the wilderness. We backpack fifty miles through Yosemite and filter creek water and fight off black bears at night. We lay sleeping bags in meadows and sleep under a dome of stars. We explore Desolation Wilderness and swim in alpine lakes and throw freshly caught trout on the fire. We build high elevation snow shelters and sleep in subzero temperatures. We hike the Pacific coastline and shoot class four white water on the Russian River and sail yachts down Hawk Channel in the Florida Keys — like Don, Margaret, and Gypsy did fifty years before.

THEY RENOVATED AN OLD bugeye yacht and made her seaworthy. They cruised around Chesapeake Bay under the shadows of blue heron. They rammed a shallow mud bank and got towed clear. They anchored the yacht, boarded a canoe, and ventured into the Everglades. They explored Fort Jefferson on Garden Key, meditated on the sea's "cathedral quiet," and found happiness in simple pleasures — white sand beaches, aquamarine water, and "that graceful form on the skyline that is our home."

Soon the family's stories drew to an end. They sailed to Miami and prepared for their next great adventure. Don bought supplies. Gypsy and Margaret fastened ropes to cleats. Onward and forward! They were off to see what "the Bahamas looked like from the decks of the *Gypsy Waters*." And, just like that, my book ends too.

The binding is separating. The pages are dirty with my notes. It's been an incredible read. Through this series of linked narratives, I've watched Don and Margaret care for their child, and I've seen a happy girl grow up. Is it unreasonable to feel a small pinch of jealousy? I imagine a childhood like hers, where both parents, both present, instilled fortitude and self-esteem, where a sense of calm and well-being flourished instead of a constant state of hypervigilance.

I wonder about Don and Margaret. I wonder about Gypsy. She must have become a fabulously interesting person.

I want to know what became of them. I'd like more than a story in a book. But how do you bridge a chasm of nearly seventy years?

Over the past several months, I've prepared folders labeled "Don," "Margaret," and "Gypsy." The folders contain the earliest information. I know Don was well known in the nautical community. He was invited to speaking engagements. And whenever the family sailed into a new harbor, the local paper usually dispatched a reporter.

I open my computer and search through Florida newspaper archives. Sure enough, the family left a trail of inky crumbs.

Newspapers described Don as "a gracious and affable person by nature" and Margaret as "an ardent seawoman . . . tanned by southern sun." Another reporter, from St. Petersburg's *Evening Independent*, wrote: "He has been to every group of islands in the Bahamas, roamed throughout the waters along the Atlantic. He hasn't stopped yet—and he doesn't intend to." Now aboard the yacht was a trained "jarakeet" named Eve and a baby alligator.

Each news item offers a feeble peek into their daily lives. But without Don talking to me through his book, it's as though I'm looking at them through a telescope. Concrete details are missing. Mysteries surface. For example, the Sarasota *Herald-Tribune* hinted at a forthcoming book called *Gypsy Waters Cruises Foreign*, about the family's Bahamas adventure, but I don't think the book was ever published.

Despite the difficulties tracking them, I have a firm understanding of their whereabouts up to 1940, when Don's stories began appearing in mainstream publications. The first appeared in the *Saturday Evening Post*, which introduced his sea hero, John Pindar, to a wide readership. In 1940, according to that year's census record, the family was still living aboard *Gypsy Waters*, docked on the Hillsborough River near Tampa Bay.

The 1940 census lists Don's occupation in two slots: "Writer" and "Magazine." He was fifty-three, Margaret was forty-two, and Gypsy, who pretty much only knew life at sea, was sixteen. Don's annual reported salary was $1,200. That's not bad, considering the median income for a single man at that time was $956. The family remained in the harbor until the wind blew them elsewhere. And I lose sight of them.

"YOU'RE LUCKY, KIDDO," Mom says, one bright Sunday in November. "You're really lucky, you know that? My dad painted houses. I never received gifts like this. Never forget that." She hands me a set of keys.

"I know," I say. "Thanks."

We're standing in the driveway on my sixteenth birthday. Mom's present is a black Toyota truck.

"Don't ever say you're not lucky," she says.

"Okay, okay," I say. "I'm lucky. You're right. I'm lucky."

It's odd how Grandma's death improves our lives. Suddenly, there's money—an inheritance. After Grandma's funeral we relocated from the downtown duplex to a four-bedroom tract house in a subdivision named for the Donner Party. Our house sits inside the late afternoon shadow of Rattlesnake Mountain, a large brown hill across the street from my bedroom window. At the base stands a plaque. The Donner Party camped here before their final, fatal ascent into the Sierras.

It's taken me decades to understand how that minor move, from downtown to subdivision, from cigarette butts on the sidewalks to a ticky-tacky oasis, was actually a massive shift in fortune. Relocating separated me from unruly friends and possible life paths. The rundown brick duplex and Boy Scouts and skating alleyways slid into things of the past.

When Gypsy was sixteen, she was still at sea with her family. At that same age, I'm making new friends, excelling academically, and sliding between extremes—okay but not okay, carefree but restless and unable to understand emerging spells of overwhelming sadness. At school I join clubs, play soccer, and stealthily absorb the advice of my friends' fathers—like snatching invisible radio waves from the air.

Mom showers me with gifts as though making up for lost time. A truck on my birthday. New clothes, a guitar, a snowboard.

As some kind of ongoing parenting lesson, she also brings home photocopied mugshots of the gnarliest drug-addled inmates. The photos always show a progression, from first arrest on, highlighting the incredible damage drugs can have on the human face.

"Just look at that," Mom says. "Just look at those scabs. See. That's what speed does. Don't ever do speed. Don't *ever*."

Sadness implants inside me like some diseased organ that periodically awakens. I mask its twinges by staying extraordinarily active. I lie about my father whenever faced with that stupid, tired question. Where friends have rough outlines about their origins, I carry questions. Who is he? Where does he live? Does he care? I don't know whether he has another family, or other sons. Without a father the transition into early manhood bewilders me. School becomes a laboratory for adopting different identities—skater, preppy, soccer jock, snowboarder, cowboy, punk, cowboy punk, skater preppy, cowboy jock, and perpetual forger, because I'm obsessed with making the perfect fake ID, as though the finest ID will not only lead to beer but to my truest self. One month, I dress like Garth Brooks, boots and cowboy hat. The next month, it's Diego Maradona, with a touch of the Clash.

I try convincing myself the fantasies are common, typical of all hormonal teenagers, but my sadness somehow seems deeper, more vivid, and scarier. Whenever the sadness descends, I draw perverse pleasure from the thought of no longer living and breathing. This person or that comment will no longer hurt because I'll remove myself from the equation. I won't be around for anything to hurt me again. Fantasies of my death give me a sense of control and stability. The movies I play in my head are complex, luscious, and soothing. Death is the one reliable thing. Sadness rudely interrupts my life at unexpected times. And when it appears, I feel worthless. After all, aren't I? My father tossed me aside. At school I play the happy teenage role while secretly enlarging gruesome kingdoms in my mind.

One night, we're at the dinner table, forking meatloaf and potatoes, passing iced tea and paper napkins. I don't feel well.

"Have you thought about a winter job?" Mom asks.

"I don't care," I say.

"Well, you should."

"Who gives a fucking shit."

"What? Don't talk like that," she says.

"Whatever."

"Why are you being like this?"

"I don't feel right."

"Everything's okay," she says. "You're fine."

"I don't think I want to live anymore," I say.

Her eyes widen. She slams her fork on the table. "And what do you mean by that, mister?"

"I feel like slitting my wrists. Or jumping off a building."

I want to hurt her. I want to be heard, and I need help. I need her help. I'm furious and don't feel well and don't know why.

Mom stands. Her chair topples over. "Don't ever say that," she says. "Never, *never* say that."

"I don't care."

"But you're fine. Yesterday, you played a good soccer game. You're okay."

"I am not okay! I don't know why you ever wanted me."

"What? Of course I wanted you."

"You should have aborted me!"

"Oh, I could have, mister," she says, her voice rising. "But I didn't. I wanted you. I love you. I wanted to have you."

"I wish you didn't!"

For a week the house remains still and silent.

One day, not long after our fight, I corner a friend at school. His name is Jason. As the most ambitious in my friend circle, Jason recently applied to a foreign exchange program. I demand answers. How did he go about it? What kind of special information does he have that the rest of us don't? He explains the process, and I follow his advice, mailing away for brochures. I'm itching to leave Reno. To leave Nevada. To *leave*.

Seven months later, I'm living on a country estate with a smart Danish family. Søren and Hanne, host parents. Jakob and Anette, host siblings. And two German shorthaired pointers. And ducks. And sheep. And a nearby forest. And a pond!

My world inverts, as though some rascally God reaches down my throat and grabs my guts and turns me inside out. The inheritance from Grandma helps us purchase a house, and it also launches me across the globe. The shift from Reno's sun-soaked streets to the orderly and well-planned Danish village is disorientating.

"Remind me. What is it your father does?" Søren asks soon after my arrival.

I've avoided the topic of my father. "He lives in California," I say, spreading my lies to another continent.

"Interesting," Hanne says. "California."

"But what is it he does?" Søren asks. "His occupation."

"He's an architect," I say. An architect seems decent and honorable. Manuel was an architect. Mike Brady, father on *The Brady Bunch*, was a California architect, a factoid implanted in my brain early on.

"An architect," Søren says. "Wonderful! Remind me to show you the different forms of Danish architecture."

For the next six months, Søren points out architectural flourishes on houses and buildings and castles, saying, "Your father would be interested in that. We Danes know what we're doing."

While living in Denmark, I hear about a stranger now living in our house. Over the phone Mom mentions that a man is staying in the spare bedroom. He needs a place, she says. Just for a little while. It's temporary. "He's going through a rough patch," Mom says. "His name is Chuck."

"But who is he?" I ask from thousands of miles away. "I don't want some stranger living with us."

"You're not even here," she says, with irritation in her voice. "Besides, he was around when you were a little boy."

"I don't remember him."

"It's only for a short time."

"How short? Tomorrow? Next week? Will he be gone by the time I return to Reno?"

"He's a good man," she says.

"I don't like this."

"Want me to ask him to move out? I can do that." Her voice rises. "I'll ask him to move out tomorrow. Want me to do that?"

"No, no. It's fine."

When I return from my Danish fairytale, I notice romance happening out of the corners of my eyes. Roses on the countertop and secret dates. Chuck has not moved out. In fact, he's completely moved in. Together, they disappear for lengthy weekends in Tahoe. That's why a strange man has been living in the house: they're dating.

Another man in the house. At night we lock our bedroom doors. Mom has a deadbolt on her bedroom door. Every night, I hear the metallic lock snap into place.

Several days after Christmas I bring home a pile of college brochures and spread them across the dining room table. The inheritance from Grandma has opened a door. Money offers options. A larger world. I've already seen it. I grab at the chance.

"I want go to New York," I say.

"Because I'm from there?" Mom asks.

"Because it's far away."

Mom flinches. "What about those colleges in California?"

"You told me I could make the decision."

"Well, okay, you're right, I did," she says. She looks at me strangely and tips her head. "You know, Grandpa would be proud. He worked hard for that money. You'll be the first one of us to go to college."

"Yeah."

"I'll miss you, kiddo," she says. "We've certainly gone through some stuff, me and you, haven't we? It's always been just the two of us."

I nod.

Judging by the quiet way she's looking at me, I believe she understands what I understand. My decision will take me away from her, and not only in distance. Just then, I hear the rumble of the garage door opening. Chuck has returned. He's not my father. None of them is my father.

"Hey, you okay?" she says. "What's going on, kiddo?" She puts her hand on my face. "It's okay. You're just going away to college. Everything's going to be all right. It's okay. Why are you crying?"

I bury my head in her neck, momentarily unable to hide from the pain.

———————

DOCTORS DON'T KNOW what to make of my list of symptoms. I visit yet another doctor, hoping the third time will be the charm. He's a large man, with close-set alligator eyes and a solid handshake. The exam room is decorated with black-and-white photos of Paris.

"So, my nurse tells me you're a student at the college," he says.

"Sophomore," I say.

"What's your major?"

"English and sociology."

He nods. "You know, I wanted to be an English major once. I always loved reading. Instead, I ended up in medicine. You know—made my parents happy. But anyway," he says, folding his hands. "Tell me about these headaches."

"They don't stop. I'm always dizzy."

"Hmm."

"And my jaw hurts, and my upper back. I wake up in pain. Even the tissue behind my eyeballs feels full, if that makes any sense," I say.

"How do you sleep?"

"Why?"

"Those black half-moons beneath your eyes tell me something."

"I think I sleep okay, I guess. I don't know."

"Tell you what. Let's put you on Ambien. Get some sleep, and we'll take it from there."

We'll take it from there—they say that. Let's watch, let's wait, let's see about this, and we'll take it from there.

Later in the week, I fight through the headaches and dizziness and ask my friend Andy to help with an important errand. We drive over to the local newspaper printing plant to retrieve my recent order: five thousand newsprint copies. My fanzine is small, only sixteen pages, the approximate size of a television-listing insert, and now five thousand copies sit bundled and stacked on wooden crates.

"Oh, my God," Andy says. "This is insane. We're going to need another car. Or make another trip. What did you do? Why did you order so many?"

Five thousand is an unbelievable amount. "That was the smallest order I could make," I say. "But you're right. This is a lot."

"A lot? Oh, my God," Andy says.

All five thousand newsprint copies nearly fill my small dorm room, stacked in columns, floor to ceiling. I wanted to make the effort count, but this seems a bit extreme.

"We did it," I tell my best friend, Josh, over the phone.

"And?"

"There are a lot of them. And I mean a lot. But we did it."

"Hell yes," he says.

I recruited Josh to help with writing articles and reviewing punk records. I asked him to be my coconspirator. We grew up together. On the masthead we have "offices" in Nevada and New York.

Writing comes at me like a bullet by way of punk rock. The angry music of my late teens introduces me to the world of photocopied fanzines made by fans of the angry music of my late teens, and I fall in love with the punk subculture and its angry, screwball, anything goes attitude.

The first time I flipped through one of these stapled, photocopied, cut-and-pasted amateur magazines at my local record store, I felt heat rising off the paper. Zines dominated three shelves below the regular glossies. Curious, I examined them one by one. Each had a personality; each gave a glimpse of a different town; each was united by a shared appreciation of punk rock. They were far from professional, but that was the point.

They were lone bullhorns aimed at a corporate, consumerist, and bloated American culture. I bought a handful. I rabidly consumed zines written by Aaron Cometbus, Bob Conrad, and Dishwasher Pete, an odd man whose odd goal was to wash dishes in restaurants in every American state. His goal struck me as supremely noble—a big, hard middle finger to the American middle-class dream. In these cheaply produced pages, I discovered the names of Noam Chomsky and Howard Zinn, two lefty luminaries who provided the kind of nourishment I was seeking. It was extremely comforting to discover others out there who were as outraged as me.

Freshman year, I slapped together my first zine, a hand-stapled, xeroxed pamphlet of such magnificent buffoonery that my older self feels embarrassed even mentioning it. Thirty printed copies went to friends and record stores. Ten typed pages full of rants calling the establishment—"the man"—fascists. The zine was filthy with *fuck yous*.

But now, now, sophomore year, Operation Ivy and Propagandhi wake me up in the morning on my stereo. Now I strut around campus acting in a way my older self recognizes as furious and shielding deep insecurities. Now I'm a poseur defensively locked in a pose. Purple hair, leather jacket, and facial rings round out my developing angry persona. Add several tattoos to the mix. Now I wear the typical accouterments of the fuck-you-I-hurt psyche. And I do hurt. My fucking head is killing me.

I nurture the idea that my father's long absence gives me significant punk rock cred. He left. Now he's sending letters to my campus mailbox. He sucks. Fuck him. Fuck *everything*.

My friend Andy helps me distribute the zine around campus. It's like a brochure loudly advertising my fury at everyone and everything.

I sprinkle copies around town like some crazed, defiant Johnny Appleseed. Friends take the newsprint bundles to their hometowns and scatter them. I mail copies to *Maximum Rock'n'Roll*, praying for a positive review in that punk rock bible. I toss them in dorm lounges and carpet bomb the student union, hoping others will appreciate my Marxist viewpoints, perhaps enjoy the interview with the touring punk band, and connect with my vibrating indignation.

The dean of student affairs soon leaves a message on my dorm phone, summoning me to his office. When I traipse in, he plucks my zine off his desk. Seeing him hold a fresh copy makes me unreasonably proud. He doesn't look pleased. "Mind telling me about this," he says.

"It's just a small project of mine," I say.

"Jesus is a black lesbian," he says. "And that's just the first sentence. There's more."

I nod.

"Well, do me a favor," he says. "Will you please let me know the next time you decide to drop this kind of publication around campus? I'd like a little warning. We might get phone calls."

More and more, I wake up with ringing in my ears. I wake up dizzy. I wake up with my eyeballs feeling full and my jaw burning.

I return to the doctor and wait in the exam room, staring at a shadowy, black-and-white photograph of Sacré-Cœur at night.

The doctor pops his head in. "Hey there, sophomore," he says. "Mind joining me in my office?"

In his office? I hop off the exam table and follow him down the hall, where he shuts the office door. He asks me to sit. I've never been asked into a doctor's office before.

"So you say you're still dizzy all the time?" he says. "Your ears ring?"

"Yes."

"Headaches?"

"Yes."

"I've looked through your chart. Your symptoms haven't gone away for months," he says. "There's nothing in your blood work. Let's do an MRI. We might be looking at a brain tumor."

My breath leaves me. "I don't have a brain tumor," I say quickly.

"Well, let's hope not," he says.

I call Mom from my dorm room. It's drizzling outside, and my hair's wet from the trek back. Chuck, who's still living with Mom, answers the phone. Chuck quickly and unceremoniously relays the news. At first I think he's joking. Apparently, he's not. I ask to speak with Mom. Her crimped voice confirms it. I hang up and stalk to the dining hall.

I slide my tray next to Andy's. "What's new?" he says. "Did you end up making it to your class?"

"My mother just got married," I say.

He doesn't respond.

"Last weekend," I say. "His name is Chuck."

"And you didn't go?" Andy asks.

"I didn't know about it," I say. "Nobody told me. Nobody tells me shit."

"Weird," Andy says.

"Yeah, weird."

Not long after Mom's fourth marriage, a slip of paper appears in my mailbox at the student union. I bring the slip to the mailroom office. There's a package from Mom, but I know from the return label it was mailed through Chuck's machining business. Sometimes Mom sends care packages. Maybe it's an apology gift for not telling me about getting married.

I set the package on a table in the student lounge. A classmate from my Milton class is sitting nearby, his tennis shoes propped on a table littered with fliers.

"Care package," I say.

"Sweet," he says. "It's been like forever since my parents sent me anything."

I slice through a layer of tape with my dorm key and open the flaps. Resting on top of a bundle of fresh T-shirts and a new sweater is a stack of *Playboys* and *Penthouses*. My classmate glances over before I shut the flaps. His eyes are wide. "Your *parents* sent you *Penthouse?*" he asks.

I've escaped to New York to get away from my mother and her men. But now that I'm in college, I find myself resenting these excitable rich kids and their outwardly perfect lives. But shit, when I do return to Reno during breaks, I yearn for the familiar collegiate atmosphere and safe leafy pathways and green ivy on red brick buildings.

I head back to the doctor's office. This time I get the Eiffel Tower exam room.

"Well," the doctor says. "Your temporomandibular joint is dislocated."

"So, no brain tumor?"

He chuckles to himself. "No brain tumor," he says. "I hope I didn't scare you."

He explains everything. Clenching my teeth triggers a cascade of symptoms: muscle spasms, dizziness, headaches, jaw pain. Everything's connected. He says some people have heart attacks, some get ulcers, and some, like me, carry stress in the neck and jaw. He tells me I need to stop worrying. I need to stop clenching my teeth. But how? I clench my teeth all day and all night. I'm uptight and stressed and always vaguely outraged, and when I don't feel outraged, I feel depressed, and when I'm not depressed, I have panic attacks while waiting in line at the bank.

"You have a severe case of muscle tension," he says. "The inner muscles of your jaw feel like steel cables. If there was a sport that involved using your jaw muscles, you'd be an Olympian."

I stare at him, not amused.

"We can always try physical therapy," he says.

"I've already done that."

"You have?"

"This isn't something new. I've also tried hypnotism and acupuncture. Nothing helps."

"Well," he says, then pauses. "Perhaps you should talk to someone."

"Talk to someone?" I say. "Like who? Talk to who?"

"A therapist."

"What?" I say. "I don't think so. I don't need that."

"Are you going through anything personal? Anything difficult?"

"No, why? Why? Why do you ask that?"

"It seems you've had these symptoms for quite a while. Emotional and psychological pain can manifest in the body. Talking to a therapist might help."

Instead of talking to someone, I turn my attention on something bigger than a sixteen-page newsprint zine. For my final English project, I spend all my free time writing a 400-page novel about a boy brought up in an apartment above a porno theater by a blind father and mute mother. The boy must translate between his parents. His mother writes messages on a notepad, and the boy reads these notes to his father. He's their interpreter, held captive by blindness and the inability to speak. I model the setting after the adult theater near the old brick duplex on South Center Street in Reno. I title my novel "The Fifth Sun." When I show it to my advisor, Tatyana Tolstaya, a visiting writer from Russia, she nods approvingly and draws a lungful of smoke from her cigarette and says, in her tricky Russian way, "It's a good beginning."

A good beginning? I bind the novel into a paper brick with rubber bands, shove it under my bed, and try to forget about it.

———

ON DECEMBER 7, 1941, the Imperial Japanese Navy bombed Pearl Harbor, and the United States declared war. My father was born the following year. A year later came Mom. During that period Margaret and her family were living in the Great Smoky Mountains on a farm with "our big flock of chickens, our pigs, our cows, and a couple horses." The war ended the family's decade-long sailing adventure, and they returned to the land.

After spending a summer in Oregon, I return to Iowa City, where my search for the family's story continues. Figuring out their zigzagging trail is a pleasurable puzzle, and the hunt produces the same kind of brain-teasing buzz Robin probably gets from her late-night Sudoku games.

By going through my notes, I remember Margaret was also a writer, and after the voyage in Don's book ended, I locate the family's narrative thread by downloading Margaret's *Christian Science Monitor* articles. For twenty years she wrote about her life and her family. I download forty-nine articles, scribbling the publication date on each.

Her writing appeared in the "Women Today" and "Home Forum" sections. Margaret wrote about everyday moments, but it's obvious she yearned to use her full powers. Her opening paragraphs are sweeping portraits of landscape, but by the end of each article she's offering readers spinach and cake recipes. Margaret's full talents were obviously constrained by an era. She was limited to writing about teaching, cooking, and parenting.

Despite that, her domestic commentaries serve a purpose. They're personal. They provide color, like Don's book. These articles also give me the family's location during the war. They were living in the foothills of the Smoky Mountains, in Sevier County, Tennessee. I'm remotely familiar with the landscape because Cormac McCarthy used Sevier County as the setting for his novel *Child of God*.

One article—"School Afloat"—reminisced about Gypsy's early schooling while living at sea. Apparently, Gypsy had been a stubborn student. The girl didn't like the idea of "floating school." Margaret, who studied teaching, understood the "various theories of modern education" and the importance of the three Rs—reading, writing, and arithmetic. But other than teaching Gypsy the three Rs, the girl's early classroom had been the world. She learned geography, history, natural science, and music by sailing, visiting Spanish forts, catching fish, and playing the accordion and guitar.

By the mid-1940s Gypsy had met a man by the name of Oliver Horn. Oliver was a pacifist. He was sent to live in eastern Tennessee at a conscientious objector's camp operated by the Civilian Public Service. And

Gypsy lived nearby. The men at Oliver's camp, CPS 108, objected to military service on ethical and religious grounds. Instead of fighting, they did "work of national importance" by serving as instant park rangers. They "fought fires, repaired trails, and maintained roads."

The Civilian Public Service is a part of our national history I know little about, and it fascinates me. On an informational CPS website, I locate an old sepia photo of Oliver. He and four others pose beside a newly constructed trail sign. Oliver is a striking young man. Crouching, slight smile, hair swept back, forearms on his thighs, he wears a long-sleeve shirt and overalls.

How Gypsy met Oliver is unclear, but they soon married.

The mountains, however, couldn't hold Don and Margaret. They set off on their next big adventure: Baja California! They traveled by jeep. Off again they went, bouncing down the desert peninsula's dirt roads and pulling a luggage trailer. Margaret would soon send dispatches to the *Monitor* from the coastal city of La Paz.

As I piece together this period in their lives, I'm eager to find an even wider window. I want to feel emotionally closer. To me, they have become a totem. They seem like a perfect family. Don and Margaret met, fell in love, and drifted around North America sharing wild experiences with an intrepid daughter who married a man with a conscience.

I place Margaret's *Monitor* articles in a new folder and start looking into Gypsy. When I type "Gypsy Waters" and "Oliver Horn" into Google, unexpected information appears on my computer screen. I get up from my desk. I pace around the house. I consider heading over to the gym and running around the track, calling it a day, rubbing my eyes and making the news I just read disappear. After some time, I return to my computer and piece together a disturbing puzzle.

In March 1948, Oliver Horn died. He was twenty-five years old. According to his death certificate, he died from a perforated gastric ulcer. Gypsy became a twenty-four-year-old widow. Oliver's body was shipped back to Missouri, his home state, for burial. Gypsy followed. Soon she enrolled as a student at the University of Missouri in Columbia. A year later, she was charged with first-degree felony arson.

FOLLOWING GRADUATION I chase the cliché and move to San Francisco to become a writer.

I want to participate in the bohemian way of life to learn something deeper, and even though many of my opinions are reactive, my worldview black-and-white, I radiate a knowing vibe. Like we all do.

We love this city. We love colorful alleyway murals and first free Tuesdays at MOMA. We embrace the idea of diversity. We love open-mindedness and secret warehouse parties and women-owned sex shops and the legacy of Harvey Milk. The city beats with the drumming hearts of activists and weekend musicians and actors who stage free political musicals in the park. My friends are driven. Each has an interesting interest. Each works toward a goal. Writers, musicians, and artists, and the day jobs they hate. A doctor, a graphic designer, a lawyer, and the lights they can afford to leave on.

Anger is still the easiest emotion for me to locate, and I use it as fuel. Writing comes easily when I have a hand tightly wrapped around a live wire. My second novel, "Pimp City Cowboy," tells the story of a young Nevada man who inherits a brothel from his truant father. I write it, read it twice, and shove it under my bed.

Then I attempt to write a memoir, but writing about my absentee father is too real, too painful. So I ignore that ridiculous notion and start my own independent press, designing and publishing books by Blake Nelson and Percival Everett. In my free time I volunteer with the prison literature project in Berkeley, mailing books to inmates. I produce several record albums, one of which raises money for the prison literature project.

Punk music provides the soundtrack to a life immersed in ideas and words and weekend activism. Music isn't just noise burping from a radio. It's rousing. It's nourishment.

The soft, misty, golden light is unlike anywhere, and that's only the half of it. When the wind blows, the minty smell of eucalyptus drifts from the park and through the cracked window of my basement studio. This city has everything. Unexpected, heart-crushing views. Energetic, clothes-optional parades. The perpetual thought the ground might shake and split open. The streets are gummy and glorious, filled with businessmen and guys in skintight shirts and street artists and homeless hawking *Street Sheet*. Even though dot-commers threaten to crush the city's spirit, the kids keep coming. The kids keep coming. We keep coming! And I feel alive, part of it, part of *something special*.

San Francisco is the home of Dashiell Hammett and the Beats and the Dead Kennedys and Lawrence Ferlinghetti's City Lights. It's the epicenter of the punk rock music I worshipped in college. A rousing crew waves radical banners. V. Vale's RE/Search Publications documents outliers and pranksters and freaks. There's also *Maximum Rock'n'Roll*, the cooperatively run, elitist punk rock magazine. Over the bridge, in Oakland, AK Press publishes leftist books. And Berkeley's all-ages punk venue on Gilman Street hosts bands that pound your eardrums into permanent tinnitus. The Bay Area is full of interesting writers. Armistead Maupin. Michael Chabon. Michelle Tea. Gary Snyder. And just recently some dude named Dave Eggers dropped a nuclear bomb on the city in the form of a memoir, a book I denounce because to broadcast my appreciation will get me ridiculed in my social circle, but privately I love his memoir for its humor and heart and insistence that *young men can own their feelings too*.

When Gypsy Waters was twenty-five, she was charged with felony arson and tossed in jail, but when I'm her age, I'm traipsing to my neighborhood bookstore and feeling slightly chilled from the blanketing, afternoon fog.

At Green Apple Books I browse through fiction, beginning with A, ending at Z, until I make a final, agonizing decision. What to read? The bookstore feels like a home.

Another Nabokov or DeLillo? Who's Paul Auster? I liked those Flannery O'Connor stories, so what about Carson McCullers? John Gardner is a pompous dick, but his book about writing novels does contain some solid points. Who the hell is Knut Hamsun? Joy Williams? Eileen Myles? A. M. Homes? Next to her: Stewart Home? Marilynne Robinson? Kathy Acker? Iain Banks? Céline?

Buy them all! Put everything on credit! I *can* have them all!

On the stroll back to my apartment, I pick up a cheap banh mi sandwich, filing away what's cool and what's not cool, what to read and what to ignore, which bands to listen to and which to trash, which political policies are right and just and which policies guide power and greed. And I wonder how to impress the woman I'm meeting at eight o'clock.

Our connection was made via a friend via the internet. Her name is Natalie. We met for a quick lunch last weekend, followed by a memorable walk through the park. Her father, I learned with delight, is a well-known Southern California surfer. I told her I harbored fantasies of one day surfing Mavericks, getting swallowed by a shatteringly cold, thirty-foot wave, only to emerge with a fish clenched in my jaw. Even though I didn't know how to surf well, Natalie laughed anyway, and we made plans for a second date.

We meet that night at a chic urban restaurant too expensive for my life-style. It promotes itself as a "supper club," which worries me, but Natalie has a runner's lean body and straight white teeth, thick hair, and when we hug I smell the slightest splash of some sophisticated violet perfume in her hair. Judging by how carefully assembled she appears, Natalie is meant to dine at supper clubs.

Over drinks at the bar, Natalie mentions she's wearing two-hundred-dollar jeans, which worries me even more. I feel an urgent need to impress her.

"So last weekend you were telling me about your novel," she says, sipping her dry martini. "The one about an anarchist couple that terrorizes a nameless city. That's quite a concept."

"No, no. That was the *last* novel I wrote," I say. "The new one is much longer. It's a class-conscious novel. It's about a group of clueless ultrarich friends partying in Pacific Heights while riots burn through the city."

"Huh," Natalie says.

"It's called 'The Good and the Beautiful,'" I say. "The name is a play on that Fitzgerald novel."

"Okay."

"It's sort of but not really inspired by the work of Bret Easton Ellis."

"And you started writing it in graduate school?" she asks.

"Yeah, but I left that program. The faculty didn't impress me."

"And how's that?"

"I mean, look. First of all, when I turned in an excerpt for workshop, the professor actually said, in front of the class, that I should be in a cage."

"Hmmm," Natalie says.

"Another professor who did like my work befriended me, and he'd invite me over to his apartment," I say.

"That's nice."

"He'd invite me to his apartment and talk about contemporary art while

I watched him smoke crystal meth from a glass pipe. But he did give me John Ashbery's home phone number. He told me to call Ashbery if I ever wanted a place to stay in New York."

Natalie leans forward. "I *love* Ashbery's poetry. Did you call him?"

"Sure," I say. "I was going to New York for a week. Ashbery picked up. We talked. But he thought it was crazy this guy gave me his home phone number. Like I said, the faculty didn't impress me."

"But, well, it sounds like you write a lot," she says.

"Yeah."

After the waiter escorts us to our table, Natalie looks at him deeply, seriously, and says, "Wine. We need some wine. I think we need a bottle."

"A bottle?" I ask. "Are you sure?"

"Oh, I'm definitely sure," she says.

As the wine disappears into Natalie's glass, I spread honesty across the table. I had a birthday recently, I tell her. But it was difficult and, well, I tell her about crying off and on during it, you know, I was angry, and I just wanted the day to end. Natalie stirs in her chair, apparently uncomfortable with the seatback. She keeps one hand attached to the stem of her glass and frequently refills it.

Around midnight Natalie stands bundled and shivering outside her apartment. Her face sits on top of a mountain of luxuriant scarf. "Well, thanks for dinner," she says. "I know that place is expensive."

I lean in to kiss her, and it's good. Her lips are full and pillowy.

I pull away. "Listen," I say. I stare into her blue eyes. "I'm not into games. I think you're remarkable. I think this is great. You're adorable. This could be really good. Let's not play games, okay? You're smart. I think, you and me, we'd make an interesting pair. I'm a writer, and you write too. I know you only write copy for Barbie, but that's okay. That's a good job. That could make for some interesting stories. I hate playing games. Let's not play any games."

The next day, I send Natalie a friendly email to say hello. She doesn't respond. Several days later, I receive a long email from her.

"I appreciated your honesty, I appreciated the compliments, and I was pleased to see that you were indeed in touch with your emotions. What I was amazed at was how NOT in touch you were with mine. I believe respect, listening skills, and sensitivity are absolute must-haves in a potential romance, and your behavior during what I like to call the *good night kiss debacle* showed me that you were decidedly lacking in those areas. I felt bullied. It wasn't nice. I just don't want to date you, and I wanted you to know why."

I stare at the bright computer screen. My apartment is silent. I lean back in my chair and groan. The screensaver activates, and for a brief moment I'm propelled through a space warp. Natalie is right. I don't know anything about her. I did bully her. I talked about myself all night and didn't ask her any questions. I mined our conversation with dropped names and bullshit. Christ: I'm an asshole! To my horror, I realize I acted the same way my father did the first time we met.

But perhaps I can still, somehow, in some way, use the experience in my writing. Besides, Natalie really isn't my type. I need someone who will whisper their anxieties to me, someone who will pace the streets until our feet leave dents in this beautiful city.

The sadness, when it returns, feels like heavy silence entering my body. Thick walls of fog roll in earlier in the day during winter months, blocking sunlight, and the sky eases from blue to grey. My jaw locks. Tension burns in my face, my neck, and my back. The sadness brings me back to that known, uncomfortable, soul-canceling place.

I roam the fog-shrouded streets with emptiness as vast as Antarctica inside me. Intrusive thoughts worry me. Walking along the sidewalk, I imagine punching random strangers in the face. I run to the doctor for assurance I'm not going crazy, for meds. In fits of self-preservation I imagine driving myself to the hospital. Which is most appropriate? During the coldest months my basement apartment is thrown into darkness, and I write a novella, "Kill Purge," about a young man who roams the fog-shrouded streets with emptiness as vast as Antarctica inside him. He thinks about punching random strangers too.

My friends think I am kind, charming. How is it possible I own such vicious thoughts?

The sadness scares me. The sadness terrifies me. I feel an incredible desire to counteract it. More and more, I want to *do* good. I want to *be* good. I don't want to be sad and angry. I want to be helpful and a decent human being. I want to do everything in my power *to not be like him*.

But my moods pendulum and my decisions suck. Too much drinking at the Casanova Lounge on Valencia. And snorting bindles of coke with a trust-fund friend. And spending Thanksgiving with a self-described polyamorous dominatrix and falling into bed with her.

And then—shit!—I crash into bed with another woman, Jessica, a lovely woman, a fantastically sexy woman, and after having our fun, I wake up before dawn, face smashed into her lavender-smelling pillows, seized with panic because we didn't use protection.

After I leave Jessica's apartment, a tidal wave of worry incapacitates me. My lips feel dry and a headache blooms between my eyes. I stop in the middle of the sidewalk, stunned by my stupidity. The thought of becoming an accidental father dominates the rest of the morning. It cannot happen. It absolutely cannot happen. I cannot be a father.

Later in the morning, I call her. She doesn't answer. I leave an urgent message on her voicemail. I pace around my apartment. I try to sleep. I can't.

So I head to the nearest emergency room. I march to the desk, and the woman inquires about the nature of my medical emergency.

"I'd rather discuss it with the doctor or a nurse," I say.

"Well, I need to put something down on the form," she says.

"Just write down it's about human sexuality."

"Human sexuality?" she says.

"I want to talk to a doctor about sex."

Her eyebrows lift and her eyes jump to the ceiling. "Ooo-kaaaay."

Two hours later, the triage nurse invites me into her closet-sized office. We sit.

"So what's all this about human sexuality?" she asks me.

"Look," I say. "I need to get the morning-after pill. If you have some samples here, great. If I need a prescription, can I please get one?"

The woman's eyes look momentarily unfocused. "Sir, I can't give you that," she says.

"Why?"

"First, you're a man," she says. "And second, this is a Catholic hospital."

I'm so hungover I failed to grasp that major detail.

Back at my place, I wait for Jessica to return my call. By the froggy sound in her voice, it appears she's been sleeping.

"Everything okay?" Jessica says. "Your voicemail sounded frantic."

"I need to see you."

"Umm. All right," she says.

"In person. Like right now," I say.

We meet at a Chinese restaurant for lunch.

"Last night, you know, what happened," I say.

"I know." She stirs the noodles on her plate with chopsticks. "That wasn't smart. I should know better."

"We should've been more careful," I say. "I *can't* have a child. You *can't* get pregnant."

She nods.

I need something, a gold-plated excuse. I *cannot* be a father. I'm half hungover, emotional, and not thinking clearly. "I can't have a kid because I'm a carrier of cystic fibrosis," I say. "What I mean," I say, "I carry the specific gene." The lie squeezes through my teeth and almost doesn't come out. "I'd love it if you agreed to take the morning-after pill. I'll pay for it. I'll pay for everything."

She looks at me kindly, warmly, and her warm kindness disassembles me. After she agrees, I drive her to the nearest clinic. In the waiting room, I flip through *People* magazine, realizing I may have just reserved a special room in hell with only my name on it.

"I've never done this before," she says quietly. "You know, the morning-after pill. I hear it makes you sick. But you're right. This is a good idea."

I feel horrible. But feeling horrible is better than having an unplanned child.

———

GYPSY'S SUDDEN ARREST made headlines around the nation, including the front page of Reno's *Evening Gazette*: "Co-Ed Charged in House Fire." Papers across the country spread the news.

"Girl Student Faces Charge of Arson."

"Coed Bound Over Arson Charge."

I search through newspaper archives for May 1949, collecting scraps, and reconstruct an event that landed Gypsy behind bars in Columbia, Missouri.

The circumstances: Gypsy was charged with taking out a $2,800 insurance policy on her possessions, placing her belongings in two lockers at the university, and setting fire to her cooperative rooming house, causing $30,000 in damages. She was arrested. Police found a gasoline canister in the basement. At her arraignment, she pleaded innocent. Newspapers mentioned her parents were living in Mexico. Soon Gypsy made bail and promptly fled town.

She didn't show up for her trial date the following April. Her attorney informed the court that she was now living in Mexico and unfit to travel due to illness. Anyone with a brain could see past that lame excuse: Gypsy simply didn't want to face the serious allegations. The judge thought the same and forfeited her bond.

That June, however, Gypsy did return to Missouri for a trial. This time, her mother accompanied her. As soon as they arrived in town, both mother and daughter were immediately arrested and thrown in the same jail cell. The court charged Margaret with perjury, claiming she'd falsified ownership of the Tennessee property she'd tendered for Gypsy's bond.

A trial began. The prosecution called its witnesses. An insurance adjustor testified that Gypsy had asked him, "If I set another fire, could you tell it?"

Gypsy's attorney objected.

Gypsy, at twenty-six, faced a long prison sentence. Locals packed the courtroom. One AP photo shows her walking to the courthouse in a dress. The town buzzed with gossip: who was this brash young woman?

Now, more than half a century later, it boggles my mind to imagine Gypsy sharing a tiny jail cell with her mom. Ten years earlier, they sailed on the open ocean and lived by their own time clock. Each day, Gypsy left her mother behind in the cell and returned in the evening after court.

Luckily, Gypsy's attorney had moves. He sensed bias. He challenged the sitting judge and replaced him with a judge from another county. On July 6, 1950, Gypsy took the stand. The courtroom was silent as she told the jury she didn't burn down the rooming house. It wasn't her, she said. She didn't do it.

The jury retired to deliberate.

It's hard to imagine a more awkward, more anxious situation: Gypsy and her mom, confined to a cell, sleeping on threadbare mattresses, awaiting an unknown fate. It must have been excruciating. Where was her father? Where the hell was Don? Newspapers don't mention him.

The jury acquitted Gypsy of the charges.

Shortly after that, Margaret walked free too. Gypsy and her mom promptly left town, traveling east.

I TELL MY BEST FRIEND, Josh, about the cool woman I met. Her name is Robin.

"She's smart and incredibly well read," I say. "I think she went to an Ivy."

"Wait. Back up. How did you meet?" he asks.

"I've been giving her a ride to this writing class we're both in."

"She's a writer?" he asks.

"Yeah."

"Oh no," Josh says.

"What?"

"Two writers? Dating?"

"But she's talented," I say. "And she also has these, I don't know, crushing kinds of opinions about everything."

We're on the phone—Josh is in Reno and I'm in my basement apartment in San Francisco. Our connection hums, but otherwise, in my mind, Josh is right next door.

"Well, she sounds like your type," he says. "You like those smart-mouthed librarian chicks."

"Shut up. She's cool. And cute. She's got this sort of pixie-style haircut. Freckles. And these square black eyeglass frames with rhinestones. They kind of look like cat's-eye frames."

"What? Cat's-eye frames?" he says. "Uh-oh."

"Why uh-oh?"

"I don't know. That just seems sort of baroque, man. I mean, cat's-eye frames? That's too much like Lisa Loeb. Her music sucks."

"Who cares?" I say.

"Where's she from?"

"Oregon. She told me the other day she doesn't have any brothers or sisters."

"What?" Josh says. "Two only children, and both writers? Are you crazy? That sounds disastrous."

At twenty-six, I meet Robin, who strikes me as an enigma. She's unlike the women I know. For one thing, she's the daughter of Brooklyn Jews. Another thing, she's from the hippie town of Eugene, Oregon, and now lives in Berkeley, the hippie mecca. She rarely wears makeup and radiates a blend of East Coast sophistication and West Coast nonchalance.

In the beginning I'm clueless.

"What are you doing this weekend?" she asks during our weekly car ride. It doesn't register that she's curious—that she might like to do something, so I just say, "Oh, who knows?"

I'm recently out of a relationship. Soon I catch on to her questions. My landlady, a Giants season-ticket holder, allows me to buy tickets from her at a discount. I ask Robin if she wants to attend a ball game.

"That would be lovely," Robin says.

Lovely?

We bump into each other at a house party the night before our scheduled date. Throughout the party I notice one guy following her around like a hungry puppy. I don't like what I'm seeing. Robin looks at me from across the room numerous times. A space opens up beside her on the couch. I take a seat.

"So, are you ready for the game tomorrow?" I ask.

"Of course."

"Have you seen the Giants play?"

"No, but I've been to baseball games before."

"Oh, yeah? Where?"

"The Eugene Emeralds," she says.

"Oh. Huh."

Robin shrugs. "I played softball as a kid until a ball hit me in the face. I used to play left field, but I'd always just start dreaming out there, counting daisies. I suck at sports."

"So." I nervously peel the label from my beer bottle. "How's Berkeley?"

"Great," she says. "I love the East Bay."

"Kind of hard to imagine living over there," I say.

"Why? Better than the City. Sunnier, for one thing. We've got the hills. And all the ethnic food in Oakland."

"Yeah, I don't know. I like the City. I like being near the ocean," I say.

"Okay," she says. She sets her beer bottle down. "Then let's go."

"What?"

"Let's go to Ocean Beach."

"What? You mean, right now? It's past midnight."

"Yes. Right now," she says. "Let's go."

We ditch the party. Outside, in the foggy street, we find my car, and Robin jumps in.

"It's going to be freezing out there. We need a blanket," I say. "I have some blankets at my place."

Robin squints. "Oh, I see. You want to head to your place first."

"For a blanket. We'll be cold."

"Uh huh."

Instead of heading to the beach, we drive across the wet city streets to my basement studio. I grab a few beers from my efficiency refrigerator and throw on a Tom Waits album. Robin excuses herself to use the bathroom. When she comes out, she says, "Uh, nice bathroom."

"What do you mean?"

"It's carpeted," she says.

"So?"

"There is carpet. In your bathroom. On the floor."

I don't know what she means. "And?"

"It smells like mildew in there."

"Really? I never noticed. Want a beer?" I say.

I hand her a bottle. She sits next to me. My old droopy couch forces our bodies to meet in the center. My studio is packed with boxes of books I've published through my small indie press. There's a desk, scattered with papers, and a bed perched on a loft. Not much else.

"So, here we are," Robin says. "Kind of dark."

"Yep."

"Yep."

"I'd like to kiss you," I say.

"It's allowed."

Silence. I sip my beer. "But let's wait. I also like building tension."

She smiles. Then I lean over. And we kiss.

And I *fall*, hard. Robin charms me with her wit and caustic sense of humor. She's adventurous and full of nervous energy, always suggesting interesting restaurants and new hikes, where we have long, wandering conversations. It doesn't take long before we start spending most of our time together.

"What kind of question is that?" I say during a hike in the Berkeley Hills.

"Why? You don't have a decent answer?" she says.

"What first attracted me to you?" I say.

"Yes. A simple question."

"I thought you were sexy," I say. "That's what."

"Tsk. How dumb," she says.

"Well, I don't think it's dumb."

"You're too body focused," she says.

"Why were you interested in me?"

"Nice eyes," she says.

"That's it?"

"But your bathroom cabinet freaked me out at first."

"You looked inside my bathroom cabinet?"

"Of course," she says, "doesn't everybody? I was like, *what the fuck?*"

"What's wrong with my bathroom cabinet?"

"It's a pharmacy. It's packed with shit! I found that weird. But, you know, I've started to think of it as endearing. If anything happens to me, you'll have it covered."

We spend weeks, months together.

We stay up late and talk into the morning hours. I'm honest with her about my father. Her mother is sick with breast cancer, and we commingle our grieving, sharing our feelings. We're sensitive to each other's needs and desires. Talking with her about my confused feelings about my father gives me a sense of fullness and importance in her life. At night, we lie in her bed, burrowing. With pillows behind our heads, she reads me her writing in a voice so sweet it hurts. Her awareness of tactile and sensory details amazes me. Sometimes she wakes me in the middle of the night with important life questions, and then we settle into each other again, her leg draped over mine.

But we're from different worlds. She's the daughter of a doctor and lawyer, and I'm from working-class Reno. I'm difficult. She's difficult. She's *too* smart. She's nearly impossible to argue with, which frustrates me, because usually I find relationships where I can dominate arguments.

So we argue and make up and argue and make love.

"Stop looking at me like that," she says one afternoon when we're on a weekend trip to the Sierras. We're sitting beside an alpine lake.

"Sorry."

"What's up? Do you have something to say to me? You're making me nervous."

"I just think—I don't know. You mean the world to me," I say.

Robin's quiet for a while. "Oh," she finally says. Her eyes soften. Then harden. "That's kind of treacly."

"Treacly?"

"Syrupy," she says. "You know, sugary. Too sweet."

"Oh, sorry."

"That's the thing about you," she says. "You are sweet. I've never been with anyone so sweet."

I love her openly and without regard for myself. I put her needs above mine, until resentments about putting her needs above mine build, and we argue again.

No matter what we argue about, both of us think we're right, always, all the time, no matter what. Small snipes lead to battles lead to argumentative wars. She says I have anger issues, which I don't get. And I think she's an officer for the politically correct police, which she doesn't get.

"What the hell's the matter?" I say one afternoon.

"You know what."

"What? The strip club?" I say. "I already told you. My friends wanted to go. They're women too. And they were curious. Everyone was having fun."

"Not the women working there."

"The strippers? They chose that job. They're empowered."

She clenches her teeth. "You're talking about those women like it's cool. They're not consumable goods, Don. They're people. Haven't you ever thought it's likely they come from backgrounds of trauma and confusion?"

"Whatever," I say. "Who cares about those chicks."

"Don't say *chicks*."

"I can't say *chicks*? Why not? Why do you police everything I say?"

"You like thinking that you can say whatever you want, like words don't mean anything," she says. "But they do matter. You're a writer. You should know that."

"You're just uptight."

"And you're just posing," she says. "You're just trying to be *edgy*."

"Whatever. Just stop."

"Why? Are you going to threaten to walk out? Like last time?"

Robin has her shit together. She knows what she wants. She's determined to be a writer. She wants to teach, too. I start paying attention, watching her, studying how she systematically submits short stories for publication. She's even poured through a literary magazine directory, highlighted the addresses, and placed Post-its on the pages with useful information. She has big plans.

One evening, after telling me a story about some guy who cheated on her friend, Robin says during dinner, "God, men are such assholes sometimes."

Her pronouncement irritates me.

"What do you mean by *that*?" I say.

"What?"

"That thing you just said. The men are assholes thing."

"I said *sometimes* men are assholes."

"Men are assholes? I don't think you like men. Words matter, you know."

"Are you trying to start a fight with me?" she says.

Oftentimes, I am. Fighting is a defensive maneuver. Sometimes I hope she'll piss me off so much that it will justify breaking up with her, thereby protecting myself from enduring an imagined abandonment. I think I know myself. I think I've got everything figured out.

And then, one night, after dating more than a year, we have an epic barnburner.

Memory deceives. When I ask Robin, years later, about that fight, the fight that changed everything, she remembers a different argument from the one I remember, but we both agree on how shitty it was, and the eventual outcome.

Here's what I remember.

We're driving to the video store to rent a movie. We're in my car, and she says, for the umpteenth time that day, "But what if my computer doesn't turn on again? What if I lose everything? I didn't make a backup."

I sigh. "Robin, come on. We've already talked about this for hours. It's an endless loop. Your computer, your computer. Please, please stop pulling me into your anxiety. You'll either fix it, or you'll get a new one. Stop obsessing."

"All my writing will be erased."

"No it won't. You have hard copies," I say. "You're just being anxious."

Silence. It's a nice evening, a comfortable seventy degrees. Sunlight glistens on the bay. But Robin is nearly vibrating in the passenger seat, which is beginning to irritate me.

"I spoke to Shayna today," she says. "I think I should visit New York. I haven't seen my East Coast friends in a while."

"You should."

"Will you help with things around the house?"

"Yeah, sure."

"It's just," she says, "what if every single file on my computer gets erased?"

A fuse ignites and burns to the center of my skull. "Stop it. Stop pulling me into your anxiety. I don't want to talk about your computer anymore. We've been talking about your computer for hours. Jesus Christ."

"You can't listen," she says. "You don't know *how* to listen."

"I've been listening to you for hours."

"No, you haven't."

"Goddamn it!" I shout. "Fuck this! Fuck this!"

She releases her seatbelt. "Let me out of the car!" she screams.

I keep driving.

"Pull over. Stop being a dick. Let me out!" she says. "You're scaring me."

But men are assholes!

I swing the car across two lanes of traffic and whip around the center median. The car shudders through a violent U-turn. I stab my foot into the accelerator and speed back in the direction of her house. I stop in front of it.

"Okay, get out!" I yell. "You wanted out! Now get the fuck out!"

She doesn't.

I slam my fist on the steering wheel. Robin flinches. "Get the fuck out of my car!" She just sits there. She doesn't get out. I punch the steering wheel again. "I can't stand your bullshit! I can't stand this bullshit!"

"What's wrong with you?" she says coolly. She doesn't get out. She doesn't leave me.

What's *wrong* with me? For as long as I can remember, I've felt shattered. *Men are assholes?* Yes, men *are* assholes. I'm an asshole who's the son of the king of all assholes. I don't know how to be in a relationship. I don't know if I should ever be in a relationship. *I don't know how to be a man.* And I'm crying in the car, hiccupping, my face cupped in my hands. I don't deserve her. I'm worthless.

"Please, please get out," I say. A breakup, a small blip, yet I feel annihilated.

I can't stomach the idea of losing her. Robin is the only person I've ever been truly honest with about every single thing. And she listens. And she doesn't think I'm total shit.

Later, after days of silence and anguish, Robin wants to sit down and talk. "I've made a decision," she says.

"I know, I know. We're finished."

"No, but we can't stay together if you don't deal with your anger."

"I'm sorry," I say.

"I know," she says. "But sorry doesn't work for me anymore."

Finally, I make the decision. And make an appointment.

A week later, I enter a therapist's office with cream walls and white trim and stacks of New Yorkers on the waiting room table. I distrust the idea of therapists. Nabokov pointed out that when you pull the word apart, you get the rapist. I don't know what to expect. I'm terrified of being judged and ridiculed. I've always thought of psychologists as grown versions of the weirdo psychology majors I knew in college, the kids who sobbed in their rooms and smoked French cigarettes.

A middle-aged woman opens the door. Curly hair and flowing, California yuppie clothes.

She smiles. "Don?" she says.

It takes six months to move from the chair to the couch. At first I sat looking and not looking at the woman's leveling gaze. She intimidated me with her sharp intuition and decades of psychotherapy practice. But I learn the couch brings me closer to a dream state, a more uninhibited place suitable to communicating with the subconscious. During my weekly sessions I interlock my fingers and hold myself at my sternum. She remarks on this. She suggests I'm holding. That I am trying to keep contained.

I hear her scribbling notes over my right shoulder as I stare at small hairline irregularities on her cream-colored ceiling.

"My father sent me his autobiography," I say.

"Have you read it?"

"No."

"Why not?"

"I tried. I can't."

"How does it make you feel?"

"Curious but terrified."

"Tell me about the fear."

She'll be my therapist for the next twelve years. Twelve years, once a week, tens of thousands of dollars. She'll talk to me about my depression, anxiety, shame, and anger.

It will take years before I tell her truths I've been too afraid to admit to myself. It will take years before I'm truly honest with her, before I learn to lower my defenses instead of deflecting.

She'll scare me, shake me, and she'll do it with kindness and care. She'll help me construct a house, and I'll point out the ways in which the house is haunted, and she'll walk with me through the house, opening doors I've been too afraid to enter, showing me disheveled floors and broken windows and graffiti marking the walls. We'll talk and I'll cry, and we'll talk some more. When Robin and I move to New Mexico, I continue our weekly appointments by phone.

She'll raise the house with me, and we'll burn it down.

We'll raise it, burn it down.

Raise it, burn it down, and through the years I'll find some love for myself, some self-worth, just enough to begin laying the foundations for my own house.

———

IN MID-OCTOBER, my friend Dan says over the phone, "If you ask me, this other Don Waters guy sounds like a total narcissist."

"What? Why do you say that?" I ask him.

"Think about it. Don could've been a quasi-tyrant who dragged his wife and kid onto that yacht."

I tap my pen against my knee, listening to Dan, and keep watch for the friendly neighborhood squirrel out the window. Iowa is having a lovely fall. Plenty of sun.

"Maybe it was all his idea," Dan goes on. "I mean, living on a yacht for ten years doesn't sound fun to me at all. Maybe that's why Gypsy ended up sort of feral."

Dan's a journalist in New York. He was born in Manhattan. Of course sailing on a yacht for ten years wouldn't appeal to him. Dan also enjoys questioning every angle of a thing, preferring to probe for complicated explanations rather than settling on easy ones. That's why I like him. But after I describe my yearlong obsession with the Waters family, Dan's quick to challenge the happy fantasies I've constructed about them.

After hanging up, I swivel around in my chair, considering the papers scattered across my desk. Heaps of printouts about Don. Bits and pieces. My father's autobiography. I think about the stories we craft for others and the personas we create on the page.

My father certainly crafted a positive story about himself. He probably hoped I'd read his autobiography and fall into his interesting, glorious web. And in some ways I've done just that. I've wanted to uncover goodness in him, some golden pieces of exceptionality—like surfing. Like his "friendship" with Greg Noll. Like sailing to Hawaii.

But his character flaws also rise off the page. It's what he doesn't say. *Where's the rest of his family? Where's Mom? Where am I?*

He's evasive, dishonest. In the past I've acted the same way.

And other flaws also remind me of . . . me. His canned explanation for leaving is a habit we share: He *needed* to move; he *needed* to explore. He didn't set down roots. He moved and moved and moved. A nomad. Like me.

Though we talk about having a family, Robin and I haven't been successful, and we really haven't ever settled down. Sometimes that alarms me, as I'm sure it alarms her. For a moment I wonder what she's doing in Portland right now.

And why am I drawn to Don's story? Is it because he had a similar wanderlust and need for escape? And where is he? The 1950s is a black hole because Don's a moving target. Gypsy simply vanishes. Other than Margaret's occasional *Christian Science Monitor* dispatches from Mexico, the family disappears.

After hunting for weeks, I finally stumble on an oral history account from a botanist at the University of California's herbarium. The botanist, Annetta Carter, befriended Margaret during numerous scientific expeditions to Baja. "[Margaret] was a freelance writer and she wanted to write up these intrepid women," the botanist said, adding:

> That was the beginning of a friendship that I have until now with Margaret Waters. She lived there for, oh, another ten years, I think, in La Paz. Her husband did leave her, so she acted as a bilingual secretary to Senior Rufo of the Rufo store, La Perla de La Paz, and taught English to Mexicans and had a very good life there.

Her husband did leave her?
Those sharp lines stand out like neon.

I don't know what to think. What the hell is happening to my perfect family? First, Gypsy was charged with arson, and now, Don *left* Margaret? The story is unraveling.

Lit by my computer's blue glow, I search for Don's whereabouts, which leads to a website for the Airstream Company.

It appears that Don became known for "land yachting" late in his life. As far as I can tell, "land yachting" meant pulling an Airstream from place to place and living inside it—sort of a precursor of RVing.

The Airstream Company spotlighted Don's feats in advertisements, which I find archived on the company's website. As an avid "trailerite" and "caravanner," Don was one of the first people to navigate the full length of Baja's unpaved road system with a trailer. He also toured Canada and Alaska. The advertisements bragged about him. Don, in his seventies, was an Airstream poster boy.

I find a full-page article in the May 1959 edition of *Trailer Travel Magazine* that refers to Don as a "Pioneer Trailerite." The piece gives a fairly generic rundown of his madcap life. Then I encounter another shocking sentence: "He fell in love with Mexico and most of his later years were spent south of the border, especially after his wife passed away several years ago."

After his wife passed away several years ago?

His wife . . . passed away . . . years ago?

Impossible!

I know for a fact Margaret was alive at the time. She was living in La Paz and hanging out with botanists from UC Berkeley.

Did Don lie to the reporter? Did he remarry?

One mystery broadens into another.

For those weeks when I couldn't locate them, I imagined an entirely different scenario: an elderly Don and Margaret sitting in rocking chairs on a wooden porch, looking out onto a beautiful pond.

None of that's true. One account claims Don *left* Margaret. In another, Don says his wife *died.*

But in fact Don died first, on July 3, 1964, in Capistrano Beach, California, just down the road from the future site of Jed Noll's surf shop. He was seventy-six.

His death certificate arrives by mail from the Orange County clerk's office, and I set it on my desk. A strange, otherworldly feeling overcomes me as I stare at a death certificate bearing my name. His cause of death, written in doctor's cursive, was cardiac decompensation and arteriosclerosis. Heart problems. Like my father.

The document makes me a bit mournful because I've come to know him in a small way. I've mapped his life from birth to death and watched him find a wife, father a child, sail for ten years on a yacht, and travel untried roads. I've read his stories and looked at him staring back at me on the wall. I've admired his tenacity and sense of adventure and the beautiful way he wrote about raising a daughter to value the natural world. Even though he's been dead for nearly fifty years, I've come to look up to him. Was he a narcissist, as Dan believes? I don't know. That word gets tossed around all the time. I know I admire his lovely passages about mound builders in Florida, those ancient peoples who left behind shells. Now his books are treasured shells on my mound of books. I know he'll stay with me.

In the "Last Occupation" box on the death certificate is the word "Author." In the burial box, the word "Cremation." In the box that says "Married, Never Married, Widowed, Divorced," the word "Married."

"Married."

Does that mean he was still married to Margaret at the time of his death?

But where was she? Where was Gypsy? The more time I spend looking for them, the more my initial affections for the family transform into strained wonder.

––––––––

KENNETH BURKE was one of the twentieth century's towering literary figures. Early on in my research, I came across Burke's name because he happened to be Margaret Waters's highbrow, intellectual brother-in-law.

Burke was a fixture in Greenwich Village's avant-garde literary scene throughout the 1920s. For a time he was editor of *The Dial*, the influential modernist literary magazine that published nearly everyone of importance—from D. H. Lawrence to Virginia Woolf to Sherwood Anderson. He shared an apartment with Hart Crane and Djuna Barnes. Even though he was a college dropout, Burke was the first to translate Thomas Mann's *Death in Venice* into English. Later on, he taught Susan Sontag at the University of Chicago and influenced her work. "It was from Burke that I learned how to read. I still read the way he taught me," Sontag once said.

Mostly though, Kenneth Burke was a writer. He wrote stories, novels, and criticism. And he wrote theory. A lot of theory. As a theorist, he was a dude heavy into the power of symbols.

Human beings, he wrote, are a "symbol-using animal."

We human creatures have the extraordinary power to use symbols. We respond to symbols. We accumulate them. We study them. Symbols teach us. We use and misuse symbols. Symbols have the power to enlighten but also have the power to ignite wars. As symbol-using animals, we rearrange them to our benefit—to communicate, to connect, and to influence.

By arranging symbols on a blank page, we can create an advertisement. Or we can create art. We can create literature.

In his essay "Literature as Equipment for Living," Burke suggested that literature has a deeper purpose beyond the telling of a good story.

His essay begins by defining proverbs. Our earliest proverbs, he wrote, are wise little lessons. And the proverb delivery system is a short, enlightening sentence.

"A person who has planted a tree before he dies has not lived in vain," goes one African proverb.

Another, from Kenya: "Earth is not a gift from our parents, it is a loan from our children."

Proverbs exist to offer guidance, in other words. They contain wise kernels of truth. They're meant to be "medicine." They're meant to console and teach and foretell. Therefore, Burke proposed, isn't the whole of literature just "proverbs writ large"?

He argued that literature—novels, stories, plays—bring attitudes and situations to life and show how best to manage and cope with real life events. Literature explores and synthesizes human issues. Instead of succinct lessons offered through proverbs, novels are *long* lessons. They're equipment—equipment that helps us understand how to live.

Kenneth Burke married Margaret's older sister, Lily, in 1919. Years later, after a divorce, he married Margaret's younger sister, Libbie. It's impossible not to wonder whether Burke required any proverbial guidance during that excruciating situation.

Anyway, I poke around in Kenneth Burke's life at the time Margaret and Gypsy disappeared following Gypsy's arson trial in 1950. I familiarize myself with Burke's theories. He's a fascinating guy. He knew a lot of brilliant people. Soon I locate evidence to suggest that some of Margaret's personal letters to her sister Libbie ended up in Kenneth Burke's archives. Penn State University maintains the archive. So I get on the phone with the university's special collections department and order photocopies. When the hefty package arrives, I find typewritten letters. The letters begin shortly after Gypsy's arson trial.

There are handwritten addendums in the margins. Margaret's handwriting. I hungrily flip through them. The letters are personal, intimate. They reveal Margaret's hopes and dreams. As I scan, previously hazy details about dates and places turn into solid facts. Margaret signs each letter with her location. The letters are a gold mine.

In 1950, after the trial, Margaret and Gypsy fled to Tennessee. Soon after, Margaret returned to Mexico, settling back into her old life in La Paz. She was alive and well. She wasn't dead. Judging by her letters, it appears that she split from Don around 1957. In Don's place were men named Charles and Hugh. Margaret certainly wasn't living an Ozzie and Harriet kind of lifestyle.

"As for the drinking," she wrote, in 1962, "I had it in La Paz. Some guy would fly down to see me, we'd party all over the place, he'd go away, some other one would appear, more partying ad infinitum."

She was a fun gal.

After a time, she moved north to Tucson, Arizona, and filed for divorce from Don, but I don't know if it was ever finalized. Is this the reason he mentioned she was *dead*? Was he pissed off? Margaret reclaimed her maiden name, and from that moment on she went by Margaret Batterham Waters.

"As for Don," she wrote, "He has retired, is living in his trailer and cruising around, and seems contented."

In Tucson Margaret enrolled in a Modern Latin American Literature seminar at the university, which was held in Spanish. "We are reading *El Cid* in the original."

She rented a cottage from Rosemary Taylor, author of the bestselling novel *Chicken Every Sunday*, and complained about Arizona's "most godawful conservatism."

One theme that stands out is Margaret's dedication to writing fiction. I already knew she had published several pulp stories when she was younger, but I didn't realize she continued to write fiction later in life. The tone of her letters hints at a deep need for artistic validation. After all, her sister, the recipient of the letters, was married to Kenneth Burke, one of the most well-connected writers of his generation. It makes sense she'd want to pass along updates about her writing.

For a while Margaret went back and forth with a New York literary agent named Carl Brandt. In one letter she claimed she was "bickering" with the Knopf publishing house about her Baja California novel, *Chaparitta*. She also mentioned another book, *Beryl Maples*, her "mountain Conscientious Objector novel."

Like most writers, she mined her own life for material. Despite her agent's efforts, neither novel found a home. Eventually, Margaret threw up her hands and self-published *Chaparitta* by printing copies on the cheap in Mexico.

I browse Google Books. *Chaparitta* isn't listed. That's not surprising.

"And the writing, my own," Margaret continued, "has suffered with all the moving and guests and men about."

In the letters I discover that Margaret owned a pistol. She drank, entertained, and kept current by reading *Harper's*, the *New Yorker*, and *Esquire*. At sixty-five, she got a facelift in Mexico.

"I have cheated time . . . I am a new me," she wrote, "hair dyed, face of 45 or 50, and a matching exterior to the interior." She reported jumping rope "over six hundred times a day, taking it a hundred at a time."

And Gypsy?

She married again, a doctor this time, and lived on a ranch in Wyoming. The next time Margaret mentioned Gypsy, the news pleases me: Gypsy was now sailing around the Caribbean with her husband on a yacht named *Roamer*. She was thirty-eight years old, my age, and the same age as her father when the photo of him was taken aboard the whaling ship, which now hangs above my desk.

"As for mine," Margaret wrote, "Gypsy is a well poised woman, and is very happy. They are now in Nassau, having made the crossover a week or so ago. Apparently she is known throughout the boating fraternity as the girl who operates a boat on her own, as [her husband] does little."

And just when I believe everything's running along smoothly in their lives, unexpected events rearrange the narrative. One day, Gypsy appeared at Margaret's doorstep. She'd left her husband, who "had become an acute alcoholic, making it impossible to be with him any longer."

Mother and daughter began living together again, and they fell back into their old ways.

In a series of highly detailed letters, Margaret described a marathon road trip in a Volkswagen bug, which took the pair all the way to the Canadian Rockies. "Our safari to Canada," she called it.

Along the way mother and daughter "raided a cornfield" and thumbed their noses at park rangers looking to collect campground fees—"We evaded the camping grounds where a charge was made . . . How that gripes us, to pay when we've already paid. It's OURS! Double-taxation."

Gypsy apparently had a green thumb. She swiped slips from plants "in plazas, in botanical gardens, along the walks of campuses, at private homes where the beds spilled out into the streets." Mother and daughter were free again, a roaming duo, reliving that long-ago decade at sea.

On the return south, they meandered through Portland and visited the Oregon coast. Reading Margaret's observations is like being transported down Highway 26, over the mountain pass, and to Short Sands, my beach:

> I could not get used to its grand inhospitality. Along Oregon, the ocean pounds in cold grey waves that have strewn great balks of whitened driftwood all along the endless grey sandy beaches . . . Some of the headlands were magnificent, with wind-sculptured Russian cedars and great boulders hollowed into fantastic shapes by surf and wind . . . Lighthouses are high up on the hills overlooking the sands and sea. Dune buggies are quite a sport hereabouts and we wished we'd investigated them more and taken a ride. They say they are more fun than surf riding.

Libbie died in 1969, and that's when Margaret's letters end. I can't find anything more about her life in the Kenneth Burke's papers. So, for the umpteenth time, Margaret and Gypsy slide off my radar.

––––––––––

WHEN I WAS A KID, Mom kept our phone number unlisted. She didn't own property. No deeds, no property tax records, no trail. She worked a low-key job as a clerk at the sheriff's department jail. Like most Americans, we were pretty much anonymous and invisible and going about our daily lives. There was no such thing as Google Search. If my father had come looking, it would have been difficult for him to find me. At least that's the story I often told myself.

The Waters family, however, was marginally well known. Readers enjoyed the published stories about this take-charge, self-sufficient family who fended for themselves during the Depression and blazed a path to good times during the gloom. For decades, newspapers ran pieces about them. Later, Margaret published her own columns. Then, a rooming house burned down, and here came the reporters again.

Despite the significant amount of publicly available information, piecing together the rest of their lives requires work—and luck.

I return to genealogy websites and peruse messages left on public forums. It's incredible how many people are actively hunting for ancestral information. It seems to be a major American pastime. People want to know their larger stories. The forums contain thousands upon thousands of queries.

I notice a message from someone in Kentucky looking for information about Don. I send the man an email. He quickly emails back. It turns out he's just a fan of Don's books. He's wondering what happened to him.

Another message stands out. So I send an email.

A woman named Alethea is more than surprised to receive a letter from me. From out of nowhere, the name of her long-lost relative appears in her inbox. She's thrilled. Don Waters was her great-grandfather's brother, and in her excited response she thinks we're family. It's flattering. In my reply I tell her I'm looking into Don because we share a name and a profession, and I'm considering writing about him. Thankfully, Alethea isn't irritated. In fact, she's incredibly nice. She tells me she's putting together her family tree and confirms some of the information I've already gathered about Don. She even mails me an early photo of Don with his North Carolina family.

I work outward, identifying other names related to Gypsy. One is Tony Burke, Kenneth and Libbie Burke's son. Tony is Gypsy's first cousin. He's easy to find. He's a Harvard-educated astronomer at the University of Victoria in Canada. I give him a call. Tony has a spry, quick-witted phone voice. He kindly agrees to answer my questions.

"The last time I remember seeing Margaret and Gypsy was the early sixties, I guess," he tells me. "They showed up from time to time at our family's compound in New Jersey."

His parents' compound was fifty miles west of New York City. The family nicknamed the place "Lake Bottom."

Tony says, regretfully, he's not really sure what happened to Margaret or Gypsy. He thinks Margaret possibly became estranged from the family, possibly over money. "Margaret wasn't in good shape financially," he says.

I ask whether he remembers their visits to Lake Bottom.

"Oh sure, sure," he says. "Sure, I remember. Gypsy was a cheerful, attractive woman," he goes on. "I remember Gypsy married a man in Wyoming. I also remember she got injured by a horse. She needed facial surgery." That memory prompts him to unearth another memory. "Margaret famously had a facelift, you know," he says.

"Why famously?"

"It was unusual back then, so the family regarded it as weird."

Growing up, Tony was familiar with Don's work. He tells me the family kept his books on a shelf at Lake Bottom. Tony surprises me when he mentions Don's glass eye.

"What? He had a glass eye?"

"He did," he says.

In the photo above my desk Don's eyes look natural. But maybe everything looked legit as long as his eye was inserted. It's an interesting detail, but otherwise Tony can't remember much else.

"That was so long ago," he says.

With a slightly better understanding of Margaret and Gypsy, I thank Tony, and call the next number on my list.

The woman who answers, Mary, sounds fairly advanced in age. Her voice trembles over the phone. Mary is another one of Gypsy's cousins, but on Don's side. Mary's helpful.

"Very early on Don and his brother, William, worked for the Southern Railroad," she tells me. "And the family house, the Waters house, is still there, in Haw Creek, located off Waters Road in Asheville."

I imagine it: a stone house in east Asheville, a set of initials notched in a tree by young Don.

"When Don died," Mary says, "he was cremated. Cremation was quite controversial at the time." She says, "But you know, Don was always ahead of his time."

Like Tony, Mary doesn't know what happened to Margaret and Gypsy after the 1960s. And neither seems to know anything about another odd, disturbing piece of information that keeps popping up in my computer searches. It's the kind of information I want to ignore.

One night, I sit at my desk, turn on my computer, and put everything together.

By entering "Margaret Batterham Waters" into Google, I find citations for several books published under her name.

Waltzing Words is a word game.

Another is called *Those Upland Meadows*.

The publisher's address is in Seymour, Tennessee, which sits in a valley just north of the Smoky Mountains. I know the family lived near the Smokies. Using Google Earth, I type in the Seymour street address and hover over a small house — perhaps a cabin or a trailer — on a rural road in the middle of nowhere. When I combine the street address with Margaret's full name in the search bar, I get a hit for county tax records. Margaret's address and the publisher's address are the same. So, she self-published these books too. Something else throws me off. A separate name keeps appearing in my searches: "Margaret Waters Crane." I look back through my notes. Crane was the surname of Gypsy's alcoholic husband.

"Gypsy" is a nickname.

Her forename is also Margaret.

Margaret Batterham Waters, mother.

Margaret Waters Crane, a.k.a. Gypsy, daughter.

Tax documents place both names at the same Tennessee address on the same rural dirt road.

From all appearances it looks as if Gypsy lived with or near her mother throughout much of the 1970s, '80s, and '90s. That would pretty much be the end of the trail and the end of the story, if it weren't for Gypsy's other arrests or the time she served in prison.

———————

I RETURN to Portland in December.

During the cold winter months, I set a portable heater near the couch to warm my legs. The Oregon days get darker earlier, the sky remains uniform grey, and I print out pages thick with legalese: Gypsy's numerous problems.

I don't know much about the law or the court system. A pleasant reference librarian at a local law school helps me sort through a lot of the paperwork. I have various appeals, suits, motions, and decisions with me.

In 1979, Gypsy was living on that rural road with her mom when a neighbor accused her of stealing his tools. The man filed a complaint. Police investigated. Gypsy was indicted, convicted, and sentenced to "not less than one nor more than two years" in the state penitentiary. At the time, Gypsy was fifty-seven years old. Her mother was eighty-four.

This new kink in their story makes my head spin. I can't help but recall all the details from Gypsy's 1949 arson charge. When I read about the incident, I chalked it up to an unfortunate accident, shoddy police work, a small town, and a bungling judge. But now I'm not so sure.

There's more.

During her theft trial Gypsy made the unusual decision to represent herself while a court-appointed attorney sat beside her "as stand-by counsel." In his trial notes the circuit court judge found Gypsy to be "competent," "intelligent," "bright," and "she had done an excellent job . . . equal to, or perhaps superior to the lawyers that have appeared in my court."

But Gypsy lost.

She presented a motion for a new trial — denied. She appealed her conviction through the court of appeals — denied again.

I'm surprised by how hard she fought the courts and her accusers. Also, her tactics horrify me. After representing herself and losing, she claimed, "she had been deprived of her right to counsel."

Gypsy's behavior is bizarre. She strikes me as unhinged.

From court documents:

The court finds that petitioner remains unrepentant, continues to deny guilt, and resourcefully and imaginatively persists in elaborate stratagems to cast doubt on her guilt. The record reveals her to be a cunning and vindictive individual who has tormented the victim of the crime, wrongfully cast aspersions on the prosecutor, invented defenses, and is remorseless about the crime.

Cunning *and* vindictive? *Tormented* the victim? Remorseless?

This isn't the Gypsy I know, that girl on a yacht, that girl who sailed across my imagination.

The more I stitch together a cleaner narrative, the more it appears that

Gypsy carried on a one-woman terror campaign against her victim and his wife.

She "wrote slanderous things about their character in the newspaper" and "accused [the victim] of being a baby pornography photographer and of taking drugs. She sent letters to the district attorney, the sheriff, the governor, the FBI, and the attorney general in Washington, DC regarding the victim's character. They also believe she reported them to the IRS for investigation."

It's a shitload of shitty behavior. It's sociopathic behavior.

In 1982, the year Michael Jackson released *Thriller*, the year *Time* magazine gave its Person of the Year to "The Computer," the year I was a fatherless eight-year-old kid living in downtown Reno, Gypsy Waters was sent to prison, convicted for concealing stolen property.

I drive home from the law library, unsure whether I want to dig any deeper. But of course, I do.

For more than twenty years, Mom worked at the sheriff's department jail. Every day, she sorted and filed paperwork, reading about all the imaginative ways people fucked up. She catalogued fingerprints. She affixed mug shots to folders. I remember her explanations about the intake and processing of inmates. A thick file got created before the cell door ever slammed shut. Anyone with a criminal record leaves behind paperwork.

I'm curious what Gypsy's paperwork might tell me.

I send a formal request, along with a check, to the Tennessee Department of Corrections. Gypsy's twenty-four-page "pen packet" arrives soon enough, and it contains an extremely detailed narrative of her life. In fact, her "pen packet" contains nearly all the pieces I've spent more than a year gathering: how Gypsy never attended formal school; how she lived with her parents aboard a yacht named "Gypsy Waters"; how the family "traveled extensively and her Father wrote monthly articles about their travels and her childhood"; how she married Oliver Horn; how she married again and lived in Wyoming; and how her father died in 1964. Nearly every answer to every big question could have been solved by this simple document from the Tennessee Women's Prison.

Included in the paperwork is Gypsy's version of events: "I bought some tools at a flea market. I was later arrested and told the things were stolen and I knew about it. I pleaded not guilty because I knew it was a set up."

A set up? Again, a paranoid response. Gypsy, the convicted felon.

Naturally, when I come across information about *another* run-in with law enforcement in 1987, it doesn't shock me.

Here's good old Gypsy: Arrested again for shoplifting a can of flea spray from a drugstore. Sentenced to thirty days in jail. Handed a $250 fine.

"Much aggrieved by her conviction," she appealed, sued the Tennessee attorney general, and took her minor shoplifting case to the US Supreme Court, which denied her a hearing. She was also accused of contempt for "altering and defacing an order of this court." I assume she eventually served those thirty days and paid the fine, but I stop looking because the whole thing bums me out.

I shove the pen packet in a manila folder labeled "Gypsy prison bullshit." It's irritating. I may have spent the past year looking into a family that raised a disturbed person. What happened to the girl from Don's book, the girl who outmaneuvered grown men on the ocean?

Maybe my friend Dan is right. Maybe sailing on a yacht for ten years, away from land and away from kids her age, actually harmed her. Maybe Gypsy wasn't properly socialized. Maybe Don did raise a feral girl. Maybe having a father could be just as awful as not having one.

———————

MARGARET BATTERHAM WATERS died in 1995.

I was a sophomore in college at the time. I was busy making a zine, busy posing as defiant, and busy being confused. Eight hundred and seventy-eight miles to the southwest, Gypsy was busy saying goodbye to her mother, her closest friend.

Since I'm not a family member, Margaret's cause of death is redacted on her death certificate, which I obtain from the Tennessee Department of Health. It's safe to say she died, at ninety-eight, of advanced age.

The death certificate:

Marital status: Widowed

Occupation: Author/Writer

I have no idea what transpired between her and Don in the 1960s. Even though I found a tiny divorce notice in a Tucson newspaper, it seems they never actually obtained a divorce.

Margaret Batterham Waters was a radical to the end. She donated her body to the University of Tennessee Medical School. She made several brave but unsuccessful attempts to publish her novels, and although her dream never materialized, she lived an extraordinarily gutsy life. Born in Asheville, she attended teaching school and later Ohio State University. She sailed Chesapeake Bay and Hawk Channel. Like an inveterate explorer, she drifted across North America—Maryland, Key West, Baja, Tucson, Tennessee. As I turn her crisp death certificate over in my fingers, I feel the same complicated sorrow I felt while holding Don's. I'm grateful for Margaret and her *Christian Science Monitor* articles and the letters to her sister. I'm even grateful she gave us Gypsy, despite her troubles.

And what about her? What about Gypsy? Is she alive? Could she be? Her mother lived a long life. I scratch calculations on a piece of paper. If she were alive, she would be around ninety years old. Few people can hide in the internet age. I return to online property tax records.

Invoices lead me to the same rural Tennessee address where Gypsy got into trouble. Her name is still on the property, but the invoices are now mailed to an address in a nearby town called Maryville. The latest invoice is under a trust in Gypsy's name. The trustee is a woman named Abbie. I wonder if Abbie's caring for the elderly Gypsy.

Soon, I learn quite a lot about Abbie. She maintains several blogs and websites. She's a forty-nine-year-old single mother with an interest in gardening, Reiki, and healthy living. Abbie's phone number is easy to find.

I call her and leave a message. I state my name, hoping she won't find that odd. If Gypsy lives with her, I wonder what she might think, hearing a voice message left by a stranger with her father's name?

Abbie doesn't call back.

I find her on Facebook and send a "friend request." She doesn't accept. I discover her other hobbies. She likes crafts. She's self-published a book of dog biscuit recipes.

Over the following weeks, as I did with Greg Noll, I call and leave messages, mail letters, and send emails.

But Abbie refuses to respond.

I find her online Pinterest page with boards dedicated to Jon Bon Jovi, Gluten Free, Chick Flicks, Crafts, and others named "Mmmmmm" (food) and "Just Sayin'." I consider driving across the country and showing up on Abbie's doorstep with a Bon Jovi T-shirt as an offering.

After leaving a fifth phone message, I realize two things. Either I have the wrong person or Abbie's deliberately ignoring me.

So I retain the services of a Knoxville private investigator. I choose the only agency with a single positive online review. The investigator immediately charms me. Her name is Kimberly, and I like the way she leans on her vowels, elongating her words.

"The search shouldn't take me more than *faaahhv* days," she tells me.

I agree to her rate: one hundred twenty-five dollars. I feel weird consulting a PI, given my past experiences with one specific PI, but Kimberly puts me at ease. People hire her for far more serious reasons, she tells me: cheating spouses, child support, locating debtors.

Less than a week later, Kimberly emails me a report. I call her right away.

"I spoke with Abbie," Kimberly tells me.

"Finally," I say. "I can't believe you got her on the phone." So what, I ask, about Gypsy?

"Well, Gypsy's alive, and she's living at an assisted living facility," Kimberly says. "Abbie was very pleasant. A nice woman. She says she met Gypsy thirteen years ago in a public library. I assume that's the library in Maryville." Kimberly pronounces Maryville like *Marrr-ville*. "Gypsy has no other family. So she found someone to take on her affairs. Abbie."

"Like I thought," I say.

"Abbie said she received your telephone messages and emails."

"And?"

"Abbie passed them along to Gypsy, and even though Abbie told her there was no familial relation, Gypsy specifically told her not to speak with you."

"What?"

"Gypsy told Abbie, 'Stay away from him. Do not speak to that man.'"

"Huh."

"Apparently, Gypsy despised her father," Kimberly says. "She could not stand her father. That's what Abbie told me. Gypsy says her father stole the family farm from her and her mother by forging some documents. And it took her twenty-five years and a long court battle to get it back, which she did."

I'm quiet for some time.

"You there?" Kimberly says.

"Yeah," I say. "I just—I thought this was a perfect little family. Apparently, it wasn't."

"I know," Kimberly says, laughing. "All this stuff sounds like that *Fried Green Tomatoes* movie."

"So," I say, "Gypsy's alive and she's in assisted living and she won't speak with me because I have the same name as her father, a man she hated."

"That pretty much sums it up," Kimberly says.

All this time, all this research, and Gypsy's alive and she won't speak to me. Her family's story, which spanned the twentieth century, has reached its end. And the ending is sad, really. Gypsy hated her father. Or maybe he did his best as a father. Or maybe Don was a tyrant. But then again, Gypsy is the convicted felon. She has a good number of sketchy incidents in her past: a burned rooming house, convicted for concealing stolen property, shoplifting. Then prison. What story is to be believed?

———————

SOON AFTER, I get an unexpected lesson in differing stories when new emails land in my inbox.

Mom finally gets around to setting up her email account, and she starts sending email chains, mostly Catholic propaganda and forwards of forwards embedded with geeky, first-generation computer graphics.

When I notice her chosen email handle—*crazywoman*—I laugh, and then I cringe. While I'm glad she's participating in the twenty-first century, I'm uncomfortable she chose to use the lame suggestion from my visit.

"Are you seriously going to use *crazy woman*?" I ask her over the phone. "It was a terrible suggestion for a handle. I shouldn't have suggested it."

"What are you talking about?" Mom asks. "I don't remember you suggesting anything. I'm just using the name of that gorgeous canyon in Wyoming."

"What are you talking about?" I ask.

"And, okay, what are you talking about?" she says. "Crazy Woman Canyon. You know. In Wyoming. Near Sheridan. I have that photo book about the place on the coffee table. I've driven through it many times."

There is a canyon in Wyoming named Crazy Woman? Was the photo book on the coffee table when I floated the "crazy woman" idea?

Every few days, a fresh batch of forwarded emails appears in my inbox. One day, Mom's handle changes again, this time to *wildwomanwaters*. I guess I liked her first choice best.

IT'S QUITE REMARKABLE to share the same moment in time with another human being. Earth is 4.5 billion years old. Every life on this planet is a mote of dust in an infinite cosmos. Despite that, my one small, short life has shared the same moment in time with Margaret's and Gypsy's, and that's a minor miracle. We've felt the same yearly sunlight on our faces, witnessed many of the same historical events, and breathed the same air. We're all just stars and dust in the grand design, anyway. We're all momentarily assembled and given voice and body and free will, and eventually we return to stars and dust, but during these few precious moments of life—these brief sentient moments—we feel as though we might be able to impact the grand design and that our stories matter.

In early January, Robin travels to Asheville, North Carolina, to teach at the Warren Wilson low-residency MFA writing program. She stays for ten days, but before she leaves, I ask her to do me a favor.

Pack Memorial Library in downtown Asheville has one copy of Margaret's last self-published book, *Those Upland Meadows*. I've been unable to obtain it through interlibrary loan. I'm eager to read it.

Robin returns to Portland with a photocopy in her luggage. *Those Upland Meadows* was published in 1994, a year before Margaret died. The book is ninety-seven pages. It's Margaret's memoir.

Margaret mostly wrote about growing up in Asheville, and like my father's autobiography, hers wanders. There isn't much focus, just brief scenes and recollections.

It doesn't surprise me that Margaret's final piece of writing is a memoir. A lot of people consider writing about their experiences at the closing of their lives.

Margaret is a better writer than my father. In many ways she's a beautiful writer. She describes flying kites with a young Thomas Wolfe. She brings to life the muggy feeling of traveling in railway cars. She mentions O. Henry's memorial service. She describes seeing the Vanderbilt's elegant horse carriage around town, her tight-knit sisterhood, and the Asheville mental asylum where Zelda Fitzgerald later died.

One passage slugs me in the chest. It's a gorgeous piece of writing that strikes contemplative notes about family, impermanence, and the passage of time. I underline it.

One morning, before dawn, when she was thirteen, her father woke her up. He got her out of bed. It was dark outside. Her father wore a nightshirt. He led her over to the window, where she stood beside him as he pointed to the inky early morning sky.

Halley's comet, which only appears every seventy-six years, was just then passing near Earth. Standing beside her father, she quietly watched this galactic event.

"I want you to remember it when you see it again," her father said, and then he said mournfully, "I won't be here when it comes."

And the comet, tearing across the dome above, became a fearsome prophet.

I'm standing next to Mom on a grassy hill at the local planetarium in 1986, when I peer into a telescope and see the past and future cut a white line across the night sky. I'm twelve years old.

"Can you see it, kiddo?" Mom asks me. "Can you see it?"

Above us, Halley's comet burns through space.

DEVILS HOLE

THE WHOLE GODDAMN MESS started with Three Mile Island, with Fat Man and Little Boy, with the entire crazed Cold War buildup. Hot on people's minds were toxic ponds and birth defects and radionuclides leaking from storage tanks. Something had to be done. The solution was to isolate and bury the waste—seventy thousand metric tons—just get rid of it; just bury it inside a series of tunnels and drifts for at least ten thousand years. The task had really only begun. When Bob Waters signed on, he did quick calculations on a paper napkin, uneasy with the size and scale and timetable of the whole undertaking: Ten thousand years was around four hundred generations. Four hundred generations. Four hundred. Now that was a lot of time.

Bob knew the policy wonks in Washington chose Nevada's hinterlands because of the godforsaken isolation, and now, over a late afternoon lunch with a colleague, he wondered about the men on the other end of that decision, men like himself, men tasked with disposing of the sewage. Only a peculiar kind of creature had enough backbone to endure such long stretches of isolation in this unrelenting sun.

And then there was Carl, smug Carl, Carl Benowitz, a man who ceremoniously buffed his fork tines with his tie before meals. Bob sat opposite him, watching. When Carl finished his big routine, he set his fork down and smoothed his tie against his stomach. Carl was meticulous, bonkers, his silverware always just so.

"I heard Operations saddled you with a visitor this week," Carl said.

Bob nodded. He put a finger to his temple, rubbed. Already, he could sense an approaching headache. "That's right," Bob said. "My number's up, I guess. They tapped me to give the nickel tour."

"And of all weeks," Carl said.

"No crap. Of all weeks," Bob said.

"Well, the tunnel will still be here," Carl said.

Bob shifted uncomfortably and lifted a manila folder. "Says this one's from Cambridge," he said. "So she's one of those."

"If by *one of those* you mean smart," Carl said.

"Remember two months ago? Jimmy had to show that visiting paleontologist around? Remember that guy? Guy quizzed Jimmy up and down about mastodons. As though Jimmy knows anything about anything, much less mastodons. Guy swallowed Jimmy's entire month. You'd think Washington would know we have work to do out here." Bob fidgeted. "All I know," he said, "my ass needs to be driving north on Friday night. I have that meeting."

Carl squinted, apparently trying to read him, searching his eyes, which made him uncomfortable. Bob hated being read. At last, Carl said, "That meeting with your son."

"Yeah, yeah," Bob said, looking away, looking to land on something, anything else. "But yes. I'm going to meet my son."

"Well, your visitor will keep you busy at least," Carl said. "Besides, we could use a new face around here. All I see every day is sunburn and work boots and calluses. Maybe she's fetching. That'd be something."

Fetching? What a Carl word, *fetching*. Bob stabbed a toothpick into his half-eaten hoagie. Earlier, he'd heard the cafeteria hadn't received the weekly resupply, and his lettuce was wilted and brown around the edges. He watched Carl flip his spoon and lean it against his plate. Bob had said it before, more than once: Carl had the pallor and bone structure of an undertaker from some old Hollywood film. Outside, through the cafeteria's rectangular hobbit windows, the auburn mountain ridge looked like a jagged line sketched across the sky. They were certainly in the middle of it—in the middle of nothing. A troubling thought struck him every now and then, and now it struck again: not long ago, he was Little Bobbie, Bobbie from California, his toes in the sand, his feet on a surfboard, a boy by the Pacific. But time had a tricky way of elongating. Blink, and ten, twenty years flew right on past. Now look at him. Fifty-three. A desert rat. And he felt that lonesome fact in his knees the moment he stood. One week showing the lady around, and then the weekend would arrive. His son. He squared his watch between his fingers. He was already late.

"Tell her I'm the one with the clean sheets," Carl said.

"Keep it up," Bob said. "I might place a brick on your car."

"Oh, please. Will you give up on that idea?" Carl said. "This isn't college. This isn't a fraternity."

"It's just an idea," Bob said.

"A childish one," Carl said.

"It's a suggestion. To keep things clear. I think it might be smart after what happened last time with that land surveyor."

"Oh, sure," Carl said. "Sure! I'm about to ask her out to dinner, and you sweep in and disappear with her to Vegas for a night out. I spent weeks showing Barbara around."

"I apologized," Bob said. "That's why I suggested the brick."

Carl looked around, lowered his voice, and said, "I mean, my God, she and I shared *Star Trek*. Do you know how difficult it is to find a lady like that?"

Bob scanned the faces in the cafeteria—all men. Carl was right. It was a desert in more ways than one. Bob took the elevator to the dorm's second floor. He figured he'd shed his dungarees and slide on fresh jeans—just in case the lady was *fetching*. Though he still rented a dim, sparsely furnished apartment in Las Vegas, he spent weekdays on-site, eating salty government food and following the progress of the Dodgers in the lounge. Some nights, he took in second-run films at the theater in the Quonset hut or hit the bowling lanes with the guys.

Like always, the door to his room caught on a bent lip of industrial carpet, and he hammered it open with his boot. Inside, he looped a belt around laundered jeans. Beside his keys on the steel desk was the letter from the kid, the first. Bob had read the letter so many times the creases had softened. He unfolded it once more, attempting to suss out meaning from the six short paragraphs. On Saturday, he was scheduled to see his son in Reno—his nineteen-year-old son—for the first time in seventeen years.

Dear Father,
I would really like to get to know you too.

For a brief moment he thought about his son's choice in words. "Father" instead of "Dad." He supposed he hadn't earned the title, the "Dad" part, but all that would change. Just give it time. A little time. He knew time had a way of removing the pollutants from things.

———

WITHIN HALF AN HOUR Bob sat idling in his jeep near the installation's entrance gate. The sun was dropping behind the western ridgeline, flooding the sky with orange atmospherics, but it was still hot, in the upper nineties. Despite the air-con, the heat penetrated the window and touched his cheek. With night closing in, he knew the usual assortment of pacifists and greenies up the access road had probably dispersed. Everyone probably, except for one guy. Bob decided to drive a straight mile between the gate and the NO TRESPASSING sign to confirm his hunch. And sure enough, there he was, sitting in a beach chair beside a foldout table, alone. Bob stopped the jeep just shy of the demarcation line. The man was notable for his deep tan. He stood month after month on hot tarmac and under the sun, protesting. Sometimes he pitched a tent. Sometimes the guy had two signs clutched in doubled fists. People said the man was a priest. Anyway, it was hard not to feel for the guy and his sun-bleached signs. At least that showed resolve. One sign had an image of a mushroom cloud birthed from a pair of dice. Emblazed across the sign were the words, WHY GAMBLE WITH OUR FUTURE?

Bob considered hopping out and explaining some things, but it was too late. Or, wait, really—was it? Was it really too late? Was anything? Lately, it had been like this. Questioning things. Going over things. Thinking too much, allowing buried feelings to rise, creating an uncomfortable blend of excitement and terror that squeezed his ribs at night and made it difficult to breathe—like a smothering panic. What if—what if his son cried? What if his son hit him? A heavy, vague pressure had bloomed inside his chest the moment his son agreed to meet him; it was *right there*, below his sternum. He wondered if he should consult a doctor about the weird sensations. He wondered if he should get a full checkup. He worried about his heart. Seventeen years—gone. Like that. The only thing that helped was the same thing that helped over these past two dead decades. He told himself stories. He adopted the long view. When looked at through the right lens, seventeen years in the grand design of everything was insignificant, a blip. We were all just stars and dust anyway. We were, all of us, alone, really. Seventeen years. Seventeen years was nothing.

———

THE INCOMING'S NAME was Eve Lindy, and she arrived by shuttle bus with a burnished leather carryall and a case that held a banjo. Bob put her in the jeep and quickly escorted her through the badging office. She settled into her temporary quarters on the dorm's third floor and rejoined him in the downstairs lobby. The woman's short, spiky hair looked styled by a blast wave, but it was her glittery green eyes that worried him.

"A banjo?" he said, when she bounced from the elevator.

"You know, in the event it gets boring around here," she said. He noticed her VISITOR badge was already missing. "It is a week, after all."

"A banjo," he said again. "This isn't some jamboree. We don't sit around campfires."

"We'll see," she said. Instead of wearing the standard department lanyard—as per regulations—Eve opted for a sheer tan scarf around her neck. He decided he wouldn't mention it tonight. "Oh, wait. I have something for you. Here," she said, and she surprised him by pulling from her leather purse the latest issue of *Time* magazine. A darkened mug shot of O. J. Simpson was on the cover. "A gift for the natives," she said.

"It's not like we're in the jungle," he said.

"And it's not like this is Manhattan either. Besides, I've heard some things," she said. She was small, small but nicely proportioned, and that worried him too. "My contact at DOE said we'll be outdoors a lot," she said. "Sun year round. Dorm living. So naturally, I thought Ping-Pong tables and BBQs. Sort of like camping. So I brought my banjo." From that same purse she withdrew a spiral notebook and flipped it open. "Okay. I have three areas on my list. The tunnel, of course, a volcanic cliff face, and—"

Bob pinched the end of her notebook. "We'll get to all that. Relax."

Good God: an entire week of her frenetic energy. He just needed to grind through it. He had bigger concerns than Eve Lindy, with her dual PhDs in this-and-whatever.

He gave her the obligatory tour. She asked questions, a lot of questions. She struck him as a type, the kind with three balls always in the air—cooking a meal while exercising her calves and learning Chinese. Her green eyes, hard to look at, and hard not to look at, consumed everything as he escorted her through the cafeteria, meeting rooms, and the dorm laundry, where they ran into Carl, who was folding a pile of white socks.

For some reason Carl's nostrils flared when he introduced himself—with a strange crimp in his throat—as "Engineer Carl." Bob thought that was odd, but Carl was odd. Bob watched his friend's forehead redden, and when Eve looked away, Carl's eyes went wide and he raised an eyebrow. That eyebrow said everything.

Bob waited in the lounge while Eve visited the ladies' room. When she returned, she was shaking water from her fingers. She said, "There aren't any paper towels in there."

"Hardly anyone uses the ladies' room," Bob said.

"In any case, I've never been to this part of the country," she said. "I want you to show me everything."

"Don't get your hopes up," Bob said.

"You could show me a quartz rock and I'd be impressed."

Outside the dorm, Bob walked Eve to his jeep and saw a red brick set carefully on the hood of his jeep. Well, goddamn. A brick. There was a pile of old red bricks at the end of the lot around an abandoned desert well. It was a gift, no doubt, from Carl. Bob smiled at Eve, like this happened all the time, and tossed the brick in the brush.

He gave Eve the usual rundown as they drove around the secure town, which was arranged in a grid. Soldiers and scientists once occupied the town during the atomic tests, he explained. Officially, the town was within the test site, department land, and only accessible through monitored gates.

"And you live out here?" Eve asked.

"Well, nobody really lives out here," he said. "It's the only working town in the states without permanent residents." He enjoyed saying that. He laughed to himself. "But you know, I return to Vegas on weekends. This place isn't much, not compared to what it was. Things emptied after that final test years ago during Reagan. And now we're here cleaning up the mess." He pointed. "Oh, there's the gym. And that's my office." His office was inside an unremarkable '70s-era building that could have belonged to any suburban office park. Bob rolled the jeep down Crossroad Street to the dead end. Above the darkening creosote flats, the sky settled into deep blue.

"It's pretty out here, in a way," Eve said, before saying, "a mean, pretty way." He felt her hand squeeze his forearm, and she said, "Can we go and see it?"

"You should probably rest," he said. "Long flight from Boston."

"But it's the reason I'm here. And I'd like to drive out and see it. If you don't mind."

Though he tried to erase it, he couldn't, and he held on to the ghostly sensation of her touch as he turned the jeep around. His last on-site fling happened several years ago. She was an Austrian archeologist. The woman collected and catalogued Western Shoshone artifacts. Not many women visited town, and when they did, men noticed. Every single man, unmarried or married, noticed.

Bob turned west on the access road and drove toward Jackass Flats. In the dim half-light he noticed Eve's clean, bare marriage finger. Eve impressed him because she knew things. Her questions told him she'd arrived prepared. She asked brainy questions and listened, and he liked how she listened, so he gave her a quick-and-dirty explanation on mine ventilation and rock mechanics. There was nothing human-made that could last the necessary duration — ten thousand years — and so scientists focused on geologic depositories. A 450-foot-long boring machine, he said, had opened the tunnel, a feat of engineering that punched twenty-five-foot holes into welded tuff. He guessed Eve was ten years younger than him.

He stopped near a set of rail tracks that disappeared into the mountain's north portal. The tunnel's wide, dark open mouth ate his headlights. "Mind if I wander?" Eve asked. Her hand was already on the door handle.

Workers were back in town and it was late, but he didn't want to deny her. "Quickly," he said, and added, "Don't go far."

Lit up by the headlights, Eve approached the tunnel with eyes raised toward the ventilation shafts. She had mastered the look of messy sophistication with a carefully chosen desert outfit — khaki tank top, cargo pants with an array of pockets and zippers, and, of course, her scarf. No one dressed like that. She didn't wear makeup either, and when she passed through the lights again he noticed a bit of padding around her midsection, which he liked. Maybe he was shallow, but it had taken him three decades to find love handles on a woman erotic. And he was sure, no, he was certain she was the kind of woman who applied lotion to keep everything soft. What harm could come of it?

He watched Eve stop and put a hand on her hip. He was proud of the mountain. Yucca was the place. He knew he was, more or less, a glorified trash collector, but his mining experience was needed out here. He was needed. Plus, Congress approved, and the president signed the paperwork. When the tunnel was complete, waste would be shipped from across the country and the drifts filled and the portals sealed — for ten thousand years. Then signs would be erected, bearing whatever messages or symbols Eve and her team of linguists and semioticians and psychologists thought appropriate. He wondered how you decided what symbols might communicate KEEP AWAY over ten millennia. Mean and pretty, probably.

"Goes on and on," Eve said when she returned.

"Thanks to three-point-six million pounds per foot of torque."

"What?"

"The boring machine," he said.

"Oh. Huh. Kind of an appropriate name, don't you think?" Eve said, and yawned. "But you're right. This time difference. I need some sleep. Also need to tell my daughter I arrived. She's staying with my sister while I'm here."

Bob slowly removed his hands from the steering wheel. "You have a daughter."

"One smart, mouthy teenager who's already better than me at everything." She turned. "You have any?"

"No," he said quickly.

"Well, mine's at that phase. Hates me but loves my paycheck. I guess I did that with my parents too. Trust me, you'd know if you had any."

The low heat of shame rose in him, and he took a breath, recalibrating his attraction. She was in his orbit, sure, and it was natural to be drawn, but he understood the dangers that accompanied getting close to someone.

Sometimes people asked. And more often than not, he lied. He'd learned to stay quiet on the subject of his son. The moment the information leaked, a follow-up question inevitably came, which terrified him because he knew so little and didn't want to be exposed, and he just didn't enjoy entering that ring naked and with bare fists.

EVERYONE KNEW: Nevada didn't want it. After Chernobyl melted, citizens questioned the science on contamination and leaks and storing such awful shit so close to public aquifers. Nevadans didn't want to be the nation's nuclear dump. It irritated Bob when state lobbyists created a storm by hiring advertising agencies to discredit the project.

And then there were the protestors—famous actors, sometimes—who drove sixty-five miles from Vegas to stage public arrests in the name of civil disobedience. Even the Shoshone tribes said Yucca Mountain was holy land. All that mess to cover up a mess! And, not to forget, good Lord, Bob's former professor, a former *friend*, who phoned him last winter and asked him how he could continue working on such an incompetent project. Bob felt differently. He was a government man. Sure, at one time he was a young fuck-up surfer, but the navy had pretty much squeezed the fuck-up out of him — except for that one thing, about leaving his son. Anyway, he had opinions. And he knew geology. He knew rock.

Yucca Mountain was one of the most studied, picked apart, and debated pieces of real estate on the planet. Geologists, hydrologists, and biologists often scurried through Bob's peripheral sightline like lizards, collecting data. They measured earthquakes, corrosion, soil, and volcanic activity. The waste wasn't going anywhere. The waste was just sitting in tubs in eastern Washington, in South Carolina, all across the country. Something had to be done. A stable solution was necessary. That's what drew him here, really. Finally, he was part of a solution.

Two days before Christmas 1977, the boy's mother served him divorce papers with his dinner plate. He stood up, enraged. He'd already been traveling back and forth on a temp job, Reno to Battle Mountain, Battle Mountain to Reno, living out of a suitcase. Next up for them was a well-paying gig in Arizona. So when he returned to Reno for the holiday, when she gave him papers, he said fuck this, *fuck you*, and he left. The mother, that bitch, deserved nothing. A court date loomed, which he skipped. And then somehow time rolled by, and he kept skipping through Idaho, South Carolina, New Mexico, Ohio, Washington, and Nevada, not one goddamn person binding him down — only rock. He had rock. That brief marriage long ago was just a two-year transfer point on his way to the next destination. Left behind in his long zigzag was a young boy.

Sometimes he wondered if the mother poured special poisons into his son's ears as he grew from a boy into a young man. Bob didn't care to think about that. He refused to think about her for a number of years, but then eventually he allowed himself to think about the marriage, and he thought about her and acknowledged to himself how the mother had taken his heart and chiseled it into useless scraps. He never would have turned it over to her in the first place if she weren't such a goddamn beauty. Long brown hair fell like a shiny waterfall down her back, like Crystal Gayle. Still, she had a tongue like a knife, that woman. After he left, he vowed to never let anyone like her happen to him again.

It took two years to firm down a meeting with the boy. The boy's mother had reached out to Bob's parents around the boy's eighteenth birthday, and she'd provided an address. The address was passed on to Bob. After mailing his son a birthday card on his eighteenth, with a check enclosed, he believed the door would fly open. It didn't. The boy was eighteen, now an adult, free to call his own shots. His son's first response was a short, rigid, polite six-paragraph letter, informing Bob he couldn't meet anytime soon.

Dear Father,

Included with the letter was a wallet-sized photo—his son in his high school soccer uniform. Whenever Bob looked at the photo, it cut him down the middle. He was almost unable to comprehend how quickly that baby had turned into that boy. Yet the boy in the photo was a stranger. He could be any kid at the Vegas mall. His own son could traipse right past him, and he wouldn't even know it.

Bob mailed another letter. He waited months for a response before his son wrote back. More short letters passed between them. It carried on like this, incrementally, like flirting, and Bob found himself getting excited at the end of each workweek, eager to return to Vegas and key open his mailbox. Often, he found nothing but junk mail and bills.

I can't meet you because . . .
But I would really like to meet you.

Six months passed. Bob grew antsy. He felt sick when he learned that his son had decided to attend a four-year college across the country in New York. His son was a Nevada boy. But of course: The mother was from New York. Made sense. Part of him wanted to give up, say *fuck it*. He didn't know what to do with the warring feelings of shame and need, or how these complicated, developing feelings fit into his everyday life. Contact had been made. He tossed a rope, his son reached back, but with his son in New York, the rope soon stretched into a long, frayed thread.

Then another birthday. Bob continued sending periodic notes—news of himself and of relatives the boy didn't know anything about. Their back-and-forth was a long-distance wooing operation. Bob admitted to himself he was equally frightened. When they met, if they ever met, what would the kid expect from him? Money? Advice? His time? He didn't know what brand of love to give, since that kind of love had been cauterized and undeveloped. He decided to sprinkle small anecdotes about himself into his letters that he believed a young man might find interesting. Like the time he was deputized by the sheriff in a dusty Podunk town. Or the night he walked alone across Black Rock Desert, unaware that a rattler had taken a chance at his cowboy boots. Gradually, Bob grew emboldened and offered life advice in his short letters, but his son was unappreciative, and the kid shot back his snotty teenage opinions. Bob just didn't know how to respond to a letter that quoted Karl Marx alongside some wacko named Noam Chomsky.

Dear Father,

Finally, Bob said *fuck it* and went for it. He was headed to Reno for a conference at the Mackay School of Mines. He asked the boy to meet again. He knew the kid was shuttling back and forth between Reno and New York. He was tough to pin down. But his son agreed, at last. He was going to be in Reno for the summer, staying with the mother. It was an eight-hour drive. Bob was closer than he'd gotten in seventeen years. Things would change. His life would have to change. After so many years he might find a way to earn the right to be called Dad. Maybe there was time.

———————

YEARS RAN BY and his life narrowed into a series of routines. For most of the year, he lived in a dorm room with white, utilitarian, cinderblock walls. A lonely life, sure, but he had the sky. He had the desert, he had rock, and he had his tunnel, which he showed Eve Lindy over the following days.

He accompanied her as she walked half a mile of tunnel, wearing an ill-fitting hardhat. She stood under high-intensity incandescent lamps to scribble in her notebook. Already there was a five-mile U-shaped tunnel punched through the mountain's hard volcanic tuff.

"Some say Yucca isn't the right place for this kind of waste," he said. "But let me tell you. It is. Some scientists want a salt rock repository, since salt is anhydrous and self-healing. But I can tell you now, volcanic tuff will last the required time." He looked over, hoping she'd write that nugget down.

"Never seen anyone care so much about something no one wants," Eve said.

"I can't imagine what you're writing."

"Words."

"I can't imagine why you need to spend a week here."

"Why?" she said. "Tired of me already?"

In the evenings Eve drew out the men from their messy dorm rooms with the plunky sound of her banjo. Her instrument was a magnet, and Bob watched her deploy her magic, slightly unnerved by her overdeveloped social skills. The men in town were social isolates, nerds fascinated by rock, yet Eve was kind, and she seemed truly interested in people. Usually, he and the guys sat around the dorm TV, watching baseball, solemn as monks.

In the middle of the week, Bob looked out his window after dinner and saw Eve sitting under the covered outdoor patio. She had her banjo in her lap and a beer between her sandals. Carl and three visiting engineers orbited her like isotopes. Bob hadn't seen anyone use the patio in years. Now people were laughing out there. The men even looked showered. Their usual pit-stained work shirts were gone.

Eve stopped playing when he joined them. She reached for her beer, and Bob noticed her red toenails. The big one was slightly chipped. "Too nice a night to spend alone in these ugly stockades, wouldn't you say, Bob?" she said.

"Suppose," he said.

Carl excavated a bottle from an ice chest and handed it to Bob without making eye contact. Carl had already emptied two, and both empties were standing neatly side by side.

"Play the Dolly Parton again," one of the engineers said.

"Another request," Eve said. She put her beer down. "I wonder what my friends would think. Seeing me surrounded by handsome desert cowboys."

"Right," Bob said. "Hardly cowboys."

"And hardly handsome," Carl added.

"I haven't had this much attention since my older brother's eighteenth birthday," Eve said. "It was a sleepover. I'm a year younger."

"We're just enjoying the music," Carl said.

"I'd like to hear some music," Bob said.

"What's it like spending so much time out here?" Eve asked. "Surrounded by superirradiated wasteland? You must have stories."

"It's just a work site," Bob said.

"But tell," she said. "How close is Area 51? How many miles away?"

Bob glanced at Carl. Carl looked enchanted by Eve. He gazed at her as though she'd hung the moon. It was a question nearly every visitor wanted answered.

"I don't know what conspiracy shows you've been watching," Bob said.

"Oh, come on," Eve said. "Tell."

So-called Area 51, or Groom Lake, lay several tan valleys to the east. It was a military production and proving facility. Even more secret was Papoose Lake, another dry lake bed, but he didn't mention it. Both were military, nothing more. "Look," he said. "NTS cut the land into thirty zones. You're sitting in number twenty-five. There is no fifty-one."

A shallow well formed between Eve's eyes as she squinted. There were lines beside her eyes he hadn't noticed before, little reminders of her age. He liked them.

"Anyhow, Bob's going to show me the petroglyphs tomorrow, aren't you, super nice Bob?" she said.

"I don't see why that's on the agenda," he said.

She pressed the banjo against her stomach. "Stop being such a wet blanket, Bob," she said. "Our group is tasked with creating permanent signage. Don't you think studying native symbols that have lasted millennia might be a good place to begin?"

It was a solid point. He hadn't considered that.

After three beers he felt a buzzing in his ears. Bob set his bottle down and reached for another. As Eve played Earl Scruggs, he watched how intensely Carl watched her moving fingers, as though she were on a stage. Later, when Carl told his old standard about getting lost and going off road and getting stopped by military police, he seemed to be talking only to Eve. Bob watched his friend's Adam's apple rise and drop, wondering what game Carl was trying to play. Carl had used the brick, sure, but he'd also made it clear it was a ridiculous idea.

Eve didn't seem to notice how much attention Carl paid her. Or maybe she did, which bothered Bob. She smiled at everyone. She certainly wasn't stingy with smiles. Even later, after the visiting engineers said goodnight,

Eve said she felt like a smoke. Like she *really* wanted a smoke, she said. She stood and put her hands on her hips and pushed them forward in a stretch. Her tank top lifted, and Bob saw a quick flash of skin. Carl did too.

"I think I have an old pack in my room," Carl said. "Wait here." He hustled off toward the dorm, the soles of his boots scuffing the concrete.

Bob saw his chance. He grabbed Eve's hand, walked her to the lot, and opened the door to his jeep. She looked at him, squint-eyed. She knew how to embrace a certain mischievous and overemphasized expression. She shrugged and hopped in. After several miles he went off road. They bounced over a gully, dropping onto a hard, dry pond basin. He pressed the accelerator.

"Watch this," he said. At sixty miles per hour he turned off the headlights. The moon was up and illuminated the flats. Pebbles pinged against the undercarriage. It was like coasting across a distant moon.

He slowed and allowed the jeep to roll to a gentle stop. Dust drifted past the windows. In the distance lights flickered in town. They were as alone and as separate from the rest of the world as they could be: in the dark, in the middle of a dry pond, in the desert, and technically within the test site. Bob rolled down the window. The heat was fading.

"This is stupid," Eve finally said. "Maybe we had too much to drink. So dramatic. Just driving away like that."

"A wet blanket," Bob said.

"It's like summer camp out here," Eve said. "It's the same. Small infatuations. But some things are different, I guess."

"For instance," he said.

"You're digging a grave for nuclear waste," she said.

He thought about that for a while. "Well, if I'm the gravedigger, then that means you're making the headstone."

"Oh, Bob. You should know when to stop. Extended metaphors don't suit you."

Bob sat quietly.

He watched Eve unzip a pocket on her cargo pants and remove a plastic baggie. The skunky, pungent aroma opened his sinuses. He knew what she had. And on federal land. Now he understood what she meant earlier by *smoke*. She was so small, so slight, but in her small body she held stores of energy, enough to ruin him, like some bomb.

———

BOB LAY IN BED, stoned, staring at asbestos popcorn nubs on the ceiling. If anyone from DOE found out, he could lose his job or get reprimanded or reassigned, but right now he was loose, floating, as he'd been, really, for decades.

He'd left the windows in the jeep down to air wash it. He hoped there wasn't a sudden downpour. Highly unlikely. He'd only been high one time, despite all his early surfing years. He was unsure if he liked the feeling. There was a twinge of paranoia in it. So he laid still, waiting it out.

His son was born in the evening, an evening birth. In the dark he tried to remember as best he could. He was unbelievably comforted by his pillow, and he tried to tunnel back to that night. He remembered Washoe County Hospital, the clinical yellow walls, the mother's suffering face, cramped by birth pains, and of course the guilt that pummeled him each fifth of November, his son's birthdate. With every passing year his memories of that night dimmed until he was unable to summon the smallest details. He didn't know what kind of man his son was hoping to meet. He didn't know much about the boy. His son — smart, interested in sports, outdoors, music. What else? A good kid, judging by his letters. Yet other than inherited genetics, he hadn't sculpted the boy in any way. More and more, he thought about the boy he'd shoved from his thoughts for two decades. He didn't know what his son's life was like, who his friends were, what he laughed at or cared about. Bob hadn't paid a penny for his upbringing. Things would change, and life would go on, only differently.

Well, I'll tell you a bit about myself . . . I am very outgoing and a basically happy person.

———————

MERCURY HIGHWAY was a ribbon of asphalt stretched across prehistoric landscape. It was the most isolated road he'd ever driven on. Vast alluvial seas of scrub rose into rocky spines padded by yucca and sage, and in the transition zone, here and there, were scattered forests of Joshua trees. They entered the controlled area through secondary gates, where a uniformed guard checked Eve's name off a list and passed her a radiation badge.

Eve turned the thick plastic card over in her fingers, apparently alarmed. "Really? I have to wear this?" she said.

"You'll receive a letter in a month informing you about your levels of exposure," the guard told her.

Her eyes widened. "My levels of exposure? A letter in the mail?" she said.

"Don't worry," he said. "You'll be fine."

They drove past dust-covered load trucks and military vehicles headed toward staging exercises. Bob felt a shade emotional, from drinking too much, from smoking, and he concentrated on the road. These desert flats, these distances between ranges, gave him a deep sense of stillness. The car seemed to remain at a standstill. At seventy miles per hour, the looming mountains didn't appear to move any closer. Spread across Frenchman Flat, an old testing range, were low man-made hills full of transuranic waste, but Eve was more interested in the fire-damaged buildings and Buicks half dissolved by after blasts.

"Army engineers put cars out here every half mile to see what the detonations would do," Bob told her. It was getting hot. He flipped on the AC.

"Wait. Let me get this straight. The army wanted to see what a nuclear explosion would do to a car," she said.

"Yes."

"Sounds quite testicular," she said.

Bob laughed. He slowed when they neared an abandoned encampment surrounded by fencing. Two guard towers stood pitched at severe angles. The place looked as if it were from an old World War II film, like an antiquated German camp or something. Bob couldn't answer Eve's questions. He didn't know why it was used. When they reached an upslope in the road, Bob pulled over. He wanted Eve to get a prime view of the valley — or what was left of it. Subsidence craters had turned Yucca Flat into a rutted moonscape.

"Underground detonations left those pockmarks," he said.

"How many?" Eve asked. She didn't blink.

"Nearly a thousand," Bob said. "All this was open-air laboratory."

"Nearly a thousand detonations," she said, shaking her head. "It's hard to imagine."

It was like this with visitors. The legend was as intense as that first hotshot over the southern New Mexico sky. And he didn't even show her Sedan Crater, a massive cylindrical hole opened by a 104-kiloton blast.

"Tourists visited Vegas hoping to see the flashes," Bob told her. "Newspapers even announced detonation times."

Staring out at the valley, Eve brought her hand to her mouth. She was silent for a time before she said, "Good Lord, what did we do?"

"Built the world's greatest defense system," Bob said.

"I look at this, and I can only think of Jenny."

"Jenny?"

"My daughter," Eve said.

"Right, right." He nodded. "Jenny."

For a moment he wondered whether Jenny shared her mother's features. He wondered about Eve's cozy East Coast life. He put in his mind the image of cobblestones and row houses and leafy tree-lined streets. Puffy jackets and wool mittens.

A few miles northwest of Skull Mountain, he found a dirt access road that brought them to the canyon Eve wanted to explore. An archeologist from the University of Chicago had provided Eve with detailed directions, and now Bob held the directions between his fingers as he steered around runnels in the dirt road. At last they stopped. The heat hit him when Eve opened her door.

Halfway up the slope, Bob put his hands on his hips, breathing hard through his teeth. He felt his heart in his throat. Fifty or so yards above, Eve called for him to catch up. He hadn't signed up for this. Eve, small, pretty Eve, didn't stop—she pecked and pecked and pecked, and he snorted as he wondered if that's how she was between the sheets. What felt like a needle entered behind his knee, and he turned. A leafy dagger from a Yucca was stabbing him. Above, the rocky outcropping jutted from the hill like an amphitheater's roof. He toed a hole in the dirt and readjusted his backpack. Eve's nonexistent path was nothing but loose talus, and it felt hotter now. He was winded, and his lungs burned from the previous night. He hadn't slept well.

When he ascended the hill, Eve was already snapping photos. Boot on a boulder, she steadied the camera with her knee. Etched into the black volcanic rock were lines, symbols, and shallow carvings. One appeared anthropomorphic, a person, both arms crook'd, square head—a simple, blunt design that looked vaguely Egyptian. The rock outcropping must have been a beacon for ancient peoples.

"Aren't they beautiful?" Eve asked him.

"I never knew these were here."

"Why would you? Our own government is too busy keeping everyone out." She gently ran her fingers along the rock's surface. "Dates back eight millennia, I'm told."

"So maybe you should just carve a skull and crossbones into the rock, set it outside our tunnel, and call it a day."

"It's not that straightforward."

"I know. I joke."

"Ever heard of Kenneth Burke?"

He looked at her. "No."

"He was a theorist," she said. "He said humans are wired to use symbols. We communicate through symbols. We're the only animals to do that. But now we have to devise a symbol to keep people away. We might speak different languages in ten thousand years. If we're even around."

Eve wandered, scribbling notes, and took more photos. He sat in the dirt and dug a twig out of his sock. Then he located a nice, flat boulder. Flat enough, at least, but they'd have to stand. He unzipped his backpack and arranged the sandwiches, chips, and warm cans of Diet Rite. All around him were symbols, evidence of expired centuries, traces of past peoples, their scratches, their claw marks. It was all done as if to say, *I was here. Remember. Don't Forget.*

Eve walked over. "You brought along a picnic." A gust of wind pushed her pointy hair sideways. Her eyes looked whiter—and larger—in daylight.

"The cafeteria made it for us," he said. "Government standard."

Eve crossed her arms. "You're nice, Bob."

"About last night," he said.

"Let's not." She touched his arm. "Last night was fun. Let's leave it right there."

They'd sat in his jeep, smoke swirling out the windows, talking, and then not talking, watching midnight dust funnels form, touch off, and dissipate. They'd just sat and smoked, and he was okay with that.

Eve chose the egg salad and peeled back the wax paper. Bob opened chips. He watched her eat in silence, little almost cute bites disappearing from her sandwich. He felt comfortable around her. He liked her. This was the closest he'd come to a proper date with a woman in years.

———————

TO BRIDGE THE TIME between late afternoon and Eve's sudden plans for an evening BBQ, Bob suggested bowling a few rounds. Eve brightened at the idea. Eight slick lanes had been installed in a former ordnance depot, and the moment he stepped inside he felt transported. He noticed the hairs on her arms prick from the air-con. The place had the look and smell of any other bowling alley in any suburb in America. But of course, tromping in with Eve was like escorting a celebrity across the red carpet.

Quickly enough, three beer-buzzed contractors descended, like wasps circling a hive. The men had the bright glistening eyes of numerous downed pitchers, and they asked Eve questions, trying to make her laugh, and trying to put Bob down to improve their chances. Eve was one of the only women within ninety square miles. But when one of them compared Bob's balding head to a bowling ball, Eve threw out a chill with her eyes, and the men returned to their lane.

"I swear, that doesn't happen back home," she said, when they were alone. She smiled. "But I sort of like it."

Bob saw Carl come through the door, lugging his bowling bag. Carl walked over as they were lacing their clown shoes.

"Thanks for waiting," Carl said.

"We thought we'd get the lane ready," Bob said.

"We're sorry," Eve said.

"We?" Carl said. He bore the look of the injured.

"I'm sorry I didn't wait," Eve said.

"Reminds me how both of you waited for me last night," Carl said. Bob didn't respond. These things happened. Carl was an adult. Carl knew life wasn't fair. Carl removed his bloodred ball and buffed it with an old Vegas tourist T-shirt. "Care to place any bets?" Carl said. He popped his silver Timex off his wrist and shoved it in his bag.

"Okay," Eve said. "I bet one dollar I win."

"A dollar?" he said. "Keep it." Then his eyes drilled into Bob. "How about a brick? Want to bet a brick, Bob? How about a brick?"

Bob sighed and looked away. He knew Carl. Carl could get like this when he was disappointed. And he knew that when Carl put his nose in the air, he was filling his lungs with his special brand of arrogance. Carl, after all, was the better bowler.

It was clear his friend was on some kind of mission. Carl's face showed all the hints; he may as well have painted warrior stripes across his cheeks. Even though Carl wore pleated slacks and a short-sleeve button-up and a striped, fork-cleaning tie, he delivered his red ball down the lane with accuracy and force. Eve commented lightheartedly about the tragedy of it all, the unfairness. How Carl was clearly superior because this was how he spent all his free time. After Carl cleaned up in the third frame, Bob shared an inside glance with Eve. She smiled at him. She shook her head. She tapped her knuckle against his chin.

Nothing could deter Carl from his systematic slaughter. He manhandled his ball. His determined stare was like an Olympian's. His game was excellent. But Bob struggled. He forked the ten count and bombed the follow-up. His pins, it seemed, were greased and full of gaps. Eve bowled properly yet poorly, tossing more than one dead ball down the gutter.

"Okay, fine, we give up, you win," Eve said to Carl. "But don't think this is a sport."

"It's more of a sad hobby than a sport," Bob said.

"There's skill involved," Carl said, swiping his hands dismissively. He sat down.

"All you need to know is how to walk, shake a hand, and aim," Bob said.

"More to it," Carl said.

"And to think there are professional leagues built around this nonsense," Bob said.

"Boys," Eve said.

Later, a light, unexpected rain stirred the smell of creosote in the air. Then the clouds disappeared, and it was warm again. Though the rain tamped down the heat to the midnineties, Eve spritzed herself with a water bottle. She invited anyone and everyone, and eight men accepted. She scrounged together a humble spread with supplies from the town's meager grocery store. She served beans and hotdogs and mustard and relish. The men sat around the patio, eating cross-legged off paper plates.

"One more day and you'll be rid of me," Eve said, and handed Bob a toasted bun.

"What if I don't want to get rid of you?" he said.

"It's been nice," she said. "But we still haven't seen any of those wild horses you tell me about."

"It's too hot right now in the lowlands," he said.

"Wrong, wrong," Carl said. He sat nearby on the picnic table, arms outstretched, feet crossed. The other men sat in a tight conversational circle a good distance away. "I saw a stallion and his mares the other day near Frenchman," he said. "Even saw a small colt."

"Oh, I wish I'd been there," Eve said.

"Well, they must be starving to come down from the hills this time of year," Bob said.

"Let's go find them. I could stay an extra day," Eve said. She looked hopeful. "Jenny will be fine with her aunt. I can manage it."

"But that won't work for Bob," Carl said. "Bob's seeing his son."

Eve blinked, and her head pulled back. "Your son?" she said.

Bob said nothing.

"For the first time," Carl said. "Bob's meeting his son," he said, and then he said, "Bob wasn't around. Ask him."

Eve blinked again. She was silent. Her eyes narrowed as she looked down at the glowing coals. Bob watched her calculate an equation. She pinched her pretty chin. By her downturned eyes, he knew he was losing her. Carl's bony, defined jaw moved camel-like as he chewed his hotdog. He stared at Bob like one of those tourists from long ago, wanting to bear witness to a detonation, but Bob was too old for that, and he just stood there and took what came to him.

Things happened. And it had happened like this before. Not long ago Bob had a good thing going with the Austrian woman. They even used the word *marriage* one night when the moon was full and his room was cool and her leg was slung over his. Living together on-site made for a pressurized environment, like being trapped on an island. Relationships formed quickly. He remembered their long, meandering drives in the desert. And when he eventually decided to come clean, to attempt honesty, the woman asked the expected questions, good questions, and Bob admitted his mistake: He had left his son. There were reasons, many reasons, relationships-are-complicated kinds of reasons, but the only thing that mattered to her, she said, was the fact that hit her in the face like a fist. He had left his son. And soon after, the woman left too. Other than a few postcards, they hadn't kept in touch.

Later in the evening, a faint orange glow graced the sky, and Eve sat on the far end of the picnic table, away from him, with her banjo in her lap. She fiddled with the tuning pegs, twisting them back and forth. The others gathered around, and now Carl sat beside her, their hips nearly touching, and Bob knew it was over. She picked a solemn song, and Bob leaned back on his hands, feeling splinters dig into the meat of his palms, feeling the throbbing, happy kick of surrender. Now he wouldn't have to try. He knew he belonged to the great species of losers who found comfort in occasional failures. The pressure in his throat released and he felt okay, really, and corrected, and he listened to Eve's song until the coals burned out and darkness came and until he could only see her teeth in the moonlight.

I am very much into alternative music and I play guitar myself. I believe music opens our minds and helps us think about how we can solve some of the problems of our troubled world. Well, enough rambling on and on . . .
Love,
Donny

p.s. I spell my name with a y and not ie

Bob remembered heat gathering in his stomach when he read the postscript for the first time. A *y*, not *ie*. He had addressed the birthday card to Donnie. Such a little thing. He felt another whiff of anger and shame. When he was a boy, his nickname was Bobbie—Little Bobbie—spelled with an *ie*. In that first birthday card he sent, he assumed his son spelled his name the same way. The mother—oh he knew the mother had something to do with the spelling. It was a fifty-fifty chance, and he fucked it up. Perhaps he would have stayed if the mother had wanted him. Or if she'd devised a comfortable living situation, but all she ever did was yammer on and on about her first husband, a naval officer, refusing to extinguish that flame. And she drove him to near madness. So much of that marriage drove him to near madness. And so he left—he left! Their brief marriage, that bright flash, produced a kind of fallout he still lived under.

THE NEXT MORNING, the sun hit the blinds and striped his pillow. He woke up thinking about time. He hoped there was time. He was desperate for more time. He was ready to endure the long drive to Reno, but he wasn't looking forward to Eve's questioning morning eyes.

He assumed her schedule called for another half day at the tunnel. Then a shuttle would retrieve her. Then she'd be gone. But after waiting for forty-five minutes in the dorm's lobby, he took the elevator to the third floor and knocked on her door. She didn't answer. Bob took the stairwell to the second floor and considered knocking on Carl's door but didn't. He didn't want to confirm his suspicions.

He wasn't surprised to find another red brick on the hood of his jeep. Placed there, no doubt, by Carl Benowitz, that son-of-a-bitch. He tossed the brick on the passenger seat and slammed the door. At 8:00 a.m., the heat was already rising. Bob felt it behind his eyeballs. He'd heard the weather was going to jump to 109 degrees. Part of him wanted to skip out on Eve and just head north, bathed in AC.

But he went looking for them.

Carl had screwed him over because Bob had once screwed Carl over. Bob wondered if their friendship could survive these repeated breaches.

He rolled through town, scoping for his friend's blue coupe. His wheels scraped against a curb. He drove half hungover, one hand gripping the wheel. What, anyway, was he doing? What did he hope to accomplish? To win Eve back? He didn't sign up for this, hunting around town for some East Coast linguist flirt. He drove the access road toward the north portal, and for a moment, driving on a road as barren as any he'd ever known, none of it mattered. The next day, he'd be with his son and Eve wouldn't matter, and none of the dark, dry tunnels would matter either.

At the north portal, an engineer told him he'd seen Carl and the visitor leave through the main gate, so Bob backtracked to the guard station.

"Carl said they were headed to some desert aquifer," the guard told him.

"What aquifer?"

"I don't know. Some place called Devils Hole." The guard shrugged. "That's all Carl said."

Bob hopped out and unfolded his tattered hydrologic map, and together they leaned over it until Bob found the spot. It was twenty miles west across Amargosa Valley. Bob had once overheard two hydrologists discussing the aquifer. He didn't know much about it. Could just be a place where they measured depth levels. In the desert, people paid attention to water sources.

"Maybe it's some kind of desert hot spring," the guard said, and smiled.

The image of Carl in his skivvies came to him. He saw Carl's skeletal hands reaching to assist Eve—nude—into an isolated spring. The thought shuffled anger around his stomach. As he drove off in pursuit, he swiveled the AC to full, blasting his sinuses with chemical-smelling air.

The long, straight highway zippered the Great Basin and Mojave deserts together. Bob drove straight up the middle. The closer he got, the more annoyed he became. In his emotional, hungover state, he felt tired of losing.

It stung. Eventually, he saw a wooden road sign for Devils Hole. He slowed and took a dirt road. He spotted Carl's coupe parked beyond an open gate. Other than some random fencing, the place was in the middle of nowhere. He parked. He got out, carrying the brick with him, half considering putting it through Carl's windshield.

In the clearing sat a yellow domed tent. There was also a tarp, held taut between steel poles, which provided shade for a collection of kitchen equipment. Carl wasn't the camping kind, and Bob knew the items weren't his. The camp was near a small aquifer pool ringed by twenty-foot cliffs. Bob stood on the precipice and peered down at the cistern. The water was black, calm, and accessed by an aluminum ladder, so that someone could safely crawl down. He wondered where everyone had gone.

He heard voices. He heard distant talking. Sound carried in the desert. Voices caromed through the thin knife valley. Bob thought he could make out Carl's deep, lungy boom. He was at the base of a hill and he figured they were on the other side.

At last he spotted them at the top. He saw three people, slowly maneuvering down the hill, sliding every few feet. He watched Eve balance herself against Carl. He wondered whom Carl and Eve had adopted. With them was some guy wearing what looked like a straw hat with a wide, ridiculous brim.

Bob felt foolish holding a brick. So he dropped it. Then he kicked it over the cliff and into the water. A loud splash rose up from below, louder than he expected, followed by what sounded like a deep suck, and then shouting. Bob looked up. The brim of the stranger's hat arched back as the man took wild, bounding leaps down the hill, seemingly unconcerned with his safety. Bob heard him yelling. "Stop! Stop!" The man nearly tumbled over. "Stop!"

He made out a blond beard, big wilderness boots, and white bared teeth. No doubt the man was the desert camper, and now he was really coming, skidding down scree and hopping over brush.

"Are you fucking mad?" the man screamed as he closed in. "Are you homicidal?" The man's face looked to be in agony. Bob backed away from the cistern's ledge, suddenly afraid the guy might hit him or shove him over.

Instead, the man rushed past Bob and used the ladder system to shimmy twenty feet to the pool below. Then he crouched on the travertine ledge, gazing into the water as though looking into some holy fountain.

A lost soul, obviously, the kind who retreated to the desert in search of visions. Bob knew men like him existed out here. He'd heard stories. Military police detained people like him all the time, desperados caught trespassing on the bombing range.

Bob watched Eve slide down a half-buried boulder. Then she coaxed Carl off it. Finally, Carl leaped and winced on impact. They walked over.

"That was no good, Bob," Eve said. She was wiping the dust off her hands on her pants. She peered over the cliff. The man below had his chin to the waterline. "We heard the splash from way up there. What in the world did you throw in there?"

"I don't understand," Bob said.

"You could kill the damn pupfish," Carl said. "Jesus Christ."

"What fish?"

"The pupfish!" Carl said.

"There are only about a hundred left," Eve said. "They're endangered. They've been living in this pool for ten thousand years. I wanted to see them on my last day."

"Only a hundred left, and Bob decides to nuke them," Carl said.

Bob didn't know. He didn't mean it. He was just nudging a stupid old suggestion into the water, drowning it. That was all. He felt sweat seep between his shoulder blades and collect in his lower back. They were only twenty miles or so from the nation's nuclear dumping grounds, and this existed? A desert hole full of endangered fish? Here? Who knew? Lately, everywhere he stepped seemed to be a step into the past. Ancient volcanic tuff. Rock drawings. And now fish? He blinked and rubbed the salty sweat from his eyes.

Carl followed Eve down, and Bob shadowed Carl. They took the ladder slowly, crabbing down, their hands gripping rock joints for balance until they joined the man on the travertine ledge. It wasn't a remarkably large pool of water, but it looked quite deep.

"Sam's the site biotechnician," Carl said. "He's a scientist."

Sam was on his knees, still peering into the water, and he said, "I count the fucking fish. I make sure the fish don't fucking die."

"And is that bad?" Bob said. "Causing that splash? That's bad?"

"Is that fucking bad?" Sam said in a voice so high it cracked. "Put it this way. The fish respond to vibrations from earthquakes that occur in Mexico." His dirty fingernails scratched against the rock. "They live in a snow globe, and you just shook it. Yes, that was bad."

"I didn't know," Bob said.

"You'd think I was the one who needed the fences and the military guard shacks," Sam said.

"These pupfish are one of the world's rarest species," Eve said.

Everything would change. Soon, tomorrow. From now on he'd change, and he'd become a different man. He was not the same person who left behind a son, but he understood the waste was still there, would always be there, buried below the surface of things. Just acknowledging that truth nearly disassembled him. He felt a sudden rush as blood ripped through his chest and throbbed in his neck, and he grabbed Carl's shoulder for support. It was not unlike the sensations he'd been having lately. He dropped to his knees and peered into the water. Carl bent over, and Eve did too. He desperately wanted the tiny things to be okay. A shiny blue fish — an inch long — darted from beneath the watery shelf and then disappeared. One was alive. He wanted to father it, if only he knew how. He didn't know much other than how to pack a suitcase, how to move, how to bore a hole into rock, and how to hide inside it. He didn't know that, in a few years' time, he would suffer near-fatal cardiac arrest, which would require emergency six-way bypass surgery, leaving him with only 60 percent use of his heart. He didn't know how his long absence — or his sudden reappearance — would throw a menacing shadow over his young son's life. He didn't understand the power of that kind of impact, but his son would later explain it to him in a furious letter: Like a meteor strike! Bob didn't know that the very next day, during their first face-to-face meeting, he would talk too much, fail to ask questions, and his self-involved tap dance would only remind his son he was a nonentity. Bob would never know, during their brief get-to-know-you-drive around Lake Tahoe, that his son would briefly consider grabbing the steering wheel and taking them both over a cliff and into the freezing, aquamarine water. And he could not know the Yucca Mountain project would reverse course decades later, leaving his tunnel abandoned and the portals sealed. He would never know the ways his son would closely examine his life, turning his decisions over and tracing his movements on a map — the places he lived, his activities. He couldn't know his son would speak with an aquatic ecologist and an environmental scientist to learn more about pupfish and the legacy of Yucca Mountain. On this searing, bright day, Bob didn't know that he'd only see his son five short times before dying in a hospital overlooking the Puget Sound. And, of course, he didn't know the lengths his son would go looking for answers or that his son would one day write about him, showing him kneeling on the brink, overlooking one of the most delicate species on the planet.

Sam removed his frayed straw hat.

"So what's the word?" Bob asked.

Sam wiped from his forehead. "Lucky, that's a word," Sam said. For the first time Bob noticed specks in the man's hazel eyes. "You're lucky. Looks like the little guys will be fine."

AND IN THE BEGINNING

A YEAR PASSES.

In that time Robin decides to join me in Iowa to work on a novel after I accept a temporary teaching position at the University of Iowa, which extends the Midwest adventure. My novel gets published by the university press, accompanied by a few decent reviews, and then quietly disappears from shelves.

When the teaching job ends, we roll westward, back to Portland, this time to the east side of the Willamette River, the younger and hipper side, where we move into an old craftsman bungalow built in 1922. We paint walls, arrange furniture, discuss what should be done with our new bloodred kitchen, and tend to Mercy's leg injury, which happened while she chased after a tennis ball at the beach.

It's summer again in the Pacific Northwest, and when there's time, I drive to the coast and surf. A finished room in the basement becomes my workspace, where I've been writing this memoir. I'd like to complete a draft before I begin work as a visiting assistant professor at Lewis & Clark, a liberal arts college in Portland.

Robin and I still talk about it. A small room beside our bedroom would make an ideal nursery. We imagine installing a crib and hanging a mobile. For now, Robin uses the space as her office.

It hasn't happened naturally. We've made an appointment with a fertility clinic to discuss options. We make a plan. We want a child. Our new home is large enough for a family. At least that's our growing hope.

A LAB TECH in a white coat calls my name. I look up from my magazine. She's young, midtwenties, with bright blue eyes, and sharp strawberry blonde bangs against snowy skin. Many of the office bees are pretty young things, I've noticed, and for a moment I wonder whether the doctors hire them to inspire a clever atmosphere of health and fertility.

I stand. "Hi, I'm Heidi," she says with an open smile. "Follow me."

Of course her name is Heidi. She may as well wear pigtails. Heidi escorts me down a series of nicely carpeted hallways adorned with cheap, blocky, maroon artwork that reminds me of Rothko. At the end of the hall, we pass through a heavy steel door. Heidi shows me a room with a plastic couch, sink, toilet, TV, and five-disc DVD player.

The room is in the rear of the clinic, off a concrete hallway, and near the back exit, where I'm supposed to slink out anonymously after I complete my task.

Heidi hands me a plastic cup with a twist lid.

"After you finish up, just place the cup in there." She points to a small steel door inset in the wall. "Have you done this before?" she asks. Her cheeks immediately redden.

"Sure, I've done this plenty of times," I say.

"I mean, what I mean," she says.

"I get it. After I finish, I put the cup inside that door. And you'll retrieve it from the other side. Easy."

She leaves me alone.

Inside, I shut the door and lock it. I've been tested before at another clinic in Iowa, but this time they're going to really examine everything, even though I don't know what they could possibly learn. First thing, I spread a sterile blue medical sheet over the plastic couch. It's impossible not to visualize the incalculable number of bare ass cheeks that have sweat all over the couch. This room serves only one purpose.

The TV is on a wood console and looks supremely out of place in the medical setting. I hunt through the drawers to see whether the lab techs left anything interesting. But it's just the same typical boring porn. At the bottom of the stack are several gay mags. I close the drawer. Five porno DVDs are already loaded into the player. It doesn't play. And the remote is busted. I wash my hands.

It's ridiculous to think that one ingredient in creating a human life begins in this weird den of iniquity. I sit on the sterile blue sheet.

This part is so peculiar. The walls are uncomfortably thin. Each small shift on the couch produces a low discordant plasticky burp. Not to mention I can hear nearly every word of Heidi's conversation with her co-worker on the other side of the wall. And I'm fairly certain, if they stopped talking, they'd hear me. The clinic is nice enough to provide earphones for one's porno-viewing pleasure, but there's no way in hell I'm touching them. Coated, most likely, in an invisible veneer of seminal fluid. For a moment I wonder whether there are men out there — and I'm certain they exist — who loudly traipse into this room, yank the headphones from the TV, and shamelessly whack away at full volume.

I'm an expert at the job. There's no need for mags or the TV, but after I finish and seal the lid on the plastic cup, I suddenly feel strange placing the cup in the little steel cubby. I know I shouldn't be embarrassed, but I am. What might my speedy expertise communicate to the pretty blue-eyed lab tech?

What if I have to do this again?

What if I have to see her again?

And what will she learn about my semen?

But then, who really gives a shit about my stupid feelings on the matter? We're trying for a child. Robin's already been through far more invasive procedures than jacking off in a Portland medical complex. From now on, I need to stop thinking about myself and start thinking about the future.

———————

AT HOME I toss my tennis shoes in the closet and slip on flip-flops. The summer sun pushes through the basement windows, and I sit at my desk, open a notebook, and consider my notes from two years ago. On the first page is that old, arbitrary list:

Sleep aboard a submarine.

Sail on his former yacht

Walk around Yucca Mountain.

The list now strikes me as eager but ridiculous. During that long-ago interview on *Talk of the Nation*, I told Neal Conan and his listeners that I wanted to sleep aboard a *Balao*-class submarine because my father served aboard a *Balao*-class submarine. But I never really had much interest at all in sleeping on a *Balao*-class submarine. What the hell, anyway, does "*Balao*-class" even mean?

Strewn across my desk are the things between us. My first letter to him.

His autobiography. His business card. His US Submarine Veterans membership card. His small Bible with the gold-edged pages. A plastic baggie of ashes.

I don't know what I'm supposed to divine from these items. I don't even know why I keep them.

Years have passed since I built a surfboard with Greg and Jed. In that time I've written a short story from my father's point of view, looked into the life of another writer, woven together three parts of a memoir, and forced myself to stare hard and unblinking at the man who came before me. Now I need an ending.

I hear Robin walking around the house above me. She owns a collection of colorful leather clogs, but they all sound the same against the hardwood floor. *Tock, tock, tock, tock.* She descends the stairs and appears in the doorway.

"Can you help me carry the bags to the car?" she asks.

"Sure, in a minute," I say.

"Why aren't you ready?" she says.

"I'm still deciding what to bring."

"You look like you're just sitting at your desk."

We're planning on spending seven days working and relaxing at her father's small beach house on the coast.

"We should get going," Robin says. "If we don't leave right now, we'll get stuck in traffic." She leans against the doorjamb, lingering, lingering. "Also, the stick has a smiley face on it. I just checked."

It's time, midcycle.

"Well, if the stick has a smiley face on it," I say. I close my notebook and stand.

"God, you're too goal oriented sometimes," she says.

"But we should do what the stick says, right? Right?"

"Probably."

Later, after sluggish stop-and-go traffic near Salem, steady rain pings against the windows. Oregon skies are sometimes schizophrenic. During the three-hour drive the sun disappears, and the sky becomes as grey as concrete. I approach the coastal highway's curving bends at thirty-five miles an hour. Mercy stares wide-eyed at the long empty beaches, balancing on the flip seat behind me. Her wide eyes are full of anticipation. In the rearview mirror I notice a loose strap on my surfboard bag snapping like a flag. With the Northwest summer soon drawing to an end, my thoughts wander to Southern California, to the sun, to the way misty white light settles behind the trees and the dry desert air, and the crinkling, crepe paper sound of swaying palm fronds.

"Okay. So what do you think about the name Jack?" Robin asks me.

"No, no, no," I say. "My friend Joe already named his son Jack."

"Well, it's close to my mom's name—Jacquelyn," she says. "I also like the name Lena. My great-grandmother's name."

"Lena's pretty. It's better than a name like Bruce."

"Bruce, ha."

"I know, right? Who names their little kid Bruce? That must have a psychological impact."

"Or what about the name Derek?" Robin says.

"Derek. You'd have to make sure your kid always wore a mullet."

"Yeah, but. Who are we to talk?" Robin says. "I mean, *Don* and *Robin*? Robin is just so seventies. I should be wearing a polyester blouse with a pointy collar. And Donald? I mean, come on."

"I'm sure it was a popular name in the forties."

"Try the twenties." Robin sighs. "Don and Robin."

"I know," I say. "We got hosed."

"Okay. What about Hannah?" Robin says. "I like Hannah."

"Or Lily," I say.

"No. My mom's cat was named Lily."

"Robin, maybe we should stop," I say.

It's quiet for a time. After a while I say, "I brought his ashes."

"What?" Robin says. "What are you talking about?"

"His ashes. My father's ashes."

"Nice non sequitur."

"Sorry."

"They're in the truck?"

"In my backpack," I say. "I'm thinking about leaving them at Agate Beach."

"Why?"

"I don't know. I've been hauling them around for years. I can't just keep schlepping them place to place and keeping them in a cardboard box. It doesn't seem right."

"So you're going to leave them at one of your surf places," Robin says.

"That's the idea."

After unpacking the truck and running Mercy at the beach, I settle in a chair overlooking the sunless coastline and open "The Story of My Life." Robin heads to the store, searching for fresh salmon cuts.

I turn to my favorite chapter. Seven pages in California. Manhattan Beach. Hermosa. Santa Barbara. Surf spots nicknamed Trestles, Rincon, Miramar, Hendry's Beach, and Overhead. Balsa-wood boards and ten-foot Styrofoam noseriders. His surfing years.

I read about Santa Barbara locals forming a surf club for the purpose of accessing the privately owned Hollister Ranch. At the time, in the early 1960s, word was spreading about the world-class breaks there. Surfers from Los Angeles were driving north, creating "destruction and mayhem," so the owner restricted access. Locals, however, came up with a plan. They formed a surf club and convinced the owner to allow admission to club members. Membership dues paid for a year-round guard. "I am among one of the earliest members," my father wrote.

His description of the Ranch summons visions of tan hills sloping into cool blue water, where incoming swells hit points at perfect angles only to bend into frothy tubes. If I'm honest with myself, one of the only things my father did in his life that I'd actually enjoy doing is surfing Hollister Ranch. But the place is nearly impossible to access.

Through my father's words I imagine what it was like at the Ranch during the '60s.

"Hot summer days surfing, lying around the beach with my friends, and girlfriend, sitting around the fire at night, where we roasted hot dogs, and snuggled with our girlfriends to keep warm at night." Though some of his details strike me as prudish—"snuggled with our girlfriends"—everything about the Ranch seems idyllic.

I study the Ranch using the satellite map on my phone. What I see—thousands of acres of uninhabited landscape—supports his claims. Santa Barbara has a unique coastline because it faces south. Highway 101 runs through town east-west, horizontally, along the Pacific, and then abruptly cuts north near Gaviota State Park. Continue west on a narrow road, and you'll find Hollister Ranch, nearly nine miles of pristine coastline. There's a scattering of large homes on the Ranch, but not many. Thirty-eight million people live in California, and virtually no one has access. A guard shack blocks entry.

I zoom in on Hollister until my phone connection disappears and the map freezes.

In 1972, the California Coastal Commission was created by a public vote over concerns about the state's coastline. Four years later came the Coastal Protection Act, which essentially handed the public the right to set foot on any beach below the mean high-tide line—in other words, anywhere the sand is wet. But that's still the major issue: getting to the wet sand.

At Hollister, there's still no way in. A well-funded homeowners' association has vigorously opposed past proposals to build trails and bridges into the Ranch. Hollister is exclusive, and residents want to retain privacy. So far, they've succeeded. The only way to access those hidden beaches and coves is to launch a boat from Gaviota pier and motor in. Or one could always trespass, but trespassing carries draconian fines. Isolated from the rest of the state, protected by lawyers, the Ranch is a surfer's Xanadu, but you just can't get there.

I'm cautious about believing everything my father wrote in his "Surfing" chapter, things such as: "I really excelled at surfing then, and was considered one of the best." I question statements like these, since he obviously overstated his "friendship" with Greg Noll, but after the magazine article appeared, his family members insist—yes, yes—my father was a good surfer, even a great surfer. He was one of the first to surf the Ranch. He and his friends hung out in beach shacks. They slept in the sand and built bonfires. Pioneers.

I get in touch with Matt Warshaw, a well-known surf historian. Warshaw's gargantuan book, The Encyclopedia of Surfing, claims a prime spot on my bookshelf at home. I reach Matt by phone at his home in Seattle. I'm interested in his thoughts about the Ranch. Is it really what people say? Is it like stepping back in time?

Matt says sure, sure, he's been twice, and the place is indeed "set in amber," he assures me. "You drive through the gate and enter a different world. It's everything you'd dream of it being. When it's just right, you can surf perfect shoulder-high waves in one of the most beautiful North American settings. The place is a ridiculous counterpoint to what's just below it, which is all of Southern California, where everything has been commercialized and commodified."

"What about access?" I ask. "How do you even get out there? Is it possible?"

"The rules are crazy," he says. "It's not a free and easy place to move around. You need to know someone."

Only landowners, it seems, have access. Nobody else.

"I have hugely mixed feelings about that," Matt tells me. "It's a crime they've been able to keep this whole area cut off. But part of me feels that when they open the gate it will all be ruined."

When I tell Matt my father surfed the Ranch back in the day, he sighs audibly, seemingly impressed, giving me a small, strange touch of pride.

"I can't think of a better time to be a surfer than that time in surfing history," he says.

Daily life at the coast house is spent in a near dream state. Mornings are grey, but skies improve in the afternoons. We wake up and eat breakfast at a long wood table with a clean view of the Pacific. Then we retire to separate bedrooms and work for a few hours. In the afternoons we walk Mercy on the beach. At night, fish and salad and wine, and reading. It's an ideal place to spend time together and work.

Each morning, I study the surf report on my phone. The quality of a wave depends on height, duration between swells, and the wind's direction and speed. Tides are important too. In Oregon, late summer and fall is prime surfing season because decent swells usually approach from the northwest. It's been a spectacular summer, sunny and temperate, and a sort of collective amnesia makes people forget where we live. I know these nice Pacific Northwest days are slowly creeping toward winter, and soon we'll be drenched by rain. I need to take advantage.

Several mornings later, the report looks good and I claim a surf day. I throw my board into the bed of my truck and toss my wetsuit in the cab. At the last minute, I grab the small baggie containing the ashes. Robin makes me promise her I won't go out if no one else is surfing. The forecast is small, I tell her, but it's impossible to know what conditions are like without seeing for myself.

Fog cloaks the ocean as I drive north to Newport. A hundred miles north, Short Sands gets crowded on nice days because it's near Portland, but Agate Beach in Newport is far from any urban center. A headland at the northern end of the beach shelters surfers from the wind. It's a pretty okay place to surf.

I park on the bluff overlooking Agate Beach. Thankfully, the fog has blown out to sea. From above, the surf doesn't look like much, nothing but choppy closeouts. It's disappointing. Along the bluff stand several homes. There's a secluded dirt trail that winds down through the trees and empties at a beach clearing, where locals have arranged driftwood benches around a scraggly fire pit. I follow the trail.

Two guys in their midtwenties, fully suited up, approach from the water carrying boards. Their long, strong arms and black wetsuits make them look like lean gorillas. I ask about the surf.

"Don't even bother," one of the guys says. "It's awful."

"It was better earlier," his friend says.

They move up the dirt path. I'm alone. There's no one else on the beach. That's another reason I love Oregon: an entire beach can be yours. I sit on a flat section on the makeshift driftwood bench. Even riddled with closeouts, the surf is beautiful. I still want to go out.

I remove the plastic baggie from my jacket pocket. Two years ago, I was unable to leave the ashes at Manhattan Beach, and now I'm unable to leave them here. Neither place feels right. But I know I don't want to keep them around forever, just stored in a cardboard box.

I've moved around this big, absurd country as often as he did. California remains important to the story—to our story. He was from there. It's where he fell in love with the ocean—Manhattan Beach, Santa Barbara. California is where I met Robin and where we fell in love. My therapist lives in California. Our dog, Mercy, is from a shelter in California's ranching country. California helped shape my love of the outdoors.

I start wondering about Hollister Ranch again. How preserved is it? I wonder whether I might feel something different there. I wonder if it's truly a place set apart, timeless and unchanged. Perhaps the sand has special properties. Perhaps I need to see for myself. Accessing the Ranch is difficult, but I hate being told no.

Over the past few years, I've pulled open a heavy door, stepped inside an old haunted house, and loitered in the dim hallways. I've gone door-to-door, airing out the rooms and scanning for shadows. One door remains unopened: one last door down a long hallway. I need to lay these last pieces to rest. Not according to what he wanted. Not according to church ritual or family obligation. According to me. According to what I want.

———

SOME PEOPLE find the idea of throwing on a skintight neoprene wetsuit, venturing into the ocean, and straddling a board that sinks below the waterline a terrifying idea. Others can't get enough, and surfing becomes a lifelong quest. For some the sport fuels competitiveness and localism and greed. And then there are the soul surfers who rarely talk about going in the water. For them surfing is a ritual, a quiet communion with the natural world. I know a number of people who head to the beach to make decisions and solve problems.

For me, surfing forces me to give over. And this giving over is total. The water washes obsessive, neurotic thoughts back to shore. This immersion puts me in the life of the body instead of the life of the mind. On the water, an unfamiliar but deeply familiar environment, it's possible to feel alone yet enveloped by a field of energy greater than myself. But even trying to describe the feeling of paddling through waves and joining one is futile. To understand it, you must experience it.

I'm not the first to recognize the ocean's transformative powers. A lot of people have experienced firsthand the wondrous, tactile vibrations that flood the body while standing waist-deep in stampeding ocean waves.

Recently, I've been dipping a toe into the scholarship of mind-body wellness in connection with the ocean. The research into the subject doesn't seem to be extensive, but it exists. It's a cool idea.

I find mention of one interesting study authored by a man named Ryan Pittsinger. His study is quoted in an article on a health and wellness website.

I lasso Ryan by email, and we set a date to talk.

"I grew up surfing in Manhattan Beach," he says, when I speak with him. "And I still consider it my home."

Ryan, a doctoral candidate in psychology, conducted his study several years ago, when he was working on his master's degree in California.

"I sat at the beach and polled over a hundred surfers," he tells me. "I administered a questionnaire before and after a session in the water. After people surfed, I found a marked improvement in mood levels."

A link between surfing and improved mood? I like it.

Sure, a surfer graduate student dreamed up the study, the conclusion seems obvious, and the sample seems skewed, but I think it lends a little credibility to a concept that surfing has undeniably curative benefits.

In his spare time, Ryan tells me, he volunteers with a nonprofit group—the Jimmy Walker Foundation—that sponsors surf sessions at Camp Pendleton for wounded marines suffering from posttraumatic stress. The foundation also conducts surf programs for underserved youth. They believe surfing and ocean therapy is a useful therapeutic tool.

It's a forward-thinking idea. Instead of dousing brains with chemical cocktails, you take a kid from a broken home or an Iraq veteran who's unable to sleep, and you show them how to paddle, how to ride, how to have fun again—and how to feel better.

Other healthcare professionals are embracing the same idea. When I discover more groups with similar goals, I begin wondering whether surf therapy can be considered a growing mental health subfield.

Halfway across the world, in Truro, near the Cornwall coast in England, Sarah Colpus and Laura Bond, both physicians, conducted a study comparable to Ryan's. They too found the same easy link between surfing and well-being. Like Ryan, Drs. Colpus and Bond surf. Also like Ryan, they volunteer with a regional nonprofit with similar aims. The Wave Project, whose motto is "Changing Lives through Surfing," was founded in 2010 with the goal of helping the emotional lives of troubled kids.

I get in touch with the project's coordinator to find out more.

The project began when local social service agencies sent them a pilot test group. The results spoke for themselves. Now, years later, the Wave Project has expanded across the UK. Besides helping build kids' self-esteem (it's hard to stand up on a surfboard), surfing can also help with anxiety, depression, and other mood disorders.

Projects such as the Jimmy Walker Foundation and the Wave Project keep popping up. The more I look, the more I find. In the Mexican state of Chiapas, Misión México puts neglected and orphaned kids on surfboards and shows them the ropes. Another program in South Africa, Waves for Change, shares the same therapeutic goals as the others.

All the anecdotal evidence suggests that surfing boosts mood levels. Sure, it's fun. Sure, spending a day at the beach makes you happy. There may even be a scientific explanation to explain the rad feeling you get riding a surfboard. Maybe it has to do with something we can't even see. Something called ions.

An ion is an atom or molecule that's gained or lost an extra electron, giving it a positive or negative electrical charge. Ions are abundant in nature and found in changing, dynamic environments. Wherever you find turbulent and disturbed water, there's also a profusion of negatively charged ions. One place heavy in negative ions is at the bottom of a waterfall. Another place: a breaking wave.

Psychiatrists and researchers have long studied the effects negative ions have on mood, cognitive performance, and sleep. Some researchers have charted positive biochemical changes when the body is exposed to negative ions. Other research suggests contact with negative ions even triggers the release of endorphins and serotonin.

There's a lot of random evidence to imply negative ions are beneficial, but then again, maybe the benefits are from being outdoors in the water.

Still, who could argue that paddling toward a wave, duck-diving below it, surfacing, and choosing a perfect, glassy wave doesn't affect the body's natural chemical state?

I know surf stoke is real. And it isn't quantifiable. And I don't know whether it should be quantifiable. Simply thinking about some study published in a dry scientific journal about surfing makes me cringe.

Surfing is so much more than draping oneself in salty spray and supposed negative ions. For many it's spiritual.

––––––––––

EVERY TUESDAY NIGHT, I receive an email from Drew Kampion. After the sun sets, every Tuesday, an email with the subject line "Walt Whitman ::: Tuesday Evening" appears in my inbox. Each message contains a snippet from Walt Whitman's body of work. Drew adds additional lines below Whitman's black-and-white photo:

> Life is a wave. Your attitude is your surfboard.
> Stay stoked & aim for the light!

Drew was the editor of *Surfer* magazine in the late 1960s. He's also published nine or ten books on surfing, and much of his writing, I've noticed, touches on the sport's spiritual aspects. Drew has decades more exposure to the ocean than me. Somehow, I ended up on his email blast list, and I've grown to appreciate his Tuesday evening Walt Whitman communiqués. By coincidence, Drew now lives on Whidbey Island. He knew my father. They were island neighbors.

On the Tuesday after Robin and I return from the coast, another

Whitman poem lands in my inbox, and I decide to call Drew. I have a few questions he might be able to answer. I've been thinking a lot about the Ranch and about the almost sacred feeling of being on a wave.

"I asked Matt about the Ranch," I say. Drew knows Matt Warshaw. It seems everyone who writes about surfing knows one another. "What do you know about that place?"

"Hollister?" Drew says. "Oh, I've only been a few times. Even back then, there was a guard shack. The cowboys who worked at the Ranch were armed. And they did not mess around. They shot at people."

"Seriously?"

"Yep," he says. "People would come back from the Ranch, and they'd have holes in their boards. Those guys didn't like trespassers."

That's not the kind of information I'm hoping for. I want to go to the Ranch. But the idea of getting shot doesn't comfort me.

I mention his weekly emails and ask, you know, why Walt Whitman?

"Because he was writing for the future," he says. Drew vibes about the confluence between Whitman and morphic fields, which I try to follow as best I can. A morphic field, Drew explains, is like that seamless zigzag movement of a school of fish. Whitman's art shares the same fluid spirit with that concept, he says. I like what Drew is saying, but after a while I steer the conversation back to the reason for my call.

"A lot of your writing deals with the transcendent and transformative nature of surfing," I say. "What is it about surfing that nurtures such other-worldly feelings?"

"First of all, it's a gravity sport," he says. "You're basically using your body and exploiting this natural force. What differentiates surfing from other sports is that your medium is in motion. There's something about that moving wave, man. It's all this force, and you're riding a wave that's in its death throes."

"In its death throes?"

"The wave is at the end of its life cycle. Waves come out of winds, frictional forces, which grow into ripples, then larger ripples, which form into swells, and they travel for thousands of miles. The Southern Hemisphere produces the waves at Malibu. That's six thousand miles. That's a long wave. You're riding all that energy."

All that energy. Is that why surfing can feel spiritual? It's like being in an open-air cathedral. Often I get butterflies before heading into the water, and then, when I'm out there, everything just drains away.

"Right," Drew says. "The real experience of surfing is, you know, getting up early, seeing that sunrise, smelling the chaparral floating off the hills, feeling the eastern wind gliding across your arms, sitting in the water, and the waves, backlit by light, breaking around you. The aesthetic side is wonderful. Surfing's got this majestic environment."

"Totally."

"Then you have the zen of it. Just waiting for the waves. You can be alone with the surf and your thoughts. A lot of the time surfing is spent in meditation. It's a space where you can have a meditative relationship with yourself and the waves."

"And that can be, in its way, a spiritual practice."

"Oh, sure," he says. "Say there's this thing called consciousness, an awareness of yourself in the moment. To become aware of higher things, your higher potential, you have to be aware of yourself. Being present in the moment is what happens while surfing. Classically, consciousness-raising had to do with being solitary and alone. But there are other approaches too. With surfing, you have three parts. It's fun. That's one. Connecting to the environment. That's the second. And then there's the meditative aspect, which makes it possible to work on presence. Surfers often move into an alpha state while on the water."

"An alpha state?"

"You know. That relaxed, open, and receptive state of mind," he says. He pauses. "I think that's what you're asking about."

He understands. He gets it. What Drew says about surfing's spiritual elements aligns with pretty much everything I feel on the water. Negatively charged ions may enter the bloodstream during the wave's crash, but there's also the conscious experience of waiting, of lingering, of watching, hearing, smelling, feeling.

Before hanging up, Drew surprises me. "You know, it was a pleasure knowing your dad."

"Oh yeah?" I say.

"I really enjoyed talking to him about the Ranch and surfing," he says. "You know, I liked him a lot."

WEEKS AFTER SPEAKING with Drew, I'm back at my desk in the basement, waiting to place another phone call and listening to early Waylon Jennings. "Slow Rollin' Low" is probably the greasiest, funkiest cowboy tune ever recorded.

As I wait for nine o'clock to roll around, I swivel in my chair, not entirely sure why I want to talk with a sociologist, but I'm curious and I have questions. I'm interested in the social science on fatherhood. A former professor suggested I contact University of Florida professor William Marsiglio, who researches fatherhood and the formation of male identity as influenced by fathers. So I emailed him, and we set a phone date. He asked me to call at 9:00 p.m., after he finished putting his six-year-old son to bed.

For years I've collected news items that touch on fatherlessness and the effects of fatherlessness. Stored inside folders in my desk are computer printouts, clipped magazine pieces, and newspaper articles.

One article declares that men with pasts like mine—that is, fatherless men—are more likely to have the impulse to destroy others. Fatherless women, however, are more likely to have the impulse to destroy themselves.

I squirrel away articles whenever I randomly happen across them, as though the complicated feelings I've had throughout my life will someday make sense as soon as I've compiled enough data.

I save news stories about behavior, health, and criminal tendencies. I save news stories about early childhood attachment theory and stories about genetics: Not only does a father pass his Y chromosome, whole, down to his son, a father also sets the example for being a man, both behaviorally and emotionally.

And the statistics—the statistics are alarming, sobering, and mind numbing. Fatherless boys have far higher rates of delinquency, addiction, aggression, and, later in life, psychological problems. The majority of prisoners in the country emerge from fatherless homes—80 percent, according to the Centers for Disease Control. A third of children presently live in homes without fathers. That's a lot of boys and girls. And if these confused hordes of fatherless boys survive the teenage gauntlet, they're still at a greater risk for violence and suicide. As these boys grow into adults, they have higher rates of divorce and substance abuse. The hits go on and on. The statistics make me want to shed my skin. My personal story happens to be a shared societal catastrophe. We are legion.

Whenever I read another shocking statistic, I think, *Shit, that could have been me . . .* Over there is a burning house, but I escaped, and over there is another burning house, but I escaped that one too . . .

Millions and millions of kids have little or no contact with their fathers.

Another study I found suggested, "Paternal deprivation during development affects the neurobiology of the offspring."

Jesus. Affects neurobiology? What does that even mean?

But statistics and studies cited in newspapers aren't conclusive. Nothing's ever really conclusive. Homes are dynamic environments. Each is different. If there isn't a father at home, there might be a father figure living next door. Or there might be an uncle who provides the fatherly role.

Every person, besides, has unique genetic qualities and different nurturing environments. You can take two fatherless boys, both from working-class homes, raised by single mothers, and from this background information you might reasonably predict similar life outcomes, or at least that's what statistics suggest. But life is full of chaos and surprise. Charles Manson, Saddam Hussein, and Ted Bundy never knew their fathers, but neither did Jack Nicholson, Eric Clapton, or Edgar Allan Poe. Gene Simmons's father abandoned him when he was three, and he ended up forming KISS, one of the greatest and cheesiest rock bands of all time. Even the coolest of the cool, Arthur Fonzarelli, Fonzie, the Fonz, didn't know his father.

Of course, there's also the complicated idea of fatherlessness in regard to adoption and donor sperm. Kids raised in these situations might not actually *know* their fathers, but I think it's pretty clear that adoptive parents—say, a lesbian couple—can offer a powerful buffer to alleviate this absence. In this case the absence has little to do with rejection and everything to do with love.

Anyway, I'm not even sure what the term "fatherless" means in the articles I save and keep.

Does it mean the father lives a half block away?

Does it mean there's no contact with any father at all?

Does it mean the father died?

Or does it mean the father simply vanished, like mine did?

At nine o'clock I pick up the phone. William Marsiglio has a calming phone voice, and right away he asks me to call him Bill. I find Bill to be thoughtful and measured in his responses. He pauses to consider each question before answering. In my email to him I sent a general outline of my personal history and the reasons I wanted to talk. I thank him for humoring me.

"So, I'm assuming your research on fathers affects your role as a father," I say.

"In a very general sense, yes," Marsiglio says. "A lot of my experiences with my son certainly influence my research. I'm thinking about him all the time. I'm highly attentive and sensitive to his needs. I'm invested in helping him."

"Tell me about your research. It seems to be about the importance of fathers and stepfathers. In terms of the formation of male identity."

"In my work I interview adult men and ask about their childhoods and their father's involvement in their lives," he says. "From this information I write a light history analysis. For instance, I'll study how a father's work pursuits motivate the way a person now views his work. Or I'll study how a father's care influenced them. In my latest project I ask men about how their father's health and lifestyle choices — exercise, eating, that kind of thing — impacted them."

"But you must come across men who didn't have fathers around."

"Of course," he says.

"And what do they say about how that experience affected them?" I ask.

"It depends," he says. "Men have told me — those who never had fathers, in circumstances like yours — that they don't want their children to go through what they went through. These men want to compensate. They want to treat their children how they would have wanted to be treated."

"That makes sense," I say.

"Sure."

With the phone pressed against my ear, I flip through my notebook, where I've written a series of questions.

What are the psychological and emotional consequences of not having a father around?

What are the larger trends?

What are the statistics?

Isn't it true a young boy in this situation will struggle?

And doesn't that struggle later manifest as confusion and anger?

Isn't it true a young boy like this will grow into a man with all-consuming questions about fathers and sons?

Bill, silent on the other end, waits for my next question. I've called because he's an authority. But I've also called because I'm fishing for some kind of solid confirmation: That not having a father around is fucking shitty. That not having a father naturally produced in me blind anger and occasional depression that I've had to deal with and ward off.

I attempt to float a question along these lines but stop myself. Bill's smart, and he picks up on the real reason for my phone call. He knows he shouldn't state something as Bible truth. In his line of work, he collects data and presents it. He doesn't have a clear-cut, scientific response for what I'm after. Bill reminds me that during the course of my life, I've been exposed to a particular cultural discourse, which has an influence on me.

"You're thinking about the idea of fatherhood during a specific time and in a certain cultural context," he says calmly. "Your interpretation of your own story has been influenced by a larger framework about how we think about fathers now. These days there's a much larger discourse in our culture about fathering. Over the past two decades, there's been a change in thinking about fathers as having a more nurturing role. There are higher expectations now. Part of this cultural discourse also has to do with words, like the term 'deadbeat dad,' which affects your personal story."

"Deadbeat dad. That term influences my story? Or how I think about my story?"

"Yes," he says. "Of course."

He's right. In my mind I turn time back and think about the '70s, the early '80s, how social attitudes were wildly different back then. I could hang with Mom in bars and no one said a word. People smoked inside airplanes. My friends and I roamed the streets like a pack of wild animals. Robin once remarked that all kids raised in the '80s either had a BB scar or a BB embedded under the skin. Back then, a different vibe existed about raising children, which is nearly incomprehensible in the current, post-Oprah era of maximum parenting. Theories about parenting and attachment were just entering the cultural discussion in those days. Fathers weren't really expected to do much.

"Okay," I say. "But you know, you have to admit, having a father around still has a monumental effect on a son."

"Having a stepfather can also have a major impact," Bill says. "Or a male mentor. Having a male mentor around can be just as meaningful as having a father."

"But there's something powerful about a man's presence in the home, right?"

"Well, on average, men interact differently than women do with children," he says. "Fathers are more likely to roughhouse or challenge their children in certain ways. How a man talks can also affect how children use language." Bill pauses for a moment, and he asks, "Do you have children?"

"No," I say.

A long pause.

"Have you ever volunteered with kids?" he asks. "Or, say, mentored with a place like the Boys and Girls Club?"

Suddenly, I feel as though Bill is attempting to patch me up—in other words, attempting to father me from a distance.

"No," I say, "I've never volunteered. Or mentored."

"Have you ever thought about it?"

"Yes, in fact, I have," I say. "I talk about it all the time with my girlfriend. But with our lifestyle we're always moving. I've been afraid to get matched with a kid and then leave six months later. I don't want to let some kid down."

"A fear of abandoning the kid," Bill says.

"Exactly."

We share another moment of silence.

I admit to Bill I'm hoping to learn about some larger trend. I say, well, I suppose I'm looking for some sort of scientific confirmation to support the way I've always felt about not having a father.

"Hmm," he says. "Let me think."

Eventually, he tells me about a paper he coauthored. The paper summarized multiple father studies during the 1990s. One study, he says, examined different fathering styles. "The study found a correlation between authoritative parenting and positive outcomes. In other words, fathers who engaged in their children's lives with what's called authoritative parenting—providing emotional support, setting limits, monitoring— had positive outcomes. Children from this type of environment had fewer internalizing problems."

"Fewer internalizing problems?"

"Less depression, less anxiety, less poor self-esteem," he says.

Immediately, I make the assumption that the opposite is also true: children without an authoritative father have *more* internalizing problems.

More depression, *more* anxiety, *more* poor self-esteem. There. One scientific paper. That's all I want. For my own satisfaction.

"Okay, one last question," I say.

"Sure."

"What's the single most important thing a father can give to a son?" I ask.

"His love," Bill says, without missing a beat. "His nurturing love. His commitment to loving and nurturing his son."

After hanging up, I lean back in my chair, thinking over our conversation.

These days, whenever I get the slightest whiff that another man in my social circle shares a similar life experience—a shared *fatherlessness*—I circle around like a shark until I gather the courage to ask. Not surprisingly, most guys remove themselves from the conversation or change the subject. Many men just don't like discussing not having a dad. It's understandable. After all, what man wants to talk about displaced pain and sadness and rage? Or issues with masculinity and identity? Abandonment is a rarely discussed subject for those who have been abandoned.

Yet even with a father around, the father-son relationship can be tricky. Other issues arise. I've seen plenty of friends struggle with their dads.

One domineering father frequently belittled his son in front of me in an attempt, I guess, to display dominance. Another withdrew night after night to tinker with his beloved Corvette in the garage, completely tuned out. And I watched another, a grizzled Vietnam vet, put up his fists and square off against his own son. They slowly circled each other, preparing to fuck each other up, before I quickly got the hell out of that home.

In a fit of curiosity, I email several friends and ask about their dads.

"My dad?" my friend, Sam, responds. "Oh, he's weird."

I write back: "How so?"

Sam: "Well, every time I visit him, he gives me a pair of shoes."

I ask another friend, Dennis, about his father. I want to pin Dennis down to specifics. Dennis is a writer of catastrophically beautiful novels, and I've always admired his honesty and courage. So I write and ask him, "What word would you use to describe your father?"

Dennis: "Wow, it's weird. The father thing must be a very good topic because as soon as I think about mine, I get anxious. Okay. The one word I would use to describe my father: narcissistic."

Then Dennis sends back a short list of questions for me:

"If a movie was made of your life, and you were consulted on casting, who would you choose to play your father?"

I consider Robert Blake. Instead, I choose Gary Oldman.

Dennis: "Your mother and father are fighting. Whom do you secretly root for?"

The answer is obvious.

But sometimes—I want to believe *often*—a loving and present father can have a remarkable impact.

Sure, I've saved plenty of articles that claim strong links between violence and broken homes, and it's never a surprise to learn that a school or workplace shooter emerged from a fatherless household, but what about homes where a devoted father picks up his son from school, where a father teaches empathy and models decency? We should throw ticker tape parades for these wondrous men!

Whenever I think about the idea of an "ideal father," the face of one man frequently comes to mind. My college friend Andy's dad, John.

John is downright charming. He's a physician with a quick wit and sharp sense of humor. He cares about people. My memories of him—tall, with frameless professorial glasses, trim white beard—often play in the back of my mind whenever I talk to Andy. Andy's mom is great too: she reminds me of the exuberance of Christmas lights. Anyway, when I was in college, Andy's parents welcomed me into their Rockville, Maryland, home during several spring breaks. I didn't have anywhere to go, and I certainly wasn't a Florida spring break kind of guy. I was an angry, grumpy punk rocker kind of guy.

John was diagnosed with multiple sclerosis when Andy was a kid. When I visited, John was using a cane to move around. The last time I saw him, in New York for Andy's wedding, John's degeneration shocked and saddened me. He was now using an electric wheelchair. Despite his disease, he was full of smiles, and he joked around.

John fathered three sons. John Jr., Nick, and my friend Andy. The man clearly had a profound influence on his sons because all three have become remarkable men. He was a loving, supportive father. And he was so warm-hearted and so kind that Andy's older brother, Nick, decided to fight the disease crippling their dad. Nick set out to raise awareness and money in a bid to find a cure for multiple sclerosis.

First, Nick swam the length of the Mississippi River, from Minneapolis to Baton Rouge. He completed the feat in a little over three months. Minneapolis to Baton Rouge! Swimming! Andy trailed Nick down the wide river in a motorized rubber dinghy. A flotilla of larger boats welcomed the brothers aboard during their long journey. I remember watching television segments about Nick's voyage on *Good Morning America*—watching Nick, in a wetsuit, swimming, his arms emerging from the water, and Andy behind him, in a dinghy.

After Nick reached Baton Rouge, he decided he wasn't finished. For his next triumph he cycled around the perimeter of the United States, and that's close to ten thousand miles.

Nick managed to raise nearly half a million dollars, a large portion of which he donated to Dr. Steven Waxman at Yale University's Center for Neuroscience and Regeneration Research. Dr. Waxman later developed a new MS medication that aids with mobility, a drug that's helped Andy and Nick's dad live a more comfortable life. In my early twenties, even in my late twenties, I harbored uncomfortably vague thoughts about harming my father, possibly destroying him. Nick and Andy have done everything in their power to save theirs.

———

THE RADIOLOGY FACILITY is in northeast Portland. I drive while Robin worries.

"I hope this shit doesn't hurt," she says.

"Me too. Medical procedures make me nervous, even if it's not mine."

"But you visit doctors for imaginary nonsense," she says. "This is real."

"I know," I say.

Robin has undergone so many tests I've lost count. Blood draws. Testing for suspected pituitary gland issues, which can impact fertility. Hormone-level checks. Everything, it seems, can influence fertility.

Robin gives her name at the front desk. Our radiologist is a woman who wears puffy blue medical scrubs. She walks us to a room and politely asks Robin to disrobe. Then she hands Robin a sheet and leaves.

Robin wraps the sheet around her midsection and throws me her pants.

When the radiologist returns, Robin is on the table, feet in the stirrups. I find it crazy that medical professionals can't come up with a better name than stirrups.

"All ready?" the radiologist asks. The woman dims the lights. I sit in a plastic chair, holding Robin's clothes and purse. The radiologist prepares the dye. Robin closes her eyes, balls her fists, and takes long, humongous breaths. Everything happens on a screen. The procedure tests for problems or blockages in the fallopian tubes. The dye slowly spreads on the screen as it spreads through Robin's uterus. The radiologist squints, searching. It's amazing to watch. I feel myself getting emotional, but I dislike seeing Robin so uncomfortable.

"Well, everything looks great," the radiologist finally announces.

Outside, after the procedure, we quietly walk back to the car. Then Robin says, "I hate going through this."

"I know, I know."

"No. You don't *know*."

"You're a champ," I say. "Just watching that, I don't know, it was like looking inside you, and it was incredible."

"Oh, please. Are you getting teary?" she asks. "Oh, stop being such a sap."

Lately, seeing a used pregnancy wand in our bathroom has become common. It's our time. We think it's our time. We're ready. We say we're ready. Discussions around the house are about fertility, infertility, adoption, fostering, our diets, exercise, pills we're supposed to take, pills we're to avoid, and the upcoming appointment with a fertility doctor.

The appointment costs $450 for one hour of the doctor's precious time. And during that hour, our doctor, a pale horsey woman with the frenetic energy of a meth addict, talks so quickly about the process of conception and our options—artificial insemination, in vitro fertilization—that it's nearly impossible to keep up. After forty minutes my eyes glaze over, and I look over at Robin, praying she's listening. After the consultation, Robin says on the way to the car, "I don't think I like her. She's impossible to follow. She's all over the place."

"I agree," I say.

Even though Robin takes the tests and her results look great, we're unable to conceive. Sure, we're in our late thirties, but many friends our age have had success. It's possible.

Several days later, I meet my friend Pauls for an early lunch. He brings along his toddler son, Phin. Phin has a twin, but I don't ask about Beatrix because Phin is already a handful. Having an adult conversation with friends who have toddlers is an exercise in maximum patience. To keep Phin from bouncing around the restaurant, Pauls gives Phin his cell phone. Phin accidentally calls someone. Pauls grabs the phone and hangs up. Then Pauls buys Phin a giant cookie, and we watch the cookie explode. Like any normal toddler boy, Phin dismantles the cookie. Phin mangles the cookie. Phin beats the shit out of the cookie. Crumbs fall on the floor. The crumbs that don't fall get kicked in the direction of other diners.

Pauls says to me with a sly smile, "And you want children."

———

FALL ARRIVES, and I fly to Reno for a bookstore reading.

It's a bumpy landing, as usual. After the plane docks at the Jetway, I follow the slow ant line of travelers into a terminal lined with slot machines. Plastered on one wall is huge image of Lake Tahoe encircled by mountains, and for a brief moment I think about moving back to Reno to be closer to those mountains. The High Sierra, the alpine lakes, the dusty trails padded with fragrant pine needles. It's my favorite terrain.

The escalator deposits me on the first floor. Mom is waiting for me near baggage claim, dressed in black, and she's standing beside two limo drivers dressed in tuxedoes. Like them, she's holding a sign, a white foam poster board. Her sign says in large block print, DON WATERS, FAMOUS AUTHOR. Immediately, I want to swerve left and continue out the pneumatic doors. Instead, I walk over, shaking my head.

"Mom," I say.

"You're embarrassed," she says. She smiles. "Look at you. All red."

"I'm the furthest thing in the universe from a famous author."

"We're proud of you," she says. "You wrote another book."

"Jesus Christ."

"Hey, language, kiddo."

Kiddo. After all these years Mom still calls me kiddo, and she can still embarrass the shit out of me. She holds her sign higher, so other travelers see it as they pass. Her sign isn't handwritten. A professional shop made it. And well, *shit*, I am touched.

As we wait outside for Chuck to swing around with the car, Mom informs me she's also made announcement flyers for the reading. Fliers have been passed around at church and posted in public places. She's excited. *It's just a novel*, I want to say. A university press published the book. Sure, it's handsome and has a beautiful cover, but the marketing budget is nonexistent. Still, Mom knows how hard I've worked. This novel — my first published but my sixth written — took years.

"Will you please, *please* put the sign away?" I say. "People are still looking over here."

"Why? I like it," she says. "Who cares what people think? Don't act embarrassed."

Dressed in black, eyes hidden behind black sunglasses, Mom actually looks hip and happy, and it occurs to me that she's never — not once — discouraged my interests or my writing, a dubious career path that's sent me drifting across the country, always seeking out new opportunities. It was the same when I was younger. Anything I wanted to do, she encouraged it, always finding ways to scrape money together. New wheels for my skate deck. Tents, backpacks, pricey high-altitude stoves. Soccer camp. And shit, that year I wanted to be the next Greg LeMond, who was from the Reno area, and we pooled her money and mine from my lawn-mowing gigs to purchase a snazzy Trek bicycle.

Chuck pulls to the curb. I toss my bag into the backseat and shake his big, callused hand.

Mom turns. "Oh, Donny. I forgot to tell you. Do you remember Louis from New York?"

"Louis from New York?" I say. "No."

"Louis. You know, *Louis*," she says. "The lawyer from White Plains. We went to visit him that one time when you were a kid. *Louis*."

"I don't remember," I say.

"Oh, you remember."

"No, I really don't."

"Well, anyway, he's now in prison," she says.

"What?"

"Look his name up on the computer. There's a whole article about him. I was shocked. Bank fraud, it says. *Bank* fraud. We went to see him that time. In New York. You remember. He was a mob lawyer. We dated, but only for a little while."

No, I say. I really don't remember any mob lawyer named Louis from New York.

"*Louis*," she says. In the mirror I can make out her eyes behind her glasses, sweeping around the dry, dusty streets. "All the stories I have from my life," she says, and clucks her tongue. "You should write a book."

"Maybe I am," I say.

"Be kind to your mother," she says. "You only get one mother."

Mom, indeed, would make a fascinating character. For a moment I think about how to expertly portray her exuberant eccentricities, how to make her compelling and relatable. Then I remember Napoleon, her old toy poodle. Mom let Napoleon climb her shoulder and perch around her neck. She went out in public like that, prancing into the grocery store, into the video store, wearing Napoleon like a prized stole.

The bookstore reading is well attended, thanks to Mom. There aren't enough chairs, and people stand in the back of the room. Even my fifth-grade elementary school teacher is in attendance — thanks to Mom. I sign a healthy number of books to family and friends, including Sam, the retired homicide detective who once sat me down for the sex talk.

Later that night, back at the house, Chuck heads to bed early. I stay up with Mom, watching *CSI: Crime Scene Investigation*. Even though Chuck closes the bedroom door, I can hear him watching Fox News. I don't understand it. That kind of nightly ritual would give me nightmares.

One reason I enjoy returning home is the television. I hate to admit this to myself, but it's true. They have every imaginable channel, including premium stations. In Portland, we don't have many channels. Mom flips through a home decor magazine and pretends to watch the crime show she insists on watching. She's in a good, generous mood. It's time.

"Those details you mentioned, years ago, that stuff really happened?" I say. I'm unsure how to cross the divide.

"What are you talking about?" she says.

"About my father."

She inhales, clearly unprepared. "Oh, Donny. Why tonight?" I don't respond. I wait. Finally, she says, "Things happened the way I said they did."

"How did you meet?"

"A friend introduced us."

"I'm still processing what you said, though," I say. What she's told me has come out piecemeal, bit by bit. "It's hard to believe. Too many details are missing."

"I can understand," she says.

"I mean, what you said. Some of it still doesn't make sense."

"What doesn't make sense?"

"Well, pretty much everything," I say.

Over the years she's given me the formless outline of a story that's been interrupted by her sobbing or my sobbing or both our sobbing. Did she give me some of the information during a yelling match? Or did she give me some of the information as we sat and talked at a picnic table in the Sierras? Details lay scattered because they were extracted under duress, and the few solid details that flew from her mouth landed in a hole in my heart, which I quickly covered over with denial. I never wanted to believe or hear the worst of the details because of what they might say about me — about my origins — and about what was possible.

"He actually dragged you by the hair?" I say.

She stiffens. It's one of the more horrendous particulars. Mom nods. Quietly, she explains everything as she remembers it. She moves quickly — a stony, matter-of-fact summary. Finally, finally, she's finally giving me what I've been denied, and I can see in her eyes how incredibly hard it is for her and I love her for it. For the first time, her story, my father's, and mine meet. She gives me our family's story.

After graduating from college in his thirties, my father's new occupation as a mining engineer sent him to far-flung desert locations. Eventually, he accepted a job at a mine in Kingman, Arizona. Mom didn't want to live in Kingman. She didn't want that kind of lonely life. She wanted to stay in Reno. The marriage wasn't working anyway. She wanted out. Her father urged her to attempt reconciliation because there was a child involved. So she visited my father in Kingman one last time. A fight happened.

"He beat me," she says.

"Christ."

"Language," she says.

"But he beat you?"

"He did a pretty good job too," she says, allowing a nervous laugh to cushion the air between us. "He managed to rip hair out of my head."

"Oh, my God, Mom. I'm sorry."

"Why are you sorry? You didn't do it. He did. He managed to send me to the hospital."

"Jesus."

"Language," she says.

Her father, my grandfather, nearly lost his mind, she says. He wanted to fly from New York and leave knuckle marks in my father's face. Soon after, her father and his father spoke, and the divide between the families widened. Then divorce proceedings. Then my father didn't show in court. He harmed the mother of his child. He must have been angry and full of guilt. He must have been disgusted with himself.

Communication between our two families was severed, until, Mom says, she wrote his parents before my eighteenth birthday and provided our address, which is why he surfaced. He surfaced because of Mom. The details almost make me dizzy.

"And where was I?" I ask.

"Where were you?"

"During the big fight," I say.

"You were a baby. You were with me. You were right there."

The terror she must have felt—the terror and disgust at this man. I feel awful for bringing her back to that time and place. I feel awful I couldn't protect her. Then another kind of horror enters my mind—the horror of the witness. How did witnessing that fight unconsciously imprint on my brain? "Why didn't you ever tell me anything?" I say.

"I didn't want to tell you, Donny, because I didn't want you to carry that around with you. That your own father did that." In her silence, in her own way, she was trying to protect me.

"All you ever really told me was he didn't know how to be a father."

"Well, he didn't, did he?"

"No."

"He could have paid support, and he could have seen you. He didn't."

"I just—I had so little information, which made me wildly angry and confused."

"I'm not perfect, kiddo," she says. I hear exhaustion in her voice.

"I'm not looking for perfect," I say.

"Well, what are you looking for?"

"The truth."

"Well, that's the truth."

The fragments I've gathered over the years now slide into a whole, like a game of Tetris. Everything makes sense: the lack of contact, the excising of his face from photographs. At least I can understand the emotions behind that. A small part of me knows Mom could be feeding me misinformation. There's no one around to refute her story. But why, really, why would she do that? Another thing: I'm a firsthand witness to Mom's choices in men, and the men drawn to her. My father fit the bill. Mom's story makes me realize that the story I've told myself throughout my life could be wrong. Perhaps not having a father around was the best thing for everyone.

"I just don't know why you want to go over these things," Mom says. "I just don't. We turned out okay, didn't we? Look at you. You're an author. We're okay. Life goes on."

"Mom," I say. "Grandma was abandoned by her father."

"Yeah, I know. I'm the one who told you that."

"Later, she was surrounded by people who loved her."

"Yeah, I know that too."

"I need you to understand, even when you're surrounded by people who love you, a cavity forms when a parent leaves. And it never, ever goes away. Grandma was terrified of being left alone. I saw it, even as a kid."

"But I'm right here," Mom says. "I've always been right here. Can't you see that?"

Later, during the short flight back to Portland, I'll realize Mom gave me more than I've ever acknowledged. She provided access to the tools necessary to lift myself from the streets of Reno. Raised by a single mother in early periods of poverty and later periods of abundance, and surrounded by a series of violent men, alcoholic and broken men, she found a way to provide the means to leave, to free myself, to interrupt the pattern of trauma by absorbing it and having the time and funds to dissect it and shed it. Though my hometown will always exist in me, Reno and its crappy casinos and bums and stories about murder and actual murder and even old, old friends — none of that's mine anymore. I've let go. A bit of pride accompanies the thought. I know Mom failed to discuss some important details, details that mattered, details that could have helped me make better sense of my story, but it's hard to fault her faults, because she's Mom and she was there, and that was everything.

Mom sets her magazine on the coffee table and stands. "I can't talk about this anymore. I'm going to bed. Look, I've told you everything now." She moves toward the hall and stops. She doesn't look at me. "Want to attend Mass with me in the morning?" she asks.

"Okay," I say.

She turns. "Really? You'll go to church with me?"

"Yes, really," I say.

―――――――

OF COURSE, ALL THIS TIME, I've been in contact with my therapist, who I want to stop talking with, but I find her so goddamned helpful and insightful that I don't. She's my confidante, my oracle. She likes to say things like, "You're trying to become the father to that boy inside you that never had one." Sometimes I'm bothered by the idea she may know me better than I know myself.

"So I'm finally, *finally* heading to California this weekend," I tell her. We're on the phone.

"Are you?"

"After all this time, I find out my friend Erika's dad can smuggle me into the Ranch."

"Lucky," she says.

"I don't know why I didn't think of it before," I say. "Erika was raised in Santa Barbara. I should have listened better when she said her dad was a surfer."

"Perhaps."

"So that means, you know, I'm nearly finished with this thing. You know, the memoir?"

"You mention it all the time," she says.

"It's a strange beast of a thing."

"You've mentioned that too. You write about another man with your name."

"At first he was just this fascinating distraction. But the more I learned, the more I wanted to know. I decided to include him because his family provides a nice counterbalance. It's a great example that, no matter how someone's life looks from the outside, no one's life is ever perfect."

"Of course."

"But the book still worries me. I fear I make it seem as though I never stop thinking about not having a father, as though that singular thought never leaves my mind, which isn't true. I have a pretty good life. I never mention laughing with friends over beers. I don't mention getting up on Saturday mornings to watch Premier League football matches or my love for the Liverpool club. I don't talk about how much I love taking Mercy on long walks. Or hiking with Robin."

"From what you've told me, you've stopped and started the book many times," she says.

"I didn't know how to write it."

"You wrote it by using every method available to you."

"That's just how it happened. A series of happy mistakes. I used every tool in the toolbox."

She's in her office in California. I'm at home. We talk every Thursday at 9:20 a.m. She's been my therapist for more than a decade.

"But now that I'm nearly finished," I say. "I keep thinking, you know, who *cares*? I'm almost forty years old. Over the past few years, I've forced myself to keep thinking and talking about him, and with you I keep talking about early childhood trust and attachment and about that dickhead stalker stepfather, and you know, I just keep thinking, well, isn't there a point when these things stop mattering? Isn't there a point when I should just shut the fuck up about it? Doesn't the time come when you're just who you are, and you shouldn't dwell? I mean, who gives a shit?"

"I think that's the dumbest thing you've ever said," she says.

"Why?"

"Because it *is* who you are."

"Yeah, so?"

"Listen," she says. "Other people may not admit it, but don't you think everyone thinks about these same things all the time? Your relationship with your family. Your relationship with your parents. How you were cared for, how you were formed, and how that shaped you."

"But I've written this shit down in a book."

"That's exactly it. Along with talking to me, that's one of the ways you relate to it."

"I guess," I say.

"I want to tell you something," she says. "You're not alone in these feelings, Don."

I don't respond.

"You told me before," she says. "Why did you want to write a memoir?"

"I guess I wanted to create a story I could understand and live next to."

"A story about what?"

"Origins."

"There was something else."

"I wrote it for a lot of reasons. I guess I also wrote it for other men who never talk about not having a father. There are a lot of us. Because I'm not alone."

"Yes."

"And I wrote it for men who are fathers now. For them."

"Right."

"And for the fathers I've known," I say. "For the men who fathered me."

"Yes," she says. "They were important too."

Other men fathered me. They may not know it, but these men modeled decency, kindness, strength, and intelligence. These men, who sometimes acted too tough. These men, who allowed me to watch as they showed their sons how to hammer a nail and fix a bicycle chain. These men, who were there, who never left, and most of them never knew I was silently trailing in their shadows like a bloodthirsty vampire. And even now, I continue to do the same thing.

Lonnie coached me.

Michael took me skiing with his sons.

Sam gave me the sex pep talk.

Len built the fire.

Glen brought me camping with his son.

Mike fathered a large family and included me.

John lectured about injustice.

Ethan taught me writing.

Ben encouraged my writing.

John, David, Bill, Joseph, Blair, Ralph, Søren, Greg, Sam, Richard, Dennis, Terry, David . . .

There are too many to name.

———

THE AIRPLANE BANKS and turns out to sea, offering a glimpse of the Channel Islands through the Southern California haze. The plane levels out. Before landing, I'm gifted with a spectacular view of Hollister Ranch from my window seat. It looks desolate and gorgeous down there. Where Highway 101 snakes north, I trace a narrow road and follow it west to the Ranch, where foothills abruptly rise into camo-green mountains. A flutter enters my stomach as I make out the white lines of breaking waves peeling off along natural points.

We land and deplane by stairway onto the tarmac. I grab my bag and proceed to the terminal. The sun is out, palm trees bend in the breeze, and I suddenly miss California. A gust of eucalyptus washes over me. The charming airport, a smallish Spanish Colonial Revival building, suits the Mediterranean climate. My momentary daydream develops into grand designs about how to live here *and* in Portland. I could be one of those people who claim dual residences. Anything's possible. I kick the idea around. I'll return to school again. I'll study finance. I'll become a banker. I'll rob a bank.

But all is not well in the land of wheatgrass and expensive coconut water. Outside, I notice the first sign of Southern California's extreme drought. A flyer attached to a dry outdoor fountain actually apologizes to visitors. And I can feel it too on my lips: it's dry. And hot. The pepper trees look as though they might burst into flames if I stare at them for too long.

This weekend, I'm staying with my friend Erika—or rather Erika's parents, who live on the hill in Montecito, an unincorporated section of Santa Barbara County. Erika's driving up for the weekend from Los Angeles, and we're meeting at the house. Erika befriended Robin before she moved to LA, and by proxy she befriended me. For some reason it took me years to connect Erika's nonchalant statement, "Oh yeah, my dad surfs," to the fact her dad *surfs at the Ranch*. I've been trying to gain access to the Ranch for a long time. So this is a miracle. Yet again another friend's father will help.

A taxi drops me at a large gate. The gate opens. Erika's mixed husky mutt Rosie gallops up, and behind Rosie walks Erika, waving, dressed in shorts and a loose V-neck T-shirt. She's an incredibly pretty woman, tall, with short hair and interesting bangs that meet her eyes at an angle. Erika recently stayed with us in Portland for a week, and over the years I've developed a kind of big-brother affection for her. She's younger by almost a decade and in the nascent stages of her writing career.

"You do know this is ridiculously beautiful," I say. "You grew up in fairy-tale land, Erika."

"I know, I know," she says in a playfully annoyed voice. It's always interesting to learn where friends come from, and Erika comes from new California money, which seems to irritate her.

Her parents' gated compound brings to mind Greg and Laura's place in Crescent City. It's a family citadel. Along the perimeter, where the yard isn't manicured, pepper trees shield the property. There's a main house, office, pool, outdoor barbecue kitchen, outbuildings, and a fully equipped guesthouse with floor-to-ceiling windows and a jaw-dropping view of the

Santa Ynez Mountains. The windows also overlook a private putting green desiccated by the drought.

"Holy shit. I didn't know I was going to be staying at the Four Seasons," I say, as Erika shows me around. "I mean, my God."

Erika shrugs. She tells me this isn't where she grew up, so she doesn't have much connection with this house. But sure, she admits, it's nice.

"We're all going to the Ranch tomorrow," she tells me. "Together."

"Can't wait. Seriously."

"Mom too. We haven't done this as a family in years. When I was growing up, my dad used to take us out there all the time, every Sunday. He called it going to church."

"I like that."

"Come on," she says. "I want you to meet him. Then we'll go rent you a board."

For a man of sixty-five, Marc has dream hair. We meet in his office adjoining the pool, and for a moment I'm fixated on his hair. Dirty strawberry-blond, thick, a sort of schoolboy mop with bangs brushed to the side. He has surfer hair, radical hair, perfect SoCal hair. Not to mention tan, sun-scrubbed skin. At the end of his life, my father was bald, his father was bald, and in a momentary, self-obsessed fit I try to remember whether you inherit the hair gene from your father's or your mother's side. I want Marc's hair.

"So your dad surfed the Ranch way back when, huh?" Marc says.

"That's right."

"What years?" Marc asks.

"Early sixties, middle sixties, something like that. He surfed Manhattan Beach in the fifties."

"Wow," Marc says. He shakes his head. "That was before any of it. That's incredible. That was the beginning."

I've come to appreciate the power of stories among surfers. Along with being obsessed with photographs of perfect waves, surfers love the mythology of the sport's origins. That's why a Greg Noll surfboard made from Ecuadorian balsa wood sells for $6,000. Mythology.

I pull out my phone and show Marc photos of my father's Santa Barbara County Surf Club membership card and Greg Noll's woodworking shop and the gorgeous Malibu-chip. His interest in my father's early surf years gives me a feeling of hollow pride. Erika scratches Rosie's ears, not really interested in the discussion. But Marc nods, and smiles. He's a nice guy, and I like him. We rap about well-known Southern California breaks, and I name-drop some of the renegades mentioned in the autobiography, as though my father's old acquaintances might lend me credibility. Marc tells me his own stories, surfing in Baja, up and down the coast, etc. He fell into it at ten, he says, so he's been surfing for more than forty years. He can't explain his obsession.

"What else is there that's like it?" he says. "*Nothing.* I still feel the same way about it as I did when I was a kid. But," he goes on, holding out his arms as though balancing, "at least I don't stand on my board in my bedroom anymore and do this."

Marc is a successful local real estate developer. His office is full of rolled blueprints. Scattered among blueprints are surf books and surf calendars. Marc began as an artist, hocking ceramics on Santa Barbara sidewalks. Behind him on a table sits a handmade set of chess pieces with strange, whimsical faces. But early on, he knew he needed something other than ceramics to get by. First came storage units. Storage units turned into larger real estate deals, and those led to owning hotels.

I thank him for inviting me. "Of course," he says. "We're glad you're here." I think Erika told him my reason for wanting to visit the Ranch, but I'm unsure. Later, I'll learn she did, and his response to her was, "Oh, that's heavy."

"I've been trying to get to the Ranch for a while," I tell him. "Making phone calls. You know. Asking friends of friends. It's almost impossible."

"Yeah, they're pretty strict," he says. "We bought a tenth of a parcel a long time ago. It's basically a surf ticket."

What's unspoken is the surf, this weekend's conditions. I chose my date to visit at random, hoping for and gambling on waves. Sometimes the ocean doesn't cooperate. Before leaving Portland, I looked at the forecast on Surfline. Several Santa Barbara breaks reported one-to-two-foot swells, ankle to knee high, nothing special.

Laurie, Erika's mom, radiates friendliness when we meet inside the main house. "You have a lovely home," I say. "And the guesthouse? Wow."

"Let's get you set up," she says. "You need coffee? Food? What do you need?"

Laurie's an athletic woman with short black hair and perfect teeth and a busy desire to turn my visit into a family event. She's been married to

Marc for forty-two years. Recently, she's developed an interest in contemporary art and sits on the board of a local museum. After ensuring my maximum comfort in the guesthouse, she corrals everyone around the pool, where we share stories, drink Coronas, and move from hot tub to pool and back. It's a storytelling family, and I notice how, as someone tells a story, they chime in and comingle information and fine-tune the story until an agreed-upon story emerges. Storytelling is how they relate, how they share history.

Later, during dinner on the outdoor patio, the stories turn into tales about the ocean. Adventures aboard a Zodiac boat. Laurie caught in a riptide, Marc attacked by a seagull. Sharks.

"Oh, the channel is full of them," Laurie says.

"There's so much sea life out there," Marc says in agreement. "And a lot of sharks." There have been days when he's gone to the Ranch alone, found absolutely no one around, and he'll leave because he's overcome with a spooky, otherworldly feeling. This topic of conversation makes me a bit nervous. Marc leans back, laughing. The Santa Barbara Channel is "really sharky," he says. It's an office park for the creatures in grey suits. And then, of course, there was the time, he says, when he was sitting on his board and saw a three-foot fin rise out of the water and head straight toward his friend. Marc turned and paddled like hell, only to later discover the fin belonged to a basking shark. "Those things are harmless," he says. "They'd have to gum you to death."

"I think we should stop talking about sharks," Erika says. "Don's eyes are getting bigger."

A small smile drifts across Marc's face. He piles on more stories. Already, I have butterflies about tomorrow. All the shark talk makes me uneasy, and it doesn't help when later, alone in the guesthouse, I come across one of my father's eerie encounters while flipping through "The Story of My Life."

I have a memory of Danny Hazard surfing at Hollister. In a silhouette in the same wave is a 15ft white shark following him. I tried to get his attention to let him know he was being preyed upon, but he would have nothing to do with my pleading with him to get out of the water. Luckily nothing became of it.

A fifteen-foot whitey!

I shove his autobiography in my bag. I only brought the thing to show Erika's dad. I can feel tension in my jaw. I'm always flush with nervous energy whenever visiting new surf spots, so maybe that's the reason I feel tense—am I going to be able to ride? What if the waves break a quarter mile from shore, and I have to paddle through twenty minutes of chop? What if conditions are brutal? What about big whitey?

Sleep is impossible. My jaw clenches again when I pick up my phone and scroll through a surf website. A surfer, it turns out, was hit yesterday at Wall Beach, in the northern part of Santa Barbara County near Vandenberg Air Force Base. Estimates put the white shark at eight to ten feet. Park rangers closed three nearby beaches for seventy-two hours.

Unbelievably, I read about two *additional* attacks earlier in the day in the same area. Around noon, a white shark hit a kayak, dumping the occupant. He clung to the kayak before being rescued by a fishing boat. A short while later an eighteen- to twenty-foot white shark hit another kayak. One of the occupants was launched into the air. The kayak was sinking when the same fishing boat pulled the kayakers out of the water.

There were no fatalities. But the distance between Vandenberg and the Ranch may as well be a short, leisurely stroll for a white shark. Three hits in two days! I don't know what to think.

I punch the pillows and bunch them behind my head. Maybe I'm just anxious about something else. Maybe the idea of a roving white shark is a symbolic stand-in. Maybe I'm unnerved by what I might possibly *feel* at the Ranch. His ashes are in my backpack. Maybe I'm too keyed up. Visiting Hollister will mark the end of one story and the beginning of the next.

————

IN THE MORNING, I wake up anxious, and my stomach feels gelatinous. Coffee doesn't help anything, but the billion-dollar view from the guesthouse does. I join Erika outside on the pebble driveway. Marc appears wearing tortoiseshell Wayfarers. His hair looks perfect.

"You ready?" he asks, with expectant notes in his voice.

"More than ready," I say.

He rummages through a storage closet next to the open garage, yanking out beach chairs covered in spider webs. I clean them with a hose. The driveway is busy with morning activity. The dogs run around barking. It's already warm and turning into a blazing day. It's the first time in a long time that the family is on an adventure, and I'm glad to be part of it. Laurie and Erika stuff a cooler full of cheeses and cold cuts and water.

Marc's surfboard quiver in the garage is impressive. His boards stand upright, racked, like guns. All kneeboards. Shorter, fatter boards. Some are wider or shorter by mere inches. He doesn't surf standing up anymore because of knee problems. Each board looks pretty much the same as the next, but the day before Marc assured me each performs differently. Unlike my Manhattan Beach run years ago, this time I'll be riding a six-foot, seven-inch Surftech, an ugly rental, dinged all to hell. The board looks like a dinosaur used it as a chew toy.

Erika walks over as I'm inspecting the rack. "My dad says there will be waves today."

"I hope so. My phone says it's only one to two feet."

She shrugs. "He seems to know these things."

I mention my late-night phone surfing, my dreams full of sharky water, and my toss-and-turn night.

"Oh, don't mind them. My parents always used to do that to us," she says, and laughs. "They try to get you riled up before going into the ocean. Think of it this way. It's like you're now a member of the family."

After loading the back of the Range Rover with gear, Marc and I secure the boards to the top, tightening straps. I throw my heavy wetsuit in the back along with my backpack.

The drive to the Hollister exit takes half an hour. Erika's dog sits in the backseat between us, slobbering on her leg. "Rosie? Really? Yuck," she says.

After exiting the highway, we drive a short distance down an isolated access road to the guardhouse and stop. A young man asks Marc for his name. Then checks a list. The guard also takes note of a decal on the windshield. Then he signals us on.

I want to say, *That's it?*

We're in, moving, moving, moving.

Before the first in a series of cattle guards, I notice an old sign posted on a fence: PRIVATE LAND. CATTLE RANCH. The road narrows, goes curvy. The Ranch is still a working ranch, and black cattle roam freely. Several large houses sit high in the hills, surrounded by open range. I don't see any other cars. It's just us. The road weaves around canyons thick with mesquite and sagebrush. A copse of pepper trees frames a nearly hidden gate that leads someplace mysterious. Foothills, valleys, and beaches. The place is as untouched as it was when my father drove these same winding roads. A 14,400-acre fairy tale, with miles and miles of surfable waves between Gaviota and Point Conception. It's everything I hoped for and expected.

Soon after rounding a bend, we start seeing waves curling along breaks. According to my phone, the surf in Santa Barbara is nil, but out here it's break after break of spiraling, kicking water. It wasn't supposed to be like this, but it is. As soon as Marc notices what I'm seeing, his foot goes down, the SUV picks up speed, and we lean harder into the curves.

"Marc, watch the road," Laurie says. He doesn't. "Marc, slow down!"

As we pass the breaks, he names them for me, like a list—names I've only read about. First, Razor Blades, a powerful wave that pushes you through rocks if you're not careful. Then Big Drakes, followed by Little Drakes.

"Wow," I say.

"I know. It's a surfer's dream out here," he says. "You pretty much know all the surfers, and there aren't many. It's perfect." Another flawless, distant break appears between twin hills. "This is ridiculous," he says. "It's point after point. I thought there'd be waves. But, I mean. Look at them." The conditions are better than he imagined, he says.

"Where's your parcel of land?" I ask.

"Oh, it's out here," Marc says.

"Can you camp on it?"

"Well, theoretically," Laurie says. "We don't know where it is. We tried to find it one time. We didn't."

After driving a bit farther, we turn onto a small road and head straight toward low beach bluffs. The Range Rover thumps over train tracks, and before I know it the vehicle pitches and suddenly we're driving on the beach. The wheels catch, and Marc steers toward wet, packed sand. His favorite spot, Rights and Lefts, is around a bend. Parked along the beach are other four-wheel drives, families camped beside them.

"What a day," Erika says.

"It's gorgeous," Laurie says.

Marc chooses an open section against a cliff face. In four-wheel drive we climb a low knoll of sand and stop. Marc's out of the vehicle before anyone. He quickly suits up. Already conditions are ideal, little wind, swell after mounting swell throwing out five- and six-footers. Flat on the horizon out to sea is San Miguel Island.

Three years after stepping on the sand at Manhattan Beach, I open the door and step out onto the Ranch. I recognize the same beach scrub from my father's old photos, where he sat waving from the porch of a rickety beach shack.

I help Erika and Laurie assemble camp. Up go umbrellas and down go towels. It's above ninety degrees. Sunscreen and visor weather. After lugging over the cooler, I climb the nearby bluff for a better view, snapping some photos. I want evidence of my visit. Train tracks, some twenty yards away, run parallel to the shoreline. I never realized train tracks ran through here. Anyone with an Amtrak ticket can ride through the Ranch but can't stop. Other than tracks and some odd power lines, it's pristine. I understand Matt Warshaw's concerns. Open these beaches to the public, and they'll be overrun with people, strip malls, and pavement. The Ranch, this shoreline, must look the same as it did hundreds of years ago, when roaming Chumash hauled fish and abalone from the sea.

From above I watch Marc paddle out. Four low-flying pelicans glide over a small posse of black-clad surfers. Rights and Lefts is a wave that charges the reef and breaks both right and left, producing twin curlers. Two surfers launch into the same wave and shoot out in opposite directions. I notice the telltale signs of a rip current between Rights and Lefts and another break to the east called Utah's. Backwash pulls out to sea and breaks apart the waves. Utah's is more my style. Back in Oregon, at Agate Beach, I like to ride the rip like a conveyor belt, which delivers me to the lineup.

Below, Laurie and Erika are now hidden beneath umbrellas. And Marc? He's gone. He's out. He's indistinguishable from the others now, one of about eight black dots. Only a generous soul could ever marry a surf-mad person. I saw that peculiar kind of generosity in Greg Noll's wife, Laura, and I recognize it in Laurie too. It's the understanding that, during the season, a surf report might throw out all aces, and your partner could vanish for days.

What's interesting, at least at the Ranch, is you're as likely to see a sixty-year-old with a board as a twenty-year-old. No matter what age, the devotees of Rights and Lefts crush it again and again. I watch the dance for a while. One guy crouches inside a barrel, pops out, engulfed in spray, shreds the face, cuts back, pops over the lip, sits back down on his board, and gracefully paddles back to the lineup. It's beautiful, as fluid as a ballet dancer on stage. Now I understand what Drew Kampion was talking about when he mentioned morphic fields. A surfer's movements on a wave aren't choreographed but preknown in the body, an organic response of muscle memory aligned with the movement of water. Like a school of fish. Other than the game of soccer, surfing is the most beautiful sport on earth. It's too bad the popular magazines and movies depict surfers as hollow-headed buffoons. Most of the surfers I know have the calm presence of a Buddha after a session. They also have successful careers, and they're smart. After all, truly understanding when and where and how to surf, and understanding the different variables and conditions of beaches and breaks, requires a basic knowledge of meteorology, oceanography, geography, and physics.

Another guy rips across a wave.

I want to get out there.

The Range Rover lends some privacy as I wrench on my wetsuit, which is thicker, I'm certain, than anyone else's at the beach. It's hooded, five millimeters in the chest, four in the arms, and designed for colder water. It's a struggle to pull it on.

"That's some wetsuit," Laurie says.

"You look really warm in that," Erika says.

And, I want to say: I look like a seal. Exactly like a seal, which white sharks love to eat. I haven't shaken the hour-long shark powwow from last night, and the surfers now out there, thirty yards from shore, are casually bobbing on twenty-feet-deep water, deep enough for a surprise hit. Plenty of white sharks traverse the Oregon coast, but I never spend the night before a session dwelling on it.

I unstrap my rental from the roof and strap the leash to my ankle. As soon as I'm waist-deep, the first surge from a marching swell slaps my board. My concerns splash away in the cool water, and I give over.

———

ABOUT THE RANCH he wrote, "I have many good memories of surfing some of the most perfect waves."

Now I understand.

I'm flat on the board when a gargantuan wave breaks across the nose and shoves the rail sideways and salt water fills my sinuses. "Some of the most perfect waves" assault me and sweep me back. I wait it out. Wait for a better opportunity. Water leaks from my nostrils. Straight up the middle, between Rights and Lefts and Utah's, the rip current ruins waves as water channels back to sea. But the rip creates an opening. You have to time it right. Between sets I paddle through the gap, hard. A pod of dolphins appears and swims parallel to shore, their grey fins shimmering and disappearing.

Another surfer joins me on the watery conveyor belt. He's around Marc's age. Ropes of muscle line his neck. A wave comes, and he duck-dives, momentarily melting from view.

My thoughts are partially on the water and partially on the reason I'm here: the plastic baggie in my backpack. He's here. He's with us. Despite years of strained attempts to connect, he never knew me, and I only know him through the story he left. Now there's a nearly endless stretch of stunning, beige, empty beach and copybook waves to remember him by. That's another reason I'm here: to build one last decent memory.

I watch Marc. He drops in and tears across a five-footer on his knees. After several more solid rides, he paddles to shore, leans his board against the Range Rover, and hoofs it toward the umbrellas.

At last I make it out, registering the effort in my shoulders and lungs. Floating on my board, beyond the point where swells turn to corkscrews, sunlight glitters across the water, and for a while I absorb the absolute beauty, the tan, clean, unpeopled beach, and the grasslands sloping into chaparral. Again, I think about him, amazed by how far I've gone looking for answers and explanations and understanding. I never internalized the feeling of having a father. A father could have helped me think about not having a father, and my insistent questioning, my searching, my journeying, all of it, has been an attempt to construct a father. I've had to become the father of that child who needed one long ago. Leaving my father here, too, seems a good thing, the best thing. Or maybe leaving him here is a stylized way of saying goodbye, a crafted farewell, but I don't care. Stylized or not, it feels right.

Water continues rolling in, swells created by energy generated thousands of miles away. I sit. And wait. Watching from a distance, I finally choose one, kicking my feet in a turn. The second hump inside a good-sized swell rears up and rolls underneath. I paddle, grabbing the rails and popping up and catching several long glorious seconds before the wave shatters. When my head pops up from below, I look around. That was something. That felt great. I tug the board back by the leash.

After paddling back and forth for a while, waiting for another clean wave, I take a breather. I sit on my board and watch the others. Part of the Ranch's beauty is watching the surfers who visit this place — this church. In Oregon, you're almost congratulated for simply entering the frigid water. It's different here. Performance matters. On another attempt my calf cramps, and I decide to take a short break.

Marc is heading back out as I'm heading in. His hair looks spectacular when sculpted by salt and sand. He shoots me a smile.

"It's unbelievable," he says. "Right? Right?"

"It's pretty great," I say.

I walk up the sand and fall under an umbrella. It's bright and unbelievably hot, especially in an arctic-weather wetsuit. Erika tosses me a sandwich, and I slug some water. Time vanishes out there. Somehow, I've been in the water for an hour and a half.

For a while, as we sit under cool purple shade, we watch the disciples of Rights and Lefts killing it. The waves keep getting bigger and more consistent as the day goes on.

There's still something I need to do. It preoccupies me. Erika brings it up. She asks me whether I left his ashes in the water. "Not yet," I say.

Laurie asks about it too. Erika told her why I wanted to come to this place.

"This really looks like the same beach from his old photos," I say. "Or it could be around that headland, but I know he surfed here. So it's a good spot for his ashes."

Laurie listens, nodding. Then she tips her head, and asks, "Do you want kids?"

"Yeah. I do."

"I can see you being a dad," she says. "You'd make a good father."

"You would, Don," Erika says.

I scan the group floating on the water. Erika's father is right here. In one weekend Marc has been more of a father than he ever was.

IN AND OUT OF THE WATER. We're having fun, a beach day, but one thing remains unfinished.

At 2:00 p.m. I pull on my baseball cap and wander away from Erika and her mom. And Marc? He's still out there. He's still killing it with his enthusiasm and his bad knees and that bitchin' hair.

I walk alone down the beach. It's an ideal day. I step over clumps of sun-ripened seaweed and broken white shells and find a private little spot between two beach boulders and sit, overheating in my wetsuit. Before leaving, I definitely want one more session.

There's not much difference in the textures of ash and the sand stuck to my feet. I study the small baggie. Part of me wants to keep these last pieces. Through the plastic I pinch a minuscule bit of bone. Ash and sand, so similar, both composed of minerals, both remnants of mountains and bodies, both reduced by the passage of time to substances that fall easily through fingers. Just like that, time passes. Time moves. Time just rips by. How many years do we have left? In that time, will I become a father?

His final words in "The Story of My Life" envisioned it.

> Initially I set out to chronicle the events of my life for my son so that he could learn who his father was. I was absent during his formative years . . . I thought it would be good to let him know of me, and perhaps share me with his children someday.

This is the place. The man I needed walked this beach. The man I want to admire surfed these waves. By traveling here, it's as though I'm trying to embrace that struggling part of him that had the opportunity to become a good father. But I know that man is a fiction.

I've spent nearly twenty years writing stories about faulty fictional men. Each was a character study. I put my characters in charged situations and watched how they reacted and what decisions they made. So many short stories about loners and lost, shattered men. I wrote seeking clarity and hoping to locate moments of redemption. I wrote about men in an attempt to understand my father, over and over.

Now I know some things.

He was a former beach boy turned rugged outdoorsman. Or he was a selfish coward and deadbeat dad. He was an honorably discharged navy veteran. Or he was a drifter and scab at a desert mine. A sailor on the water. A surfer on waves. A miner digging holes for nuclear waste. Different lenses yield different stories. And stories are never black-and-white.

I know he was raised in Manhattan Beach and Santa Barbara. I know he grew up with his feet in the sand. I know he loved water and geology. I know he was my height. Broad forehead. Blue eyes. Crooked row of bottom teeth. I know he loved Mom and married her, and I know I don't remember anything before he left. I know I met him at nineteen inside a Reno casino, and I know I saw him four other times. I know I'm the son of a broken union, and I know he stayed away because he didn't know how to be the right kind of man.

He was complicated, average, sensitive, talented in ways and brutal in others, passionate and careless and curious and hopeless and all too human. That's all I really need to know. He was human. So let me leave it at that, because there's no such thing as closure. Closure implies a beginning, middle, and end, an arc that cinches into a tidy little bow. The most honest kind of closure is living beside the pain and the truth and knowing it will always be with you.

I look down the beach and think about the plane flight, the highway, and the interconnected roads and stories that all led here, and I can't help but wonder, if I ever have a child, will any of this remain the same? Will it survive? I realize something. Hollister Ranch is pretty, but it really doesn't compare with the exceptional, soul-crushing beauty of the Oregon coast.

I push against a boulder and stand. I scoop a handful of sand into my ball cap to keep it from blowing away. I leave it behind. Sweat has collected inside my wetsuit, and I'm eager to wade in again. I cross the beach with the familiar feeling of needles burning in my chest.

In the water I open the baggie. A wave rises up, filling it and washing it clean. His ashes puff into a cloud and disappear. I lean into the charging waves, pushing against the surge. The water washes away my tears. After spending the morning under the sun, I'm tired from surfing, tired from not sleeping, tired from traveling, and tired of searching. I'm tired of pushing. So I give over and sink under the next wave, swimming to the bottom, holding in a sore breath and clutching the sandy bottom.

Walking out from the water, I whip back my wet hair, retrieve my hat in the sand, and head down the beach, alone. As soon as I get home, I decide, I will throw everything away. His rocks, his business cards, his navy patches, all of it in boxes, all of it taking up space. Throw it all away, everything but his autobiography, a few interesting photos, his Bible, and four pages of a typed genealogy. His parents gathered the list of names. Before this trip, I sat down at my desk, studying my family's lineage and flipping through his Bible, the only book he had in his hospital room before he died.

Even though I don't believe in scriptural doctrine anymore, I know we're all connected by vast, interconnecting energy, like the continuous energy of waves, and if I know anything, I know enough to understand the energy we share with one another always comes back, and finally I'm ready to give back to myself by saying to my father, wherever his energy may be, I *forgive you.*

Forgive the sins, like it says in my father's old Bible.

In the beginning God created the heaven and the earth.

And the earth was without form, and void; and darkness was upon the face of the deep.

And the Spirit of God moved upon the face of the waters.

And God said, Let there be light: and there was light . . .

And William lived seventy and six years and begat Clement.

And Clement lived eighty and one years and begat Theodore.

And Theodore lived thirty and four years, and he begat James.

And James lived eighty and two years and begat Robert.

And Robert lived ninety and two years, and he begat Robert Stanley.

And Robert Stanley, when he was thirty and two years, knocked up Donna Lee, and on November 5, 1974, at eight o'clock in the evening in the high desert gambling town of Reno, Nevada, a.k.a. "The Biggest Little City in the World," Robert Stanley begat a son—me.

In my father's version of the story, it was a beautiful beginning.

———

IT'S NOT LIKE we haven't tried. After years we've still been unable to conceive. And now, finally, finally we pull the trigger and attempt in vitro fertilization. We've been informed IVF is a grueling and a supremely invasive process. Robin's not looking forward to it. And neither am I.

Robin's already been through IUI—artificial insemination—three times. That was moderately painless, though she'd certainly say otherwise. She took hormone pills, visited the clinic for ultrasounds, and timed her ovulation by peeing on sticks. Then the lab washed my sperm and the doctor injected them into her cervix. Even though I was a mere spectator, it felt as if I were participating in some godly origin story.

Neither attempt worked.

I've watched Robin endure test after test. After each visit to the clinic, I read pain and frustration on her face. Sometimes I consider suggesting that we just stop. It's hard on her. It's hard on us. Nothing about the process is fun. It's shitty and worrisome and stresses both of us out. It's expensive but the bigger tax is on the soul.

Plus, every test leaves Robin feeling exposed during the days leading up to the results. Every test, so far, reveals good news. Robin looks healthy. Her uterine lining looks wonderful. Her ovaries are solid. Even though she's in her late thirties, the doctor says everything looks tip-top.

"But I worry about endometriosis," Robin says one night during dinner.

"The doctor says everything looks fine. Stop worrying," I say.

"That's probably the reason I can't get pregnant," she says. "There's a history of endometriosis in my family."

"But the doctor—"

"You can't just test for it," she says. "They have to put you under. You have to have an operation to find out."

Then there are the ongoing semen tests. Before we ever visited the fertility clinic, I carried around the vague idea a sperm was a simple, fairly stupid cell that carried out its stupid job quite accurately. I also thought semen tests primarily looked at two variables: if the sperm moved and the number of them.

But in fact, there's way more, and from the moment we began testing my semen and poring over the results, I too started feeling wildly vulnerable. The way the lab technicians rattled off the results to me over the phone in such a nonchalant manner made me feel like a judged calf at a county fair.

The semen tests measure my viscosity, motility, volume, and shape. By and large, my volume and motility are in the normal range, but we worry about my viscosity and shape. I have higher than normal viscosity. And the percentage of misshapen sperm—morphology, they call it—is a bit higher than they'd like to see as well.

At night, as I drift off to sleep, I begin hoping the apple I ate or the bowl of blueberries I ate or the vitamin I took will help lower my viscosity and improve the shape of my spermatozoa.

After my most recent semen sample, I receive a phone call from the lab. Then I call Robin. "The results look the same," I say. "She said twenty-eight million."

"Yeah, but what about the viscosity and morphology?" Robin asks.

We've become experts in the lingo.

"Viscosity and morphology are the same as before," I say.

"I wonder if that's what's preventing us from getting pregnant," she says. "Viscosity and morphology matter. Maybe that's it."

It doesn't matter. Through IVF, the lab will lop off the sperm's tail and inject it straight into an egg. It doesn't matter whether my guys move or not. The whole thing makes me feel like a cheater.

"But we still need to get enough good eggs from me," Robin says.

"Oh, we will," I say. "We will."

Despite the dubious viscosity and morphology business, I'm proud of my numbers, and I walk around the house saying, "Twenty-eight million. Oh, boy. Twenty-eight million. Doesn't Shanghai have something like twenty-five million people?"

"Will you knock it off?" Robin says.

For ten days leading up to Robin's egg extraction operation, I wake up early each morning before classes and give her shots in the stomach. I inject saline solution into a small vial and then extract the mixture into a hypodermic needle.

Each morning, I bring Robin a cup of coffee and set the two primed syringes on the bedside table.

"Morning," I say. "I have coffee."

"No. It's too early," Robin says. "I don't want to do this."

I sit on the bed.

Without looking at me, she lifts up her T-shirt and pinches her belly in the usual spot, right next to her belly button.

"I'm sorry," I say, before plunging the first needle.

"I know."

"I feel like I'm stabbing you every time."

"You are stabbing me."

"I'm sorry. I love you," I say, as though that might help.

"Just put the stupid needle in."

I do.

"Ouch, fuck," she says.

"I'm so sorry."

She reaches over and touches my neck. "God, this is crazy."

At night, before bed, I administer another shot in her stomach with a fancy injection pen. The idea is to trick her body into allowing more eggs to emerge. Then the doctor will extract as many eggs as possible. To me, the whole thing is infinitely worse than thinking about a dentist needling my gums with that sharp little sadistic instrument.

The extraction takes place early in the morning at the clinic. I drive Robin to the procedure and sit with her until she's wheeled into an adjoining room.

Later that day, Robin gets a call from the nurse. She's at home. She calls me. "We got eighteen eggs," she says. Her voice is bright, tired, and optimistic.

The lab technician studies her eggs, selecting viable-looking ones, and we're actually left with twelve eggs. Nine fertilize.

"We need to wait five days to allow the embryos to grow," Robin says. "Hopefully they'll all survive. But the literature says only half usually make it."

On the morning of the transfer, we head back to the clinic, where the doctor informs us four embryos survived. We have four. Only four.

"How many embryos would you like to transfer?" the doctor asks us.

I look at Robin. Robin looks at me. We've talked about each and every miniscule detail, but we haven't decided how many embryos to transfer. We're just both amazed we've survived the process this far. We don't know. The doctor leaves us alone.

"If we transfer one, we can freeze the others," I say. "We can try again. Or we can try two right now."

"But if we transfer two we might end up with twins," Robin says. "Do you want twins?"

"I don't know. Do you?"

"I don't know. What do you want to do?"

"I don't know."

"I don't know either," Robin says. "I'll do whatever you want."

"But I'll do whatever you want," I say.

We don't know.

The doctor returns to the room with the embryologist. "We'll transfer one embryo," Robin says.

"Okay, good," the doctor says. "In the meantime we'll screen the remaining three. Otherwise, we have one good-looking, great-rated embryo waiting."

"You should see it. It looks terrific," the embryologist says brightly. She turns on a screen and lights up the room with a picture of our embryo. She's right. Our embryo does look amazing. The embryo and background are bathed in a golden hue. The embryo looks like a large, round cell with what appears to be activity happening above it. It's alive, moving, replicating. I can't remove my eyes.

Later, after the transfer, the nurse emails a digital copy of our embryo to Robin. Robin emails me a copy, which I look at on my phone. Our embryo is wondrous. Is this little Lillian? Is this little Ivan?

We have to wait five days before Robin can take a pregnancy test. Before then, we decide to head to her father's coast house for a brief getaway. Dealing with fertility issues takes an emotional toll. We're both exhausted. As soon as we arrive, we take Mercy on a walk at the beach, and then we return to the house, where we lie in bed with our books.

I'm reading about the tragedy of the whaling ship *Essex* when Robin's phone rings. It's the clinic. I sit up. Robin presses the phone against her cheek, turning away from me. I listen to the waves crashing on the nearby rocks. The sound fills the room.

I try listening to the words filtering through the phone. A father. A kind, good father. A good man.

Robin's head turns. Her lips tense. "That's devastating news," she says into the phone. She hangs up. "They've already tested the three remaining embryos. All three had chromosomal abnormalities," she says.

"What does that mean? What's going to happen to them?"

"They'll be destroyed," she says.

I feel sick. The stress, just so much unbelievable stress. Putting Robin through daily injections, the rollercoaster of emotions, the hopes and disappointments. I don't know whether either of us can handle the process any longer.

But I want to be a father. Now I'm certain. I want to hold my child. I don't care if the screaming little gremlin vomits in my face. At least I don't think I'll care. Vomit-in-the-face is part of it, isn't it, isn't that a part of life? I only know the feeling that comes over me whenever a friend's baby clutches my finger with its tiny hand. My chest absolutely dissolves into warmth. I want to teach her or him how to play soccer in the sand and how to love water and how to love one other. I want to do every kind of square thing a responsible parent should and must do. I do. I actually do. We have one chance with the golden embryo now inside Robin.

During the hopeful, excruciating days before Robin's pregnancy test, I prepare myself. I think about everything pragmatically. I use logic. And I pray. For the first time in years I pray.

I want a child. I want this child.

I think about my parents. They got pregnant and rushed into marriage. They didn't spend time considering what it means to bring a child into this world. But I have — I've spent decades thinking about what it means to be a father. I've done the personal work. I've tried to become the best man I can possibly be. I will give more than my father ever gave.

I find myself staring at the golden image on my phone, visualizing cells dividing, a bright pink newborn, carrying a baby in a ridiculously yuppie infant backpack, holding my daughter's hand, her graduation, strolling with her as adults and talking about her life on a mountain trail.

Out at the coast, Robin and I talk about our embryo nonstop, and then we try not to talk about it. It's our turn. It's now our turn.

Our one embryo. Our baby. Our future baby.

When we return to Portland, Robin's friend Laura arrives for a visit. Robin needs a friend around. She needs distractions. Several days later, Laura accompanies Robin when she takes the defining blood test at the clinic.

Later in the day, Robin gets the phone call. Laura and Robin are both on the couch when I return from teaching.

Robin says, "Not pregnant."

It will not be.

I sit across from them. I put my face in my hands.

"I spoke with the nurse," Robin says. "They suspect the abnormal chromosomes suggest something. They usually don't see a pattern to the irregularities in multiple embryos. Ours had a pattern."

We've taken tests. We've given eggs and sperm. We've given blood. We've given money. We've tried nearly every available option. We've given everything. There has to be something more we can do, something else. I head to the clinic again to extract blood for another test. I'm determined to find out more.

A week later, I visit the clinic to review my results with the genetics counselor, a woman named Emily.

Thankfully, Emily is older than the bright-eyed, dim little office bees. She's my age. She has stylish black hair, and I'm relieved to read intelligence in her eyes. I've had too many frustrating interactions with the office bees.

Emily shuts her office door. She hands me a piece of paper from the lab. I look at it. The page looks like something torn from a biology textbook. Numbers, data. I don't understand half of it.

> Cells counted: 20
> Cells analyzed: 20
> Cytogenetic result: 46,XY,t(1;14)(q21;q24)

"Your karyotype reveals balanced translocation between chromosome one and chromosome fourteen," Emily tells me.

"I don't understand," I say, scanning the paper.

"You have balanced translocation," she says.

I don't say anything. There it is, in the middle of the page. Interpretation: Balanced Translocation Carrier. "And what does it mean?"

Emily hands me another piece of paper with a color-coded map illustrating my chromosome translocation. A large green arm from one chromosome is attached to a smaller blue chromosome, and that small blue section is affixed to the green chromosome.

"Pieces of chromosome one and fourteen have traded places. You don't lose genetic material or genetic information, but they've basically rearranged themselves."

"Is this why Robin can't get pregnant?"

Emily extracts a hefty book from the shelf and opens to a section about chromosome abnormalities. She slides the book across the desk. I'm not about to sit and read her big book.

"If an unbalanced gamete is involved in fertilization, it can increase the chances an embryo or fetus will spontaneous miscarry," she says. "Or, depending on where the break in the chromosome occurs, it might lead to an abnormal liveborn."

"An abnormal liveborn?"

"Congenital deformities," she says.

"Is it possible Robin has been pregnant before and the embryos miscarried?"

"It's possible."

"So it's me."

"It's you?"

"It's me, my sperm," I say. "That's why she can't get pregnant."

"This isn't about assigning blame."

Robin has been through endless tests and appointments—ultrasounds, blood work, injections, MRI, sexually transmitted disease screening . . . Jesus, all these tests. Doctors always focus on her, the woman. No one ever thinks it might be me, the man. So many goddamn tests!

"Why wasn't I screened before we started this process? More blood work could have settled it. We didn't even know this balanced translocation thing existed."

Emily doesn't respond. Her face registers strained calm. I pick up her book and read a paragraph. As a carrier, you can be healthy, but balanced translocation could bring about miscarriages or intellectual and congenital abnormalities. It says the same thing she just told me. I close the book.

I sit in the well-lit room. And I listen.

A strand of hair falls in Emily's eyes. She swipes it to the side. She waits for my next question. What does she see when she looks at me? She's now intimate with the basic material that makes me *me*. I watch her scratch her forearm with concern in her eyes. Her nails run back and forth unevenly, imprinting her skin with little red untidy lines, the blood rising to the surface.

"As a carrier, you're perfectly fine," she says. "You're just a carrier. This is something passed down and inherited," she says. "Like so many other things."

EPILOGUE

I HAUL MYSELF OUT OF BED at 5:00 a.m. so that Robin can continue sleeping. She's often up in the wee hours of the night, so Sylvie and I spend mornings together. First thing, downstairs, I carefully unwrap her from her swaddling cloth, and she gives me a tremendous, toothless smile. That heart-melting move must be hardwired, I always think, a finely tuned evolutional behavior, because her smiles make me forget that the sun hasn't even dawned, that I've been exhausted for four months — teaching full time while learning to be a new dad. After Sylvie's crushing smile routine, she performs an overemphasized stretch, which is equally liquefying. We move to the dim living room and sit on the floor, where we gurgle at each other for a while. A game we play. She gurgles, smiles. I gurgle back, and she smiles again and releases a squeak.

After gurgling, we listen to records. In my lap she watches me place a record on the turntable. In her first few weeks, she slept soundly to Linda Ronstadt and Bill Withers. These days she's partial to the Beach Boys' *Pet Sounds*, the B side. Sylvie has excellent taste.

At some point in the middle of our music appreciation session, Sylvie begins to groan and whine and struggle until I manage to insert the nipple of a bottle into her drooling little mouth. She slurps like some wild beast. The sounds she makes!

I never knew these kinds of feelings were possible, but as I hold her and feed her, as we stare at each other, I know I'm operating on a new and unexpected plane of existence. That might be a saccharine sentiment, sure, but these days the saccharine keeps washing in, and I welcome the deluge. Few things in these moments matter more than providing the right amount of quiet comfort, food, white noise, warmth, and dimmed lighting to coax my baby to sleep.

This morning, after her bottle, I fasten her to my chest in a front pack baby carrier, bounce around the living room listening to the *Fame* soundtrack, wait for Sylvie's series of necessary burps, and then set up an ad hoc workstation in the kitchen by placing the dog food bin on the counter and my laptop on that. I bounce on my toes as I type, and Sylvie slowly falls asleep against my chest.

––––––

SYLVIE JACQUELYN was born early on a Saturday morning in August. Eight pounds ten ounces and just under twenty-one inches. After seventeen hours of labor, she arrived by a complicated birth. Intensive Care Unit doctors swept her out of the room as soon as she entered the world. In a near state of shock, I trailed the nurses first to a small observational room and soon after to a room in the neonatal ICU. Robin couldn't join us, so I removed my shirt and asked for skin-to-skin contact within her first hour. Sylvie spent an additional night in the neonatal ICU, and we took her home that Monday. Sylvie's fine, completely fine—she's amazing.

A year ago, I thought this memoir was finished: here was the story of a man trying to figure out his father; here was the story of a boy and the fathers he'd known and lost; here was the story of a man trying to become a father. After my genetic test results showed balanced translocation, I thought, mournfully, there would be no baby.

When Sylvie is old enough to understand such things, I will take her in my arms, tell her how much I love her, and explain to my daughter that I'm not her biological father. Because of my balanced translocation, we used a sperm donor. Already, even though she's only four months old, I'm concerned this information will one day cause her some amount of pain. I hope my presence in her life, my attention and care for her, will provide a cushion against any future distress. And I hope my experience wrestling with not knowing my father will help guide her when the time comes. Because here is what I know: I have never felt as in love with another living soul as I am with Sylvie.

She weighs fourteen pounds now. Her dark blue eyes are slowly turning lighter. She has a healthy, chubby face, above which wisps of light reddish hair whoosh off her head like meringue. She looks like a stunning little Irish lass. My daughter has fine strawberry blonde eyelashes, her mother's

Ashkenazi Jewish ancestry, a French name, a determined disposition, and she's completely her own charming person. I like holding her upright as she balances on her fat legs. Robin laughs when I laugh at the ridiculous shape of her baby body. Her bulbous stomach!

She's vomited on me countless times. It's absurd, really, patting her back and willing her to produce great burps, accompanied often by projectile barf the color of mother's milk. Once, when she had a minor cold, I inhaled her snot while using the nasal aspirator because I'd forgotten to insert the filter. I only cared a little.

She likes baths. I want her at ease in the water. And she's more than comfortable—she loves it. Lately, whenever I run the bath, she starts kicking, eager to get to her game. I hold her, and she stands and slaps the water, chasing a floating water-temperature thermometer, which is shaped like a turtle. A fierce look comes into her eyes as soon as the turtle enters her domain.

I RARELY THINK ABOUT my father these days. I'm busy. I'm tired. Besides, there's so little to remember about him, just a few shared moments that blink through my mind from time to time. My father in the casino corridor. My father in the hospital bed. I don't possess one skill or morsel of useful advice he passed down, other than the platitudes in his autobiography, a document that still sits inside that old, beat-up, cardboard box in the basement. And, I often think, why fixate on my father when I'm already overwhelmed figuring out how to be the kind of father Sylvie needs? I will try to be the right kind of father for her. I just hope the successes outweigh the missteps. One thing is certain. I will never leave my girl behind.

Even when I leave the house to drive across town and teach for a few hours, I'm eager to return home. Sylvie's starting to really smile now, and her smiles crush me. Sometimes I wonder whether my father ever knew the impatient feeling of waiting to see his child while sitting in bumper-to-bumper traffic during a cold, wet December afternoon? I've certainly gotten to know this kind of gnawing impatience. Did he ever feel needed and necessary? Did he take pride in knowing that a partner and baby awaited him, that they depended on him? Did he feel awe at the new story being formed?

I hope he felt it. At least once.

But as I stand here bouncing on my toes, as my daughter gradually awakens, squishing her face against my neck, I can't spend that much time hoping. There's a reason this epilogue will be brief. Sylvie needs my attention more.

Acknowledgments

I owe first thanks to Sam Moulton and *Outside* magazine, where my search for answers about my father began with a simple magazine article—thank you. A great deal of bitchin' thanks needs to be paid to Greg, Laura, and Jed Noll for building a surfboard with me, and to Erika, Marc, and Laurie Recordon for an excellent trip to the Ranch. As always, thank you to my friends and teachers for your friendship, humor, advice, and guidance, especially Josh Benke, Ireri Rivas, Scott Benke, Caleb Cage, Ben Fountain, Martha Walters, Andy Greer, David Shields, Dan Engber, Julian Rubinstein, Aaron Gilbreath, Jesse Lichtenstein, Clifton Spargo, Sam Stone, Ralph Morgan, Mary Szybist, Willy Vlautin, Pauls Toutonghi, Blake Nelson, Justin St. Germain, Andy Irons, Nick Irons, Josh Weil, Mario Zambrano, Dennis Cooper, Pardiss Kebriaei, Ann Townsend, Jillian Weise, Justin Tussing, Rus Bradburd, Sam Chang, Ethan Canin, and Marilynne Robinson. For the miraculous gift of time and space, I want to thank Martha Jessup and Douglas Humble at the Lannan Foundation. I'm delighted to work with University of Iowa Press again, and I'm immensely grateful to Jim McCoy, Allison Means, Karen Copp, Carolyn Brown, and Meredith Stabel. Huge thanks, naturally, to my agent, Maria Massie. Thanks to my mom, my stepdad, Chuck, and my entire family—Kathy, Ginger, Brian, Lisa, Jason, Katy—for their love and support. And again, and again, and again: thank you to Robin Romm. This memoir would not exist without you: xoxo.

Author's Note

Researching the life and movements of an early twentieth-century ne'er-do-well pulp writer and his family was a years-long, piece-by-piece process. I hunted for information using multiple offline and online methods, generating a patchwork of informational scraps until I created a fuller portrait of the family, which culminated with the hiring of a private investigator. Early on in my research into the Waters family, I relied on Ancestry.com, FamilySearch.org, Findagrave.com, Civilianpublicservice.org, Vintagelibrary.com, PulpFest.com, and Genealogy.com, along with material available from US Census records, US Public Records Index, US Copyright Office, National Register of Historic Places, Massachusetts Crew Lists (1917–1943), *Christian Science Monitor* archives, and the Pulp Fiction Library at the Library of Congress.

A lot of helpful information also came from the following sources: California, Office of Orange County Clerk and the California Coastal Commission; Massachusetts, New Bedford Whaling Museum; North Carolina, Asheville Preservation Society, North Carolina Digital Archives, Pack Memorial Library Special Collections, and Buncombe County Historical Society; Ohio, *The Ohio State University Announcement Catalog* (1916) and *The Ohio State University Alumni News* (1916); Tennessee, Office of Blount County Clerk and Trustee, Knox County Library, Sevier County Public Library, Office of Sevier County Probate, Tennessee Department of Public Health, and the University of Tennessee Libraries.

During my research, I often referred to documents from court cases, including *State of Tennessee vs. Margaret Crane* (Circuit Court, Sevier County, Tennessee), *Margaret Crane vs. Eileen Radeker* (US District Court, Nashville, Tennessee), and *State of Tennessee vs. Margaret Crane* (Criminal Court of Appeals of Tennessee). I also consulted Margaret Crane's "pen packet," Tennessee Department of Corrections, Women's Prison Records Office, Division of Probation and Parole. And like anyone hoping to find waves and research surf history, I often sought out Surfline.com and the *Encyclopedia of Surfing*.

So many people helped sort details and throw light into the shadows and allowed me to fully see this story's wild places. I couldn't have taken the reader to these places without the help of the following people: Laura Bond and Sarah Colpus at the Wave Project; Barry Hahn at the Surfing Heritage and Culture Center; Drew Kampion, Matt Warshaw, Ryan Pittsinger, the Jimmy Miller Foundation; Kimberly Lytton; Kevin Wilson at the National Park Service; Darwin Morgan at the National Nuclear Security Administration; Jeff Goldstein at the National Park Service; Matthew Law at the National Archives and Records Administration; Connie Miller and Lorene Smith at the Blount County Genealogical and Historical Society; and Bill Marsiglio at the University of Florida. Distant relatives of Don and Margaret helped out enormously, and I owe thanks to Anthony Burke, Alethea Gaukel, Patricia (Waters) Boyer, Greg Boyer, and Mary Rhoades. Librarians are the heroes of any well-researched book, and I owe a great deal of gratitude to the following heroes: Shelley Fridell at the Blount County Public Library, and Steve Ostrem and Janalyn Moss and the University of Iowa Libraries.